STYLE

Ten Lessons in Clarity & Grace

Fourth Edition

Joseph M. Williams

The University of Chicago

HarperCollins*College*Publishers

Senior Acquisitions Editor: Jane Kinney
Developmental Editor: Marisa L. L'Heureux
Project Coordination and Cover Design: Tage Publishing Service, Inc.
Production Administrator: Hilda Koparanian
Compositor: Compset, Inc.
Printer, Binder, and Cover Printer: Courier Corporation

For permission to use copyrighted material, grateful acknowledgment is made to the copyright holders on page 256, which is hereby made part of this copyright page.

Style: Ten Lessons in Clarity & Grace, Fourth Edition

Library of Congress Cataloging-in-Publication Data

Williams, Joseph M.
    Style : ten lessons in clarity and grace / Joseph M. Williams.—
4th ed.
        p.   cm.
    Includes index.
    ISBN 0-673-46593-4
        1. English language—Rhetoric.   2. English language—Technical
English.   3. English language—Business English.   4. English
language—Style.   I. Title.
PE1421.W545   1994
808'.042—dc20   93-30211
                                                            CIP

    94 95 96   9 8 7 6 5 4 3 2

For my mother and father

*. . . English style, familiar but not coarse,
elegant but not ostentatious.*
Samuel Johnson

PREFACE

Most of you require no convincing about the importance of a readable style, especially those of you who daily must struggle with the prose of those who never learned to write clearly. Unfortunately, most of the advice that we recall doesn't help us revise their writing, much less our own, because it consists mostly of banalities like "Be clear," or of trivia like "Don't begin sentences with *and* or end them with prepositions." To understand why anyone writes badly, especially ourselves—we have to understand how sentences work, how we—or another writer—distributes parts of an idea through the parts of a sentence, and then we have to understand how to revise it.

To develop that skill, we have to be specific about sentences and ideas, and that means we have to use a few of those terms we may remember from junior high—*verb, object, noun, active, passive,* and so on. Every subject has its special vocabulary. It's the same with style: If you want to improve yours, you have to control the vocabulary. There aren't a lot of terms, they're not difficult, and they are all defined in the Glossary. Don't memorize them. Learning to define nouns and verbs doesn't help anyone write better. But you must develop a sense of how nouns and verbs differ. Then you'll understand why some writing seems clear, and *that* will help you write better.

To Students in Particular

Nothing is more tedious than working on a skill that seems to have no immediate application. You've already learned to write well enough to get as far as you've come. And if you are reading textbooks, journal articles, and scholarly monographs written in a style so difficult that it makes your head throb, you've probably decided that the penalty for bad writing must not be especially severe. If people can write unclearly and get published, why spend time learning how to write well?

The answer is one that I ask you to take partly on faith: The value of clear writing is increased by its scarcity. Though unclear writing does not bar writers from getting into print, a person who can write clearly and gracefully goes into the world with a rare skill. One common reason people do not achieve their potential is their inability to communicate, to get their ideas on paper quickly in a way that lets others understand those ideas easily. Whenever professionals are asked what they wish they had studied more diligently, their first or second answer is always communication, especially writing.

True, you might compensate for a turgid style with great ideas, with an original and creative mind. The more common truth is that most of us have minds closer to merely good than to brilliant. And ideas that are merely good need all the help they can get. So if we weren't born brilliant, we can at least learn to be clear; it is, in fact, an ability as rare as genius, and usually more useful.

I know how unpersuasive this kind of "let-me-tell-you-what's-good-for-you" argument is before you've tested it against your own experience. But in fact, you may already have: How often have you wanted to toss aside a textbook or journal article because every paragraph was an ordeal? How often have you read a dozen pages only to realize that you can't recall a thing? You have to read that kind of writing now, perhaps because it's an assignment, perhaps because you need it for a research paper. But suppose for a moment that you supervised someone who wrote prose as difficult as the prose you find in academic monographs, and that you'd just received one more unreadable report? What would be your first impulse?

The tone of this book is prescriptive. In its lessons I will tell you straight out what I think you should know if you want to be judged as a clear and concise writer. I think the advice is sound. Do not, however, take what I offer here as Draconian rules of composition. They are intended as diagnostic principles of interpretation. Use these principles as the basis for questions to diagnose your prose so that you can anticipate how readers are likely to respond to it, a kind of knowledge usually unavailable to you when you unreflectively reread your own writing.

Don't be reluctant to experiment, to play with different styles. Try the ponderous bureaucratic style that this book condemns, just to get the feel of it. Try creating a passage in a style elegant beyond your needs, just to see whether you can pull it off. Try writing the longest sentence you can, just to feel when you've stretched it to its breaking point. Do not let language box you in. Use your language to *choose* what you want to say and how you want to say it, even if that means choosing to say it obscurely.

If you are working through this book on your own, go slowly.

Devoured in large pieces, it will be indigestible. It does not have the leisurely pace of an amiable essay that you can read in a sitting or two. Take the lessons a section at a time, up to the exercises. Do the exercises; find someone else's writing to edit; then edit some of your own that you wrote a while ago. You will be surprised at how much worse it has gotten since you wrote it. Then look hard at what you've written today. Look first for elements in your writing that are addressed by the lesson you are on. Then go through it again, looking for another point, and if you have the time, again for others. If you try to revise everything at once, a sentence will dissolve into a confusion of words.

As you learn these principles, you may find that at first, you are writing more slowly. That's inevitable. Anytime we reflect on what we are doing as we do it, we become self-conscious, sometimes to the point of paralysis. It will pass. But in fact, you can avoid that paralysis if you remember that the principles offered here have little to do with how to write a *first* draft. I don't have the faintest idea how to teach anyone to draft a clear and graceful sentence off the top of the head. I think I know how to teach you to revise a first draft sentence into one that is clear, and with some work, even graceful. So don't try to apply the principles during that creative moment when you are struggling to get words on the screen or on paper. When you draft from scratch, produce whatever you can as quickly as you can. Then start the most productive part of the writing task—revising.

To Teachers

This book addresses only one aspect of composition: style. It does not take up matters of intention, invention, or all of organization. Nor is this book intended for basic writers. I intend it to be a short book that focuses on a problem that *mature* writers wrestle with: a wordy, tangled, indirect prose style. I know that many undergraduates have a different problem—a style characterized by one fifteen-word sentence after another. But that problem does not endure for long. I have yet to meet an adult writer whose major problem was a style as immature as it was in his or her basic composition course.

You might object that there is still no reason to address a problem that does not yet afflict your students. Three points: First, dealing with this matter now prepares them to deal with it later. Second, by writing out revisions in the exercises, students will feel what it is like to write a sentence longer than ten or fifteen words. Copy and imitation, time-honored ways of teaching writing, help less advanced students feel the rhythm and movement of a long but clear sentence. If we cannot lead our students through what they are supposed to learn to do, we should not be surprised when they do not learn to do it. And third, by analyzing and revising examples of mature prose, students come to realize that their failure to understand what they are reading may result not from their lack of intelligence or reading ability, but from the failure of those who do not write clearly. And when students realize that they can revise turgid professional prose into something more readable, they experience a sense of empowerment that is both exhilarating and liberating.

All this is intended to anticipate an objection that some readers of earlier editions have made: The material is appropriate for advanced students but too difficult for first year students, even those who already write reasonably well. They assert that their students do not understand some of the terms I use here, even that they have never heard of some of them. I understand how severely underprepared many students are in matters of style and grammar. And true, I do use terms of grammar here, even some new ones. But I have always assumed that we are in the business of teaching students what they do not know, and that if they do not know what *subject, verb, predicate,* and *object* mean, we tell them. If we are teaching beyond the banalities, we can no more avoid using new terms than a physicist can avoid using terms such as *lepton, quark,* or *charmed particle.* In fact, nouns and verbs are substantially easier to understand than chemical reactions or double-entry bookkeeping.

Those of you who have followed the incarnations of this book will recognize that its organization is almost back where it started. I have been persuaded that the lesson on Concision should follow the material on agents and actions. I have split the lesson on agents and actions into two, because it has grown with material that I hope teachers and students will find useful. It addresses the matter of why good writers can seem to lose their style when they are writing about complex matters in a new field. I have deleted the lesson on cutting down long sentences but incorporated parts of it into the lesson on managing long sentences. I have also replaced a good many of the more difficult exercises with new ones. I was also persuaded that the lesson on Correctness should come earlier.

In that lesson, I again may disconcert a few readers by claiming that some widely promulgated "rules" of usage may not be as widely observed by careful writers as some might think or wish. I did not base that lesson on quirky notions of personal usage, but on a good deal of reading aimed at finding whether those "rules" have any force among careful writers. I can only assert that in the writing of excellent writers, there are a good many singular *datas,* a good many *which*es for *that*s, a good many prepositions at the ends of sentences, split infinitives, sentences beginning with *and.* Indeed, all these so-called violations of good usage appear in books that have been scrupulously edited.

Some readers will notice that I discuss a point of style in one lesson, then return to it in later lessons. That redundancy is intended. Some of these matters are difficult to grasp on first reading, so I decided to approach them from different points of view, sometimes three or four times.

So many have provided support that I cannot possibly thank them all. But I must begin with my English 194 students, who, many years ago, put up with hundreds of badly typed and faintly dittoed pages and with a teacher who was at times as puzzled as they. Their interest compensated for the hours spent on their papers. They were a pleasure to teach, and their comments about the importance of what they have learned have been gratifying. I am still grateful to them all.

I have considerable intellectual debts to those who have broken ground in psycholinguistics, text linguistics, discourse analysis, functional sentence perspective, and so on. Those of you who keep up with such matters will recognize the influence of Charles Fillmore, Jan Firbas, Nils Enkvist, Michael Halliday, Noam Chomsky, Thomas Bever, Vic Yngve, and others. I know I have been influenced by Robert Graves and Alan Hodge, H. W. Fowler, H. L. Mencken, and surely by E. B. White. I would like to think that I have made explicit what Mr. White advised writers to do and what he himself did for so long. Maine air must be, I think, a powerful astringent to style. More recently, the work of Eleanore Rosch has provided an explanation for why verbs should be actions, why subjects should be doers and what the sentence should be "about." Her work on prototype semantics is a powerful theoretical account for the kind of style I urge here.

I am grateful to colleagues who have taken time from their own busy lives to read the work of another. At such times, the word *community* in Community of Scholars takes on a special meaning. Whatever quality this book may have is due in large part to their care, time, and energy. For reading earlier versions of this book, I must thank in particular Randy Berlin, Ken Bruffee, Douglas Butturff, Donald Byker, Bruce Campbell, Elaine Chaika, Avon Crismore, Constance Gefvert, Maxine Hairston, George Hoffman, Ted Lowe, Susan Miller, Neil Nakadate, Mike Pownall, Peter Priest, Margaret Shaklee, Nancy Sommers, Mary Taylor, and Stephen Witte.

For this edition, I must thank the following reviewers for their thoughtful and useful feedback: Lydia Fakundiny, Pamela Gardner, Rodney Keller, Charles Lave, Sarah Liggett, Shirley W. Logan, Linda R. Mahin, Celest Martin, Janet Marting, Lisa J. McClure, Christina Murphy, Carol S. Olsen, Carol Pippen, Karen Rodis, Jan Spyridakis, James Stokes, Bill Whaley, and Bob Winters. I would like to acknowledge the assistance of Frederick C. Mish, editorial director, G. & C. Merriam Company, in locating the best examples of three citations in the lesson on Usage. I would like to acknowledge that Charles Bazerman's work on the Crick and Watson papers led me to the first paragraph of their DNA paper. I have used Bill vande Kopple's Hart Queen paragraph in Lesson Six. Also thanks to Mike Day.

The editors of HarperCollins have saved me from more than a few stylistic gaffes. Dave Ebbitt's editing pen appears not to have lost its sharp point. I would like to thank most profoundly the editor who first urged me to write this book, Harriett Prentiss, and my current editor, Jane Kinney, who has certainly preserved her steely good humor in the face of my often less than delicate requests. And my thanks to Marisa L. L'Heureux, who has skillfully guided this edition from the soft copy of the third edition to what you now hold in your hands.

For several years now, I have had the special fortune to work closely with three who have been both good colleagues and good friends: Greg Colomb, Frank Kinahan, and Don Freeman. Don's exquisitely careful reading saved me from more than a few howlers here, and I am indebted to him for the quote from William Blake in Lesson Eight. It has been a pleasure and a privilege to work with them for many years, and I value their friendship highly. Frank's untimely death leaves us all the poorer.

And again, the five who by their inimitable styles have contributed so much to the quality of my life: Oliver, Megan, Joe, Dave, and Chris.

And still at beginning and end, Joan. If I knew the secrets of her patience and good judgment, I could write a book that would make us all rich.

J.M.W. April 1993

CONTENTS

Lesson One

Understanding Style

Essentially style resembles good manners. It comes of endeavouring to understand others, of thinking for them rather than yourself—or thinking, that is, with the heart as well as the head.
SIR ARTHUR QUILLER-COUCH

Have something to say, and say it as clearly as you can. That is the only secret of style.
MATTHEW ARNOLD

Everything that can be thought at all can be thought clearly. Everything that can be said can be said clearly.
LUDWIG WITTGENSTEIN

Most people won't realize that writing is a craft. You have to take your apprenticeship in it like anything else.
KATHERINE ANNE PORTER

The great enemy of clear language is insincerity.
GEORGE ORWELL

In matters of grave importance, style, not sincerity, is the vital thing.
OSCAR WILDE

PRINCIPLES AND AIMS

This book is based on two principles: it's good to write clearly, and anyone can. Few would argue with the first, least of all those who have to read much prose like this:

> Better evaluation of responses to different treatment modalities depends on the development and standardization of an index allowing accurate descriptions of learning disorder behaviors.

But that second one may seem optimistic to those who hide their ideas not only from their readers, but sometimes even from themselves. Hard as they struggle, they can't get closer to this:

> We could better evaluate how those with learning disorders respond to different treatments if we could develop and standardize an index that accurately describes how they behave.

Your prose can fail for reasons more serious than its style, of course. It will confuse your readers if your subject confuses you. Your explanations will bewilder them if you do not prepare them to understand new and complex ideas. Your arguments will fail to persuade them if you do not anticipate disagreements with your most contestable claims. But as important as those problems are, this book addresses a different matter: Once you've gathered information and thought it through, once you've formulated your claims and supported them with good reasons, you still have to express yourself in a style that is readable. Before readers can decide whether to agree with a claim, they have to understand it.

That's the aim of this book: to explain how to overcome a problem that has afflicted generations of writers—a style that, instead of revealing ideas, hides them. When we find that kind of writing in government regulations and directives, we call it *bureaucratese*; when we find it in contracts and judicial pronouncements, *legalese*; in scholarly articles and books that inflate modest ideas into gassy abstractions, *academese*. It is the style of pretension and intimidation. It is a kind of writing that a democratic society cannot tolerate as the standard of its public discourse.

Unfortunately, since it is also a style so common that it seems to bespeak institutional success, many writers adopt it not because they want to hide anything, but because by reading so much of it, they eventually learn to imitate it. It is an old problem in the English-speaking world. Though we have been graced with many clear and graceful writers, we have had to endure too many more who were not. The reasons are both historical and private.

A SHORT HISTORY OF UNCLEAR WRITING

The Past

It was in the late sixteenth century that English writers finally decided that our language was respectable enough to replace Latin and French as England's institutional language, but their first impulses toward elegance led them to a style complex beyond the needs of their readers:

> If use and custom, having the help of so long time and continuance wherein to [re]fine our tongue, of so great learning and experience which furnish matter for the [re]fining, of so good wits and judgments which can tell how to refine, have griped at nothing in all that time, with all that cunning, by all those wits which they will not let go but hold for most certain in the right of our writing, that then our tongue has no certainty to trust to, but write all at random.
>
> —Richard Mulcaster, *The First Part of the Elementary,* 1582

Within a century, this inflated style had spread to scientific writing. Shortly after some British natural philosophers (as scientists were then called) founded the Royal Society, its first historian complained,

> ... of all the studies of men, nothing may sooner be obtained than this vicious abundance of phrase, this trick of metaphors, this volubility of tongue which makes so great a noise in the world ...
>
> —Thomas Sprat, *History of the Royal Society,* 1667

When the New World was settled, American writers had a chance to create a new prose, not viciously voluble, but lean and direct. They let the chance slip. By the early nineteenth century, James Fenimore Cooper was complaining that "the common faults of American language are an ambition of effect, a want of simplicity, and a turgid abuse of terms":

> ... The love of turgid expressions is gaining ground, and ought to be corrected. One of the most certain evidences of a man of high breeding, is his simplicity of speech: a simplicity that is equally removed from vulgarity and exaggeration. ... He does not say, in speaking of a dance, that "the attire of the ladies was exceedingly elegant and peculiarly becoming at the late assembly," but that "the women were well dressed at the last ball"; nor is he apt to remark, "that the Rev. Mr. G—gave us an elegant and searching discourse the past sabbath," but that "the parson preached a good sermon last sunday."
> The utterance of a gentleman ought to be deliberate and clear, without being measured. ... Simplicity should be the firm aim, after one is removed from vulgarity, and let the finer shades of accomplishment be acquired as they can be attained. In no case, however, can one who aims at turgid language, exaggerated sentiments, or pedantic utterances, lay claim to be either a man or a woman of the world.
> —James Fenimore Cooper, *The American Democrat,* 1838

Unfortunately, Cooper himself seemed unable to resist abusing his own terms, for his style is a model of that which he condemned. He criticized "The attire of the ladies was elegant," but echoed that construction in his next sentence: "The utterance of a gentleman ought to be deliberate." Had he followed his own advice, he might have written this:

> We should discourage writers who love turgid language. A well-bred person speaks simply, in a way that is neither vulgar nor exaggerated ... We should not measure our words, but speak them deliberately and clearly. After we rid our language of vulgarity, we should aim at simplicity and then as we can, acquire the finer shades of accomplishment. No one can claim to be a man or woman of the world who exaggerates sentiments or deliberately speaks in language that is turgid or pedantic.

About 50 years later, Mark Twain wrote what we now like to think is classic American prose—clear, concise, direct.

> There have been daring people in the world who claimed that Cooper could write English, but they are all dead now—all dead but Lounsbury. I don't remember that Lounsbury makes the claim in so many words, still he makes it, for he says that *Deerslayer* is a "pure work of art." Pure, in that connection, means faultless—faultless in all details—and language is a detail. If Mr. Lounsbury had only compared Cooper's English with the English which he writes himself—but it is plain that he didn't; and so it is likely that he imagines until this day that Cooper's [style] is as clean and compact as his own. Now I feel sure, deep down in my heart, that Cooper wrote about the poorest English that exists in our language, and that the English of *Deerslayer* is the very worst tha[t] even Cooper ever wrote.

Many admire Twain's style, but too few have followed his example.

The Present

In the best-known essay on English style, "Politics and the English Language," George Orwell anatomized the language of twentieth-century politicians, bureaucrats, and other chronic dodgers of responsibility:

> The keynote [of a pretentious style] is the elimination of simple verbs. Instead of being a single word, such as *break, stop, spoil, mend, kill,* a verb becomes a *phrase,* made up of a noun or adjective tacked on to some general-purposes verb such as *prove, serve, form, play, render.* In addition, the passive voice is wherever possible used in preference to the active, and noun constructions are used instead of gerunds (*by examination of* instead of *by examining*). The range of verbs is further cut down by means of the *-ize* and *de-*formations, and the banal statements are given an appearance of profundity by means of the *not un-*formation.

But in the act of skewering that style, Orwell, like Cooper, modeled it. Had *he* avoided making a VERB a phrase (capitalized words are

defined in the Glossary), had *he* avoided the PASSIVE, had *he* avoided
NOUN constructions, he would have written something closer to this:

> Those who write pretentiously eliminate simple verbs. Instead of
> using one word, such as *break, stop, spoil, mend, kill,* they turn a
> verb into a noun or adjective and then tack it on to a general-purpose
> verb such as *prove, serve, form, play, render.* Wherever possible, they
> use the passive voice instead of the active and noun constructions
> instead of gerunds (*by examination* instead of *by examining*). They
> cut down the range of verbs further with *-ize* and *de-,* and try to make
> banal statements seem profound by the *not un*-formation.

If, in the act of condemning this style, Orwell could not avoid it
(I do not think he was trying to be ironic), we ought not be surprised
that today's academic and professional writers fare worse. On the language of the social sciences:

> . . . a turgid and polysyllabic prose does seem to prevail in the
> social sciences. . . . Such a lack of ready intelligibility, I believe,
> usually has little or nothing to do with the complexity of
> thought. It has to do almost entirely with certain confusions of
> the academic writer about his own status.
> —C. Wright Mills, *The Sociological Imagination*

On the language of medicine:

> It now appears that obligatory obfuscation is a firm tradition
> within the medical profession . . . [Medical writing] is a highly
> skilled, calculated attempt to confuse the reader. . . . A doctor
> feels he might get passed over for an assistant professorship
> because he wrote his papers too clearly—because he made his
> ideas seem too simple.
> —Michael Crichton, *New England Journal of Medicine*

On the language of law:

> . . . in law journals, in speeches, in classrooms and in court-
> rooms, lawyers and judges are beginning to worry about how
> often they have been misunderstood, and they are discovering
> that sometimes they cannot even understand each other.
> —Tom Goldstein, *New York Times*

Students first confront this kind of writing when they struggle through the prose in some of their textbooks. Here is a passage that is clearer than many, but less readable than it might have been:

> Recognition of the fact that systems [of grammar] differ from one language to another can serve as the basis for serious consideration of the problems confronting translators of the great works of world literature originally written in a language other than English.

That is, in fewer words,

> When we recognize that languages have different grammars, we can consider the problems of those who translate great works of literature into English.

Generations of students have labored through their readings, often blaming themselves because they thought they could not read well enough or were not smart enough to understand seemingly complex ideas. Some of them have been right about that, but most of them could have blamed the authors they were trying to understand. Some students, sad to say, give up, but sadder yet, many who learn to read that style also learn to imitate it and then go on to write their own books in the same way, causing more grief to more students, some of whom master that same turgid style and go on to write yet more books . . . Thus the style of each generation insinuates itself into the writing of the next.

SOME PRIVATE CAUSES OF BAD WRITING

Hiding Behind Language

But if the institutional causes of unclear English go back almost 500 years, other causes spring from motives more immediate and private. Michael Crichton mentioned one: Some writers use complicated language not only to dress up their thinking, but to mask its absence, hoping that opacity will impress those who confuse difficulty with substance. Others use intimidating language to protect what they have from those who want a piece of it—the power and privilege that go with the ruling class. We conceal ideas by locking them up, but we can also hide them behind a style so impenetrable that only those trained to read and endure it can find them.

Bad Memories

Others among us write badly because they are gripped by the memory of someone who thought writing was good only when it was free from those errors that only a teacher of grammar could understand: fused genitives, dangling participles, split infinitives, and other exotic *disjecta membra*. Too many of us now approach a blank page not as an occasion for discovery, but as a minefield to be traversed gingerly. We inch our way from word to word, concerned less with clarity and precision than with sheer survival.

Temporary Aphasia

Finally, some of us write obscurely not because we intend to or because we never learned to write better, but because we feel we are in the grip of a kind of stylistic aphasia, a dismaying experience during which we can no longer write as well as we thought we once could, or at all. This typically happens when we write about matters that we do not understand, for readers who do. We are most afflicted when we are learning to think and write in a new academic or professional area, for a new "community of discourse." The afflicted include not just undergraduates taking their first course in economics or psychology or philosophy, but graduate students, business people, doctors, lawyers, professors—anyone who has ever written about knowledge that seems new and intimidating. As we struggle to master unfamiliar ideas, many of us, perhaps most of us, have to pass through a period of stylistic affliction. Our floundering may dismay us less when we understand that we are experiencing an anguish shared by countless others. We usually discover that we are able to write about a subject more clearly when we more clearly understand it.

There is in all of this, of course, a great irony: When we have to write about a subject that we are struggling to understand, we are likely to write about it in confusing ways. But when we struggle with an article or book not only because its subject matter is intrinsically difficult, but also because it is expressed in a gratuitously difficult style, we too often assume that the complexity of the style reflects the complexity of the ideas, and so we make that style the model of our own prose, confounding our own already confused writing even further.

The point of this book is to cut through that confusion.

Once we understand how confused writing reflects confused thinking, we may be able to think more clearly by writing more clearly. Few of us express ourselves well in a first draft. When we revise that early confusion into something clearer, we understand our ideas better. And when we understand our ideas better, we express them more clearly, and when we express them more clearly, we understand them better . . . and so it goes, until we run out of energy, interest, or time. For a fortunate few, that moment comes weeks, months, even years after they begin. For the rest of us, it's closer to tomorrow morning. And so we have to be satisfied with an essay or report that is less than perfect, but still does the job—a document that our readers will feel is not just correct, but as readable as the complexity of its subject and the time available allow. Perfection is an admirable goal, but it is the enemy of done.

It is at the point where you have something—anything—on paper that principles of style are most useful—not as you are creating your first draft, but when you are rethinking and revising it. In fact, if we had to think about principles of style *as* we wrote, we'd probably never write anything. Smart writers get something down on paper as fast as they can just so they can revise it into something clearer.

As important as clarity is, though, some occasions require more:

> Now the trumpet summons us again—not as a call to bear arms, though arms we need; not as a call to battle, though embattled we are; but a call to bear the burden of a long twilight struggle, year in and year out, "rejoicing in hope, patient in tribulation," a struggle against the common enemies of man: tyranny, poverty, disease and war itself.
>
> —John F. Kennedy, Inaugural Address, January 20, 1961

Few of us are called upon to write a Presidential Address. But we may still want even our most modest prose to be more than just readable: We have something to say that demands special dignity, or we just take pleasure in our craft, regardless whether anyone notices. That is the object of our last lesson.

About 50 years ago, H. L. Mencken wrote,

> With precious few exceptions, all the books on style in English are by writers quite unable to write. The subject, indeed, seems to exercise a special and dreadful fascination over school ma'ams, bucolic college professors, and other such pseudoliterates ... Their central aim, of course, is to reduce the whole thing to a series of simple rules—the overmastering passion of their melancholy order, at all times and everywhere.

That melancholy judgment has hovered over every sentence I've written here. Mencken was right: No one can teach good writing by rule, simple or not, especially to those who have nothing to say and no reason to say it, to those who cannot feel or think or see.

But I know that many of us do see clearly, and feel deeply, and think carefully, but cannot write well enough to share those visions and feelings and thoughts. I also know that when we write clearly, we are better able to think and feel and see, and that in fact there are a few simple principles—not rules—that help.

Here they are.

Lesson Two

Correctness

God does not much mind bad grammar,
but He does not take any particular pleasure in it.
ERASMUS

It is not the business of grammar, as some critics seem
preposterously to imagine, to give law to the fashions which
regulate our speech. On the contrary, from its conformity to
these, and from that alone, it derives all its authority and value.
GEORGE CAMPBELL

No grammatical rules have sufficient authority to control the firm
and established usage of language. Established custom, in speaking
and writing, is the standard to which we must at last resort for
determining every controverted point in language and style.
HUGH BLAIR

English usage is sometimes more than mere taste, judgment, and
education—sometimes it's sheer luck, like getting across the street.
E. B. WHITE

CHOICE VS. OBEDIENCE

In later lessons, we will examine principles of style that can help you write clearly, even gracefully. Those principles do not demand obedience; they suggest ways to recognize choices and then to choose well. For example, which of these sentences seems the clearest?

1. There was a lack of sufficiency of evidentiary support for their claim.
2. Their claim lacked a sufficiency of supporting evidence.
3. They lacked sufficient evidence to support their claim.

Most of us choose (3), but (1) and (2) are not grammatically wrong, only less direct than we might prefer. But before we consider these kinds of choices, we should address a matter that some writers and teachers think is even more important. It is the matter of "correctness."

We must write correct English. But we must also understand that some points of grammar and usage are less important than many think (in fact, are not important at all) and that a writer who obsesses on usage can write in ways that are entirely correct but wholly unreadable. So we are going to consider this matter of correctness before that of clarity not because "good usage" is the first characteristic of good writing, but because we should to put it in its place—behind us—before we move on to more important matters.

Unlike matters of style, this question of correctness seems to address not choice, but obedience. When the *American Heritage Dictionary* says that *irregardless* is "nonstandard ... never acceptable" (except, they say, when we're trying to be funny), the choice between *regardless* and *irregardless* seems at best academic. It is not a question of better and worse, but of right and of utterly, irredeemably, unequivocally, existentially Wrong.

That simplifies things: "correctness" does not require good taste or sound judgment, only a good memory. If you remember that *irregardless* is always Wrong, its possible choice ought never rise to even the lowest level of your consciousness. The same would seem true for dozens of other "rules":

Don't use double negatives.
Don't begin a sentence with *and* or *but.*

Don't end a sentence with a PREPOSITION.
Don't split INFINITIVES.

Unfortunately, questions of correctness are not settled so easily: Many of the rules that some of us may remember are not linguistic fact, but classroom folklore, invented by eighteenth-century grammarians out of whole cloth, taught by those who repeat what they find in textbooks, and are now enforced by many among us, despite the fact that some of those rules are ignored by respected writers everywhere. Other rules are imperatives that we violate at the risk of seeming at least careless, at worst illiterate. Those rules are observed by even the less-than-best writers. And then there are rules that we may observe or not, depending on the effect we want.

REASONS FOR RULES

Two Extreme Views

There are divided opinions about the social role of Standard English and the rules that allegedly define it. To some, Standard English is just another stratagem invented by one class to repress another: a standard grammar helps keep the underclasses under. To others, Standard English is the final product of a sifting and winnowing conducted by generations of grammarians, a kind of managed linguistic Darwinism whose outcome is the best of all possible forms of English, now captured in rules that are observed by the best writers everywhere.

Both views are right, partly. The radical critics are right in that Standard English did arise from impulses toward control. For centuries, some have always believed that "errors" in grammar can identify those who are unwilling or unable to learn diligence, self-discipline, and obedience—the values that those who manage our institutions look for in those whom they screen for admission. And the conservatives are right: many features of Standard English did originate in efficiencies of expression. For example, we no longer need the elaborate verb endings that writers used a thousand years ago, and so we now omit present tense endings in five of six contexts:

I leave + 0	*you* (sg.) *leave* + 0,	*she leave* + **S**
we leave + 0	*you* (pl.) *leave* + 0,	*they leave* + 0.

So by that measure, the -*s* in, "You know**S** him," seems not just ungrammatical, but redundant and therefore in the nature of things inherently Wrong.

A MORE REASONED VIEW

The history and logic of Standard English are more complicated.

Historical Accidents

The radical critics are wrong when they claim that Standard English was *devised* to achieve socially vicious ends. Linguistic standards arise from historical accidents of social geography and political power. When a society is marked by differences in regional dialects and regional prestige (usually grounded in wealth), the most prestigious dialect will predictably be that of its most prestigious region, and that most prestigious dialect is likely to become the basis for that society's standard form of writing. Thus if a thousand years ago, Scotland had been closer to the Continent than was London and had developed great ports and become the center of Britain's economic and literary life, it is likely that Standard English today would resemble the English not of London but of Edinburgh.

But the conservative critics are also wrong when they claim that the features of Standard English today reflect an intrinsic superiority over the features of nonstandard English. It is true that many features of Standard English seem to reflect impulses toward efficiency. But most of those features are shared by speakers of all dialects, regardless of social class or geographical origin. Every speaker of Modern English, for example, enjoys (or should) the absence of nouns that are grammatically masculine, feminine, and neuter.

Illogical Logic

If Standard English is not defined by features that are historically inevitable, neither is it defined by features that are intrinsically logical, if by logical we mean regular and predictable. In fact, many features of nonstandard English are more "logical" than their corresponding features in Standard English.

— The person who says, *He knowed that* makes the same "mistake" as the first person who said, *I climbed the tree* instead of the historically correct *clum*. Both speakers apply the principle of regularity to a body of inconsistent data, an act that in any other context is taken as a sign of intelligence.

— With reflexive pronouns, we use the possessive form in *myself, ourselves, yourself, yourselves, herself,* and *its*[*s*]*elf,* so it seems "logical" (i.e., predictable) to use possessive pronouns in *hisself* and *theirselves.*

— The person who says, "I'm here, ain't I?" uses a wholly logical (and once entirely acceptable) contraction of *am* + *not:*

I am here, [am + not → ain't] ain't I?

What is illogical is the correct form—*I'm here,* **aren't** *I?,* because that *aren't* derives from an ungrammatical construction:

I am here, [are + not → aren't] aren't I?

We could point to a dozen other examples where, strictly applied, principles of logic and historical precedent should legitimize the form that we condemn as nonstandard, the form that in fact reflects a logical mind deducing and applying the principle of regularity.

I want to be clear: Though logic predicts *hisself* and *knowed* and history attests to a once respectable *ain't,* we must still reject those usages in writing intended for serious purposes, so much greater is the power of convention than of logic. But we must also reject the notion that Standard English has a natural logic or goodness or an historical inevitability that, by its nature, makes Standard English or its speakers superior to nonstandard English and its speakers. Those who want to discriminate, of course, will do so on the basis of any social difference. But since our language seems to reflect the quality of our minds more directly than do our hair styles or ZIP codes, it is easy to think that linguistic "error" is a reliable sign of mental deficiency. All of us who take language seriously must reject the idea that *accidents* of correctness connect in any way with the intrinsic goodness of language or its users. That belief is not just wrong. In a democratic society, it is destructive.

THREE KINDS OF RULES

These attitudes have been complicated further by grammarians who, in their zeal to accumulate principles of "good" English, have since the eighteenth century confounded three kinds of rules, rules that refer to the fundamental structure of English, to its standard usage, and to its most debatable points of usage, usually trivial.

1. Some rules define the fundamental grammatical structure of English—ARTICLES precede nouns: *the book,* not *book the;* verbs usually precede OBJECTS: *I see you,* not *I you see.* These rules are observed by every native speaker of English.

2. Some rules distinguish Standard from nonstandard speech: *you was* vs. *you were, I don't know nothing* vs. *I don't know anything.* The only writers who worry about these rules are those striving to join the educated class. Educated writers think about such rules only when they see them violated.

3. Finally, some grammarians have tried to impose on educated and literate people rules that they think they *should* observe. Most date from the last half of the eighteenth century:

   — don't split infinitives, as in *to quietly leave.*
   — don't use *than* after *different;* use *from.*
   — don't use *between* for *among,* when referring to three or more.

A few date from this century:

   — don't use *hopefully* for *I hope,* as in *Hopefully it won't rain.*
   — don't use *which* for *that* in RESTRICTIVE CLAUSES as in *a book **which** I bought.*

By mingling these three kinds of rules in the same book, sometimes on the same page, grammarians have led generations of writers to believe that a split infinitive is an error as important as a double negative, and that both are almost on a par with incoherent sentences.

We are going to concentrate on the third class of rules, because they are the only ones that cause educated writers anxiety. They are the rules whose "violation" Pop-grammarians endlessly rehearse as evidence for the Decline of Western Values. But since such grammarians have for centuries been accusing educated writers of violating these rules, we have to conclude that educated writers have for centuries been ignoring both rules and grammarians. Which has been lucky for the grammarians, because if educated writers did obey all the rules that all the grammarians invented, grammarians would have to keep inventing new ones.

The fact is that some educated and careful writers honor every rule; most observe fewer; and a few know all the rules, but also that they need to observe only certain ones, and that other rules they can observe or ignore as they choose. What do those of us do who want not only to write well, but to be thought of as "correct?"

ON OBSERVING RULES THOUGHTFULLY

The Worst (i.e., Safest) Case Policy

We could adopt the worst-case policy: follow all the rules all the time because somewhere, sometime, someone might criticize us for something—for beginning a sentence with *and* or ending it with *up*. And so with a stack of grammar books and usage manuals close by, or with a grammar-checker booted up on a computer, we scrutinize every sentence for "errors," until we learn the rules so well that we obey them without thought. But if we decide to follow all the rules all the time, we surrender a measure of stylistic flexibility. Worse, we may find ourselves so obsessed with rules that we tie ourselves—and our writing—into knots. And sooner or later, we will begin to impose those rules—real or not—on others. After all, what good is learning a rule if all we can do is obey it?

A More Thoughtful (but Riskier) Approach

The alternative to blind obedience is selective observance. But selectivity has its problems. First, you must learn which rules to observe, which to ignore, and which to observe or ignore as you choose. Second, you have to deal with those whose passion for good grammar seems to give them a moral upper hand: they seem dedicated to precise usage and able to identify in violations like "between you and me" sure signs of moral decay.

If you want to avoid being labeled "permissive," or worse "without standards," but if you also don't want to submit mindlessly to whatever "rule" someone can recall from ninth grade English, you have to know more about the rules than do the rule-mongers. For example, some teachers and editors chide those who would begin a sentence with *and* or *but.* For matters of this kind, it is useful to refer to the most conservative guide to British English (the preferred standard for most conservative American critics): H. W. Fowler's *A Dictionary of Modern English Usage* (first edition, Oxford University Press, 1926; second edition, 1965). The second edition was edited by Sir Ernest Gowers, who added this to Fowler's original entry on *and:*

> That it is a solecism to begin a sentence with *and* is a faintly lingering superstition. (p. 29)

To the original entry for *but,* Gowers added ". . . see *and.*"

Look also under Fetishes, Illiteracies, Superstitions, and Sturdy Indefensibles. A good summary of American authorities is Roy H. Copperud, *American Usage and Style: The Consensus* [Van Nostrand Reinhold Company, New York, 1980].

The Final Arbiter: Habits of the Literate

To be sure, every good writer commits an occasional error. We all have slipped up on the number for a verb distant from its subject, and when someone points it out, we gratefully correct it. But we must reject as folklore any rule that is regularly and unselfconsciously ignored by educated and intelligent writers and by equally intelligent readers. If otherwise careful writers begin sentences with *but* and the vast majority of careful readers don't notice, then regardless of what any teacher or editor says, beginning a sentence with *but* cannot be a grammatical error.

On the basis of two principles—how the best writers regularly and unselfconsciously write, and how their best readers respond—we can sort rules of usage into these three categories:

1. Real Rules. When we violate these rules, our educated readers notice and condemn. These are the rules of Standard Usage.
2. Folklore. When we violate these "rules," few if any educated readers notice, much less condemn. So these are not rules at all, but

folklore that we can ignore, unless those we are writing for have the power to exact from us whatever kind of writing they like.

3. Optional Rules. When we violate these rules, few readers notice, but when we observe them, some careful readers do. We can observe these rules or not, depending on how we wish to affect those for whom we are writing.

1. REAL RULES

The most important rules are those whose violation stigmatizes a person as a writer of nonstandard English.

1. Double negatives: The car had **hardly no** systematic care.
2. Nonstandard verbs: They **knowed** what would happen.
3. Double comparatives: This way is **more quicker.**
4. Some ADJECTIVES for ADVERBS: They worked **real good.**
5. Some incorrect pronouns: **Him and me** will study it.
6. Some subject-verb disagreements. **We was** ready to begin.

These and others are so egregious that literate writers never knowingly violate them, unless they are trying to be funny. They are rules whose violations we instantly notes, but whose observance we entirely ignore. (Among this group, some require discrimination: see faulty parallelism (pp. 169–70), dangling modifiers (pp. 183–84), and comma splices (p. 195).

2. FOLKLORE

A second group of rules includes those whose observance we do not remark, but whose violation we do not remark either. In fact, these are not rules, but folklore, enforced by many editors and schoolteachers, but ignored by most educated and careful writers.

The advice that follows I have based on a good deal of prose that was carefully written and intended to be read just as carefully. The quotations that illustrate "violations" of these alleged rules are from writers who are of substantial intellectual and scholarly stature or

who, on matters of usage, are arch-conservatives (occasionally both).
You may never have heard of some of these "rules," but even if you
have not yet met someone who has invoked one, chances are that you
will.

1. Never begin a sentence with *and* or *but.* Allegedly, not this (a
   passage that violates the "rule" twice):

> **But,** it will be asked, is tact not an individual gift, therefore
> highly variable in its choices? **And** if that is so, what guid-
> ance can a manual offer, other than that of its author's
> prejudices—mere impressionism?
>
> —Wilson Follett, *Modern American Usage: A Guide,*
>   edited and completed by Jacques Barzun et al.

The vast majority of highly regarded writers of nonfictional prose
begin sentences with *and* or *but,* some more than once a page.

Some especially insecure writers also think that they should not
begin sentences with *because:*

> **Because** we have access to so much historical fact, today
> we know a good deal about changes within the humanities
> which were not apparent to those of any age much before
> our own and which the individual scholar must constantly
> reflect on.
>
> —Walter Ong, S.J., "The Expanding Humanities and the
>   Individual Scholar," PMLA

They would prefer either of these:

> We have access to so much historical fact, **so** today we . . .

> We have access to much historical fact. **Consequently** we . . .

This proscription appears in no handbook, but it is gaining popular currency. It must stem from advice intended to avoid
sentence FRAGMENTS like this one.

> The application was rejected. **Because** the deadline had passed.

When we attach this introductory *because*-clause to a MAIN
CLAUSE and punctuate the two as a single PUNCTUATED SEN-
TENCE, the introductory *because* is correct:

> Because the deadline has passed, the application was rejected.

A more recent variation on this theme is a suspicion that we should not begin a sentence with a preposition, either.

In the morning, everyone left.

This kind of folklore results from overgeneralizing the "rule" about ending sentences with prepositions and perhaps the mistaken belief about *because.* It is a "rule" with utterly no substance.

2. Use the RELATIVE PRONOUN *that*—not *which*—for restrictive clauses; use *which* for NON-RESTRICTIVE CLAUSES. Allegedly, not this:

> Next is a typical situation **which** a practiced writer corrects "for style" virtually by reflex action.
> —Jacques Barzun, *Simple and Direct,* p. 69.

Yet on just the previous page, Barzun himself had written, "In conclusion, I recommend using *that* with defining clauses except when stylistic reasons interpose." (No stylistic reasons interposed.) A rule can have no force when a writer as prestigious as Jacques Barzun asserts it in print and then immediately and unselfconsciously violates it, and his editors and proofreaders and he himself never catch it.

This point of usage first saw light of day in 1906 in Henry and Francis Fowler's *The King's English* (Oxford University Press; reprinted as an Oxford University Press paperback, 1973). Henry and his brother Francis recommended the rule, because they thought that the random variation between *which* and *that* in restrictive clauses was messy. So they simply announced that writers should (with some exceptions) limit *which* to non-restrictive clauses.

A non-restrictive clause describes a noun that a reader can already identify unambiguously. In this position, *which* enjoys the full support of historical and contemporary usage:

> Abco ended its bankruptcy, **which** it had announced earlier.

Since a company can usually have only one bankruptcy at a time, a reader identifies it unambiguously as the only bankruptcy in question, and so the writer puts a comma before the modifying clause and begins the clause with *which.*

But, according to the brothers Fowler, we should use only *that* to introduce a *restrictive* relative clause, a clause identifying a noun phrase that [not *which*] a reader cannot identify unambiguously:

> Abco developed a product **that** [*not* **which**] made money.

If Abco has many products and the reader does not know the particular product the writer was referring to, then the identifying clause singles out that product from an indefinite set of other products. And so the writer does not put a comma before the modifying clause, and, at least according to the Fowlers, should begin the clause with *that.*

But this "rule" did not then and does not now enjoy the support of either historical or contemporary usage. Francis died in 1918, but Henry continued the family tradition with *A Dictionary of Modern English Usage.* In that landmark reference work, he devoted more than a page to discussing the fine points of *which* and *that,* and then, perhaps a bit wistfully, added this:

> Some there are who follow this principle now; but it would be idle to pretend that it is the practice either of most or of the best writers. (p. 635)

That observation was apparently judged still relevant to our own usage, because it was retained by the editor of Fowler's second edition.

3. Use *fewer* with nouns that you can count, *less* with quantities you cannot. Allegedly not this:

> I can remember no **less** than five occasions when the correspondence columns of *The Times* rocked with volleys of letters from the academic profession protesting that academic freedom is in danger and the future of scholarship threatened.
> —Noel Gilroy Annan, Lord Annan. "Thee Life of the Mind in British Universities Today," *ACLS Newsletter*

We never use *fewer* before uncountable singular nouns: *fewer sand,* but educated writers use *less* before plural nouns: *less problems.*

4. There is a handful of words commonly used in ways proscribed by some conservative critics, who are ignored by most careful writers.

Most careful writers do not restrict *since* to refer to an earlier point in time (*We've been here* since *Friday*) but use it with a meaning close to "We take for granted (and hope that you will too) the truth of the proposition following this word *since*":

Since we agree on the matter, we need not discuss it further.

Careful writers use *while* in the same way. They do not restrict it to its temporal meaning (*We'll wait* while *you eat*), but use it as well with a meaning close to "The fact that I state in this clause is true right now, but what I assert in the next simultaneously qualifies it":

While we agree on the problems, we disagree about solutions.

Though some critics insist that *data* and *media* must always be plural, many careful writers use them as singulars, in the same way they treat *agenda* and *insignia* as singular (*agendum* and *insigne* were the original singulars). Careful writers and careful readers distinguish between the plural forms, *strata, errata,* and *criteria* and their singular forms, *stratum, erratum,* and *criterion.*

Careful writers use *anticipate* to mean "expect"; *alternative* to refer to one of not just two, but three or more choices; *contact* as a general verb meaning "enter into communication with." Editors of some dictionaries who base their decisions on the usage of careful writers countenance *infer* for *imply* and *disinterested* for *uninterested.* Many teachers and editors disagree. So do I.

A nice point about *disinterested,* though: Its original meaning was, in fact, that of today's *uninterested.* Only in the eighteenth century did *disinterested* begin to mean "impartial." Some critics like to cite this newer usage to claim that those who use *disinterested* to mean *uninterested* encourage the demise of English. Right or wrong, the recalcitrant survival of *disinterested* in its original sense shows just how durable our language really is.

On the most formal of occasions, when you would want to avoid a hint of offending anyone who might believe in any of these alleged rules, you might decide to observe them all. In ordinary circumstances, though, these "rules" are ignored by most careful writers, which is to say that these rules are not rules at all, but folklore. If you adopt the worst-case approach and observe them all, all the time—well, private virtues are their own reward.

3. OPTIONAL RULES

These rules complement the Real Rules: Few readers notice when you violate these Optional Rules, but most readers will notice when you observe them and assume that you are signalling special formality.

1. "Do not split infinitives." Some purists would condemn Dwight MacDonald, a linguistic arch-conservative, for this:

   > . . . one wonders why Dr. Gove and his editors did not think of labelling *knowed* as substandard right where it occurs, and one suspects that they wanted **to *slightly* conceal** the fact or at any rate to put off its exposure as long as decently possible.
   >
   > —"The String Untuned," *The New Yorker*

   They would require this:

   > One wonders why Dr. Gove and his editors did not think of labelling *knowed* as substandard right where it occurs, and one suspects that they wanted **to conceal** the fact *slightly* or at any rate to put off its exposure as long as decently possible.

   The split infinitive is now so common among the best writers that when we avoid splitting, we invite notice, whether we intend to or not.

2. "Use *shall* as the first person simple future, *will* for second and third person simple future; use *will* to mean strong intention in the first person, *shall* for second and third person." Some purists would condemn F. L. Lucas, a highly regarded writer on matters of style, for this:

   > **I will** end with two remarks by two wise old women of the civilized eighteenth century.
   >
   > —"What Is Style?" *Holiday*

They would demand:

> **I shall** end with two remarks by two wise old women of the civilized eighteenth century.

They would be right, only if they needed some special formality.

3. "Use *whom* as the object of a verb or preposition." Purists would condemn William Zinsser for this:

> Soon after you confront this matter of preserving your identity, another question will occur to you: "**Who** am I writing for?"
>
> —*On Writing Well*

They would insist on:

> Soon after you confront this matter of preserving your identity, another question will occur to you: "**For whom** am I writing?"

Whom is a small but distinct flag of self-conscious correctness. And when a writer makes the wrong choice, it is a sign of anxiety.

The rule: The form of the pronoun *whom/who* depends on whether it is a subject or an object *of its own clause*. This is an example of over-compensation:

> The committee must decide whom should be promoted.

In that sentence, since *whom* is the subject of the verb *should be promoted,* that *whom* should be *who.*

4. "Do not end a sentence with a preposition." Purists would condemn Sir Ernest Gowers for this:

> The peculiarities of legal English are often used as a stick to beat the official **with.**
>
> —*The Complete Plain Words*

And insist on this:

> The peculiarities of legal English are often used as a stick **with** which to beat the official.

The second is more formal, but the first is correct. Whenever we move a preposition before a *which* or *whom* we make its sentence more formal (with the obligatory *whom* compounding the formality). Compare:

> The man **with whom** I had spoken was the man **to whom** I had written.

> The man I spoke with was the man I had written to.

We must occasionally recognize that a preposition at the end of a sentence can be clumsy and weak. (See pp. 213–214.) George Orwell may have ended this next sentence with a preposition to make a point, but I suspect it just turned up there.

> [The defense of the English language] has nothing to do with archaism, with the salvaging of obsolete words and turns of speech, or with the setting up of a "standard English" which must never be departed **from.**
> —George Orwell, "Politics and the English Language"

This would have been less awkward and more emphatic:

> Defenders of English do not preserve archaisms, salvage obsolete words and turns of speech, or create rules of "standard English" that [not *which*] a writer must always obey.

5. "Do not refer to *one* with *he* or *his;* repeat *one.*" Purists would deplore Theodore Bernstein's *he:*

> Thus, unless one belongs to that tiny minority who can speak directly and beautifully, one should not write as **he** talks.
> —*The Careful Writer*

They would prefer the more formal:

> Thus, unless one belongs to that tiny minority who can speak directly and beautifully, one should not write as **one** talks.

6. "Contrary-to-fact statements require the subjunctive form of the verb." Purists would correct this by H. W. Fowler:

> Another suffix that is not a living one, but is sometimes treated as if it **was,** is *-al; &. . . .*
> —*A Dictionary of Modern English Usage*

They would insist on this:

> Another suffix that is not a living one, but is sometimes treated as if it **were,** is *-al; &. . . .*

As the subjunctive slowly sinks into the sunset of linguistic history, it gives a sentence a faintly archaic and therefore formal glow. We regularly and unselfconsciously use the simple past tense to express most subjunctives:

> If we **knew** what to do, we **would** do it.

Be is the problem: Strictly construed, the subjunctive demands *were,* but *was* is gradually replacing it:

> If this **were** 1941, a loaf of bread would cost twenty cents.
> If this **was** 1941, a loaf of bread would cost twenty cents.

Certainly, when the occasion calls for formal English, the wise writer chooses the formal usage. But the writer *chooses.*

THE BÊTES NOIRES

For some critics, a fourth group of items has become the object of particularly zealous abuse. These are the items the columnists and commentators endlessly cite as evidence that cultivated English is an endangered species. There is no explaining why these items should excite such passion, but they have become the symbolic flags around which those most concerned with linguistic purity have apparently agreed to rally. None of these "errors" interferes with clarity and concision; indeed, some of them save a word or two. But because they may arouse such intense feelings, every writer should know their special status. However real those feelings may be, though, we have to understand that these so-called rules are largely capricious, with no foundation in logic, history, etymology, or linguistic efficiency.

1. Never use *like* for *as* or *as if*. Not this:

> These operations failed **like** the earlier ones did.

But this:

> These operations failed **as** the earlier ones did.

Like became a conjunction in the eighteenth century when writers began to drop the *as* from the conjunctive phrase *like as,* leaving just *like* to serve as the conjunction. This elision of one element while keeping the other is a common linguistic change. We might note that the editor of the second edition of Fowler deleted *like* for *as* from Fowler's original list of Illiteracies and moved it into the category of Sturdy Indefensibles.

2. After *different* use *from,* never *to* or *than.* Not this:

> These numbers are **different than** the others.
>
> We solve this **differently than** we did last year.

But this:

> These numbers are **different from** the others.
>
> We solve this **differently from the way** we did last year.

This is a case where ignoring the rule can save a few words.

3. Use *hopefully* only when the subject of the sentence is in fact hopeful. Not this:

> **Hopefully,** the matter will be resolved soon.

But this:

> **I hopefully say** that the matter will be resolved soon.

This rule is so entrenched in the popular mind that it is impossible to convince some critics by evidence alone that the rule is idiosyncratic, with no basis in logic or grammar. *Hopefully* always refers to the feelings of the speaker, when used to introduce a sentence such as

Hopefully, it will not rain tomorrow

It is synonymous with,

I am hopeful when I say it will not rain tomorrow.

It is parallel to other introductory words such as *candidly, bluntly, seriously, frankly, honestly, sadly,* and *happily:*

Seriously, you must be careful
→**I am serious** when I say that you must be careful.

No one condemns a speaker who uses one of these words to describe attitude, but many deplore the exactly analogous *hopefully.* If we adopted their line of reasoning, logic would further require that we also reject all words and phrases such as *to summarize, in conclusion, finally,* and so on, because every one of them also qualifies the voice of the writer: *I summarize, I conclude, I say finally.* But just as bad money drives out good, so does entrenched folklore drive out logic.

4. Never use *finalize* to mean *finish, complete, end.*

    But *finalize* does not mean what any of those other words means. *Finalize* means to clean up the last few small details of a project, a specific sense captured by no other word. Some think *finalize* still smacks too much of the bureaucratic cast of mind, an understandable objection. But we ought not accept the argument that the word is bad because *-ize* is ugly. If we did, we would have to reject *nationalize, synthesize, rationalize,* along with hundreds of other common words.

5. Never never use *irregardless* for *regardless.* The word is a recognizable blend of *irrespective* and *regardless,* but history doesn't legitimize it (or should I say, make it legitimate?).

6. Do not modify an absolute word such as *perfect, unique, final,* or *complete* with *very, more, quite,* and so on. Presumably, not this:

We the People of the United States, in order to form a **more perfect** union . . .

A SPECIAL PROBLEM: PRONOUNS AND SEXISM

We expect literate writers to make verbs agree with subjects.

> There **are** several **reasons** for this.

We also expect their pronouns to agree with antecedents. Not this:

> Early **efforts** to oppose building a hydrogen bomb failed because **it** was not coordinated with the scientific and political communities. **No one** wanted to expose **themselves** to anti-Communist hysteria unless **they** had the backing of others.

But this:

> Early **efforts** to oppose building a hydrogen bomb failed because **they** were not coordinated with the scientific and political communities. **No one** wanted to expose **himself** to anti-Communist hysteria unless **he** had the backing of others.

We must use a singular pronoun to refer to a singular referent:

> The early **effort** to oppose the building of a hydrogen bomb failed because **it** was not coordinated . . .

But there are two further problems. First, do we use a singular or plural pronoun when we refer to a singular noun that is plural in meaning: *group, committee, staff, administration,* and so on? Some writers use a singular pronoun when the group acts as a single entity:

> The **committee** has met but has not yet made **its** decision.

We use a plural pronoun when members of a group act individually:

> The **faculty** received the memo, but not all of **them** read it.

These days we find the plural used in both senses.

Second, what personal pronoun should we use to refer to indefinite pronouns: *someone, everyone, no one* and to singular nouns that do not indicate gender: *teacher, doctor, person, student?* Casual usage invites the plural:

Everyone who spends four years in college realizes what a soft life **they** had only when **they** get a nine-to-five job, with no summer and Christmas vacations.

When **a person** gets involved with drugs, no one can help **them** unless **they** want to help **themselves.**

In both cases, more formal usage requires the singular pronoun:

Everyone who spends four years in college realizes what a soft life **she** had only when **she** gets a nine-to-five job, with no summer and Christmas vacations.

When a **person** gets involved with drugs, no one can help **him** unless **he** wants to help **himself.**

But when we observe the formal rule, we raise another, thornier problem—the matter of gender-neutral language.

Common sense demands that we express ideas in ways that are neither wrong nor gratuitously offensive. We give up nothing when we substitute *humankind* for *mankind, police officer* for *policeman, synthetic* for *man-made,* and so on, and we stop reinforcing stereotypes. (Those who ask whether we should also substitute *person-in-the-moon* for *man-in-the-moon* are being merely tendentious.)

But generic *he* is different: If we reject *he* as a generic pronoun because it is sexist, and *they* because it is ungrammatical or potentially ambiguous, we are left with either a clumsily intrusive *he or she,* a substantially worse *he/she,* (or worst, *s/he*). The *he/she* or *s/he* constructions make anyone with a sense of style flinch:

When a writer does not consider the ethnicity of his/her readers, they may respond in ways s/he would not have anticipated to words that for him/her are innocent of ethnic bias.

So we rewrite. We can begin by substituting plurals for singulars:

When a **writer** does not consider the ethnicity of **his** readers . . .

When **writers** do not consider the ethnicity of **their** readers . . .

But to the careful ear, plurals are less precise than singulars.

When appropriate, we can substitute a second person *you* or a first person *we* (though some readers object to the royal *we*):

> If **we** do not consider the ethnic background of **our** readers, **they** may respond in ways **we** would not expect to words that to **us** are innocent of ethnic bias.

We can also drop people altogether, but that leads to academic abstraction, a problem that this book is dedicated to eliminating:

> **Failure to consider** ethnic background may lead to an **unexpected response** to words considered innocent of ethnic bias.

Finally, we can alternately use *he* and *she,* as I have done. But that is not a good solution either, because to some readers, *she* seems as intrusive as *he/she.* A book reviewer in the *New York Times* (1/9/92) wondered what to make of an author whom the reviewer charged with attempting to

> right history's wrongs to women by referring to random examples as "she," as in "Ask a particle physicist what happens when a quark is knocked out of a proton, and she will tell you . . . ," which strikes this reader as oddly patronizing to women.

We might wonder whether particle physicists who happen to be women would feel the same way.

For years to come writers of English are going to have a problem with generic pronouns, and to some readers, any solution will seem awkward. I suspect that we will eventually accept *they* as singular:

> No one should turn in **their** writing unedited.

There is precedent: At one time, our second person singular pronoun was *thou.* But by the late sixteenth century, *thee* and *thou* were considered socially condescending, even insulting, so most English speakers replaced them with *you,* originally a strictly plural pronoun. The same thing could happen with *they.* Predictably, some believe that should such a day ever come, speakers and writers of English will have surrendered all aspirations to precision. We can only wait and see.

PRECISION

We must put this matter of precision precisely: We want to be grammatically correct. We must be. But if we include in our definition of correct both what is true and what is folklore, we risk missing what is important—that which makes prose wordy and confusing or clear and concise. We do not achieve precision merely by getting straight all the *which*es and *that*s, by mending every split infinitive, by eradicating every *finalize* and *hopefully.* Many of those who concentrate on such details seem oblivious to the more serious matter of imprecision in substantive thought and expression, and it is those who will allow obtuse prose eventually to become the national standard, prose like this grammatically impeccable and stylistically wretched passage (it actually appeared in print):

> Too precise a specification of information processing require-
> ments incurs the risk of overestimation resulting in unused
> capacity or inefficient use of costly resources or of underestima-
> tion leading to ineffectiveness or other inefficiencies. Too little
> precision in specifying needed information processing capacity
> gives no guidance with respect to the means for the procure-
> ment of the needed resources. There may be an optimal degree
> of precision in providing the decision-maker with the flexibility
> to adapt to needs.

SUMMARY

The finer points of correct English are unpredictable, so I can offer no principles by which to decide whether any particular point of usage is Real, Optional, or Folklore. Indeed, if "correctness" did submit to principle, correctness would be less of an issue, because most "errors" of usage are created by someone trying to level idiosyncrasies on the basis of a general principle. But, of course, the idiosyncrasy of such rules is exactly what makes them so useful to those who already know them. Their very unpredictability guarantees that they will be mastered only by those born into the right social environment or by those willing to learn such rules as one of the prices of admission.

Actually, I think that those of us who choose to observe all these rules all the time do so not because they think that they are protecting the integrity of the English language or the quality of our culture, but because they want to assert their own personal style. Some of us are straightforward and plainspeaking; others take pleasure in a bit of elegance, in a touch of fastidiously self-conscious "class." The *shall*s and the *will*s, the *who*s and the *whom*s, the aggressively unsplit infinitives—they are the private choices that let us express a refined sense of linguistic decorum, a decorum that many believe testifies to linguistic precision. It is an impulse that we ought not scorn, so long as it is informed and thoughtful, and so long as those who believe in all the rules include in their concern for precision the more important matters to which we now turn.

Lesson Three

Clarity 1: Actions

Whatever is translatable in other and simpler words of the same language, without loss of sense or dignity, is bad.
SAMUEL TAYLOR COLERIDGE

Suit the action to the word, the word to the action.
WILLIAM SHAKESPEARE, Hamlet, 3.2

Action is eloquence.
WILLIAM SHAKESPEARE, Coriolanus, 3.2

Words and deeds are quite different modes of the divine energy. Words are also actions, and actions are a kind of words.
RALPH WALDO EMERSON

The great enemy of clear language is insincerity.
GEORGE ORWELL

In matters of grave importance, style, not sincerity, is the vital thing.
OSCAR WILDE

MAKING JUDGMENTS

We have words enough to praise writing that we like—*clear, direct, concise, flowing, readable.* And more than enough to describe what we don't: *turgid, unclear, indirect, wordy, unreadable, confusing, abstract, awkward, disjointed, tangled, complex, obscure, inflated.* We could use some of those words to describe these two sentences:

1a. Our lack of data prevented evaluation of committee actions in targeting funds to areas in greatest need of assistance.

1b. Because we lacked data, we could not evaluate whether the committee had targeted funds to areas that needed assistance the most.

Most of us call (1a) indirect and awkward, (1b) clearer and more direct. When we say that, we may seem to be describing those sentences, but in fact we are describing how those sentences make us *feel.* When we say that sentence (1a) is less clear than (1b), we are really saying that *we* have a harder time understanding it. If we say that (1a) is awkward, we are saying that *we* feel uncomfortable as we read it. If we say it is more abstract than (1b), we are saying that we can't get a good picture of its meaning.

How we feel about writing is important, of course. But if we want to understand why we feel as we do, we need another vocabulary, one that lets us connect what is *in* (1a) that makes us want to describe it as unclear and awkward, what it is *in* (1b) that makes us want to describe it as more direct, more readable.

Some measures of clarity, for example, would have us compute ratios of syllables, words, and sentences. According to most such schemes, when the ratio exceeds some set number, a sentence is supposed to be difficult to read. But if we counted every syllable and word in every sentence we wrote, we'd spend more time counting than writing. And even if we did figure out ratios, they wouldn't explain how (1a) and (1b) differ, because (1a) has the same number of syllables as (1b) and fewer words. And finally, even if numbers could tell us which sentence was less clear, they wouldn't explain how I improved it.

TELLING STORIES

We respond to (1a) and (1b) differently, not because of different numbers, but because of the different ways that those sentences use SUBJECTS and VERBS to tell their stories. From the time we are infants we hear stories, and then we learn to tell them to explain, persuade, amuse, cheat, warn, mislead, excite, inform, seduce, inspire. No other form of discourse communicates so much, so quickly, so persuasively. Stories need two elements: a set of CHARACTERS and their ACTIONS. This story is flawed:

> 2a. Once upon a time, there was Little Red Riding Hood, Grandma, the Woodsman, and the Wolf. The end.

Interesting characters, but no action. Here are the actions.

> 2b. Once upon a time, there was a walking through the woods to a house, when a jump out from behind a tree caused surprise.

Still a problem. We have to associate actions with characters:

> 2c. Once upon a time, there a walking through the woods on the part of Little Red Riding Hood to her Grandma's house, when the Wolf's jump out from behind a tree caused surprise in her.

Something still wrong. You expected this:

> 2d. Once upon a time, Little Red Riding Hood was walking through the woods to her Grandma's house, when the Wolf jumped out from behind a tree and surprised her.

Academic and professional writing may seem distant from fairy tales (some of us occasionally disagree), but those versions of Little

Red Riding Hood differ in the same way as these more academic sounding sentences:

> 3a. An explanation of the causes of the war appears in the third paragraph of the Gettysburg Address, while the fourth expresses encouragement in the continuation of the struggle.

> 3b. In the third paragraph of his Gettysburg Address, Lincoln explains what caused the war, and in the fourth he encourages his audience to continue the struggle.

In (3a), we feel Lincoln and his audience are hidden, the language complex and impersonal. In (3b), they seem present, doing something, and the language seems clearer, more direct. This pair of sentences differs in the same way that our sentences about Little Red Riding Hood differ and in the same way that (1a) and (1b) differ. In particular, they differ in the way they use subjects and verbs to tell the story of characters and their actions.

THE NARRATIVE STYLE

We can understand how sentences can tell the same story in different ways if we start with a sentence that seems clear and then change it:

> 4a. Although the Governor knew that the cities needed more money for schools, he vetoed higher state taxes to encourage the cities to increase their local taxes.

This sentence seems reasonably clear because we instantly know who the main characters are and what they are doing. The characters are obviously the Governor and the cities (a legislature is implied). The Governor is the source or AGENT of three actions:

> (1) The Governor **knew** something,
> (2) he **vetoed** taxes,
> (3) he did that to **encourage** the cities to do something.

The cities are the agents of two actions:

> (4) The cities **need** money,
> (5) they [should] **increase** their local taxes.

Each of those actions is the same part of speech—a verb.

Exercise 3-1

Stop now and write a different version of that same story, but instead of using those five verbs to express actions, use their corresponding NOUN forms. Two of the nouns differ from the corresponding verbs:

> to know → knowledge,
> to encourage → encouragement,

The other three nouns are identical to their corresponding verbs:

> to need → the need,
> to veto → the veto,
> to increase → the increase.

You might begin, "Despite his knowledge of . . ."

Here is one version. Yours may differ:

> 4b. Despite his **knowledge** of the **need** by cities for more money, the Governor executed a **veto** of higher state taxes in order to give **encouragement** to the cities for an **increase** in local taxes.

At some level, this sentence tells the same story as (4a), but at the level of directness, clarity, ease of understanding, the stories differ just as the two of the versions of Little Red Riding Hood differ. What causes the difference? First, compare the underlined subjects in (2a) and (2b):

> 2a. Once upon a time, there was a **walking** through the woods to her Grandma's house on the part of Little Red Riding Hood, when a **jump** out from behind a tree by the Wolf caused **surprise** in Little Red Riding Hood.

> 2b. Once upon a time, Little Red Riding Hood was **walking** through the woods on the way to her Grandma's house, when the Wolf **jumped** out from behind the tree and **surprised** her.

In (2a), the subjects are abstractions: *a walking, a jump;* in (2b), they are characters: *Little Red Riding Hood, the Wolf.* Now compare the boldfaced actions in (2a) with the corresponding actions in (2b). In

(2a), the actions are abstract nouns: *a walking, a jump, surprise.* In (2b), they are all verbs: *was walking, jumped, surprised.*

Make the same comparisons between (3a) and (3b):

> 3a. Whereas <u>an **explanation**</u> of the **causes** of the war is in the third paragraph of the Gettysburg Address, <u>a **rallying cry**</u> for the **continuation** of the struggle appears in the fourth.

> 3b. In the third paragraph of his Gettysburg Address, <u>Lincoln</u> **explains** what **caused** the war and in the fourth <u>he **rallies**</u> his audience to **continue** the struggle.

These sentences differ in the same two ways: First, in the clearer sentences, (2b) and (3b), the subjects are characters who perform actions. But in the less clear sentences, (2a) and (3a), the characters are shunted off someplace else (or omitted entirely), and the subjects of the verbs are abstractions. And second, in the clearer sentences, actions are verbs. In the less clear sentences, those actions are expressed in abstract nouns.

These differences suggest two principles for clear writing.

TWO PRINCIPLES

We usually feel that we are reading clear prose when sentences fulfill two kinds of expectations:

1. We expect to see central characters in most subjects.
2. We expect to see their important actions in most verbs.

In this lesson, we'll look briefly at characters and subjects, then in more detail at actions and verbs. In the next lesson, we'll return to characters and subjects.

Characters and Subjects

The most important characters are agents, the source of actions or conditions. Look at how sentences (1a) and (1b) represent agents, that is, "doers" (they are boldfaced):

> 1a. **Our** lack of pertinent data prevented evaluation of **committee** actions in targeting funds to **areas** in greatest need of assistance.

1b. Because **we** lacked pertinent data, **we** could not evaluate whether the **committee** had targeted funds to **areas** that needed assistance the most.

In (1a), there are three characters: *our, the committee,* and *areas.* Where do those characters appear in (1a)? None of them is the subject; the subject of (1a) is instead an abstraction, *lack:*

> *Our* **lack** *of pertinent data*_{subject} prevented_{verb} · · ·

One character, named by *our,* appears **in** the WHOLE SUBJECT of (1a), but *our* is only part of that subject, not the subject itself. If the characters in (1a) are not subjects, where are they?

— *Our* is a modifier of *lack:* **our** *lack.*
— *Committee* is a modifier of *action:* **committee** *action.*
— *Areas* is the object of a PREPOSITION: *to* **areas**

> Now look at where those same characters appear in (1b):

1b. Because **we** lacked pertinent data, **we** could not evaluate whether the **committee** had targeted funds to **areas** that needed assistance the most.

These characters are consistently subjects:

— *We* is the subject of the verbs *lacked* and *could not evaluate:*

> Because **we** *lacked . . .* **we** *could* not *evaluate . . .*

— *The committee* is subject of the verb *had targeted:*

> *. . .* **the committee** *had targeted . . .*

— *Area* is the object of a preposition (*to areas*), but it is simultaneously the subject of *needed:*

> *. . .* **areas that** *needed* assistance the most.

Sentence (1a), the less clear sentence, consistently departs from our first principle: it does *not* make characters subjects of verbs. Sentence (1b), on the other hand, does observe that principle, and thereby seems clearer. (We will return to characters in the next lesson.)

Actions and Verbs

As we use the word here, *action* covers more than physical movement. It also refers to mental processes, relationships, conditions, literal or figurative. Just as sentences seem clearer when characters appear as subjects, so do sentences seem clearer when their actions are expressed in verbs. These next sentences become clearer as their verbs express more specific actions:

> There has **been** the effective exercise of information dissemination control on the part of the Secretary.

> The Secretary has **exercised** effective staff information dissemination control.

> The Secretary has effectively **controlled** how his staff **disseminates** information.

The crucial actions aren't *be* or *exercise,* but *control* and *disseminate.* In fact, writers of abstract prose typically use verbs to state only that an action exists:

> There **is** the possibility of prior *approval* of it.

> He **may approve** of it ahead of time.

> A *need* **exists** for greater candidate *selection* efficiency.

> We **need** to **select** candidates more efficiently.

Now look at how sentences (1a) and (1b) express the actions their characters perform. In (1a), actions (bold faced) are not verbs, but nouns:

> 1a. Our **lack**$_{noun}$ of pertinent data prevented **evaluation**$_{noun}$ of committee **action**$_{noun}$ in **targeting**$_{noun}$ funds to areas in greatest **need**$_{noun}$ of **assistance**$_{noun}$.

In (1b), the actions are almost all verbs:

> 1b. Because we **lacked**$_{verb}$ pertinent data, we could not **evaluate**$_{verb}$ whether the committee had **targeted**$_{verb}$ funds to areas that **needed**$_{verb}$ **assistance**$_{noun}$ the most.

These two sentences differ not in some ratio of syllables/words, but in how they use subjects and verbs to express characters and actions.

Exercise 3-2

Analyze the subject/character and verb/action patterns in this pair of sentences:

5a. There is public opposition to nuclear power plants near population centers because of a widespread belief in their threat to human health.

5b. The public opposes nuclear power plants near population centers because it believes that they threaten human health.

VERB → NOUN = NOMINALIZATION

When we write in ways that seem abstract and impersonal, we typically use too many abstract nouns, particularly abstract nouns derived from verbs and adjectives. There is a technical term for these abstract nouns:

NOMINALIZATION

The word illustrates its meaning. When we nominalize *nominalize,* we create the nominalization *nominalization.* We can also nominalize ADJECTIVES: *probable > probability.* Some examples:

Verb → Nominalization	Adjective → Nominalization
discover → discovery	careless → carelessness
resist → resistance	different → difference
react → reaction	elegant → elegance

We can also nominalize a verb by adding *-ing* (making it a GERUND):

fly → flying   sing → singing

Some nominalizations are identical to their corresponding verb:

hope → hope	charge → charge
result → result	answer → answer
repair → repair	return → return

We **request**_{verb} that when you **return**_{verb}, you **review**_{verb} the data and **report**_{verb} immediately.

Our **request**_{noun} is that on your **return**_{noun}, you conduct a **review**_{noun} of the data and provide an immediate **report**_{noun}.

The frequent use of nominalizations instead of verbs results in the frustration of reader expectations. The expectation of a reader is the appearance of characters as subjects and their crucial actions as verbs. Increased frustration results from writers' dropping characters out of sentences altogether. That feeling no doubt occurred with you in your reading of this version of *Little Red Riding Hood*:

Once upon a time, a walking through the woods occurred, when a jump out from behind a tree caused surprise.

Dropping Little Red Riding Hood and the Wolf from the story became a possibility subsequent to the nominalization of the verb *walk* into the nominalization *walking,* the verb *jump* into the nominalization *jump,* and the verb *surprise* into the nominalization *surprise.*

Exercise 3-3

Here are several verbs, adjectives, and nominalizations. Turn the verbs and adjectives into nominalizations and the nominalizations into adjectives and verbs, until you are certain you understand the difference. Keep in mind that some verbs and nominalizations have the same form:

Poverty predictably **causes** social problems.

Poverty is a predictable **cause** of social problems.

analysis	*approach*	*acquisition*	*accuracy*
believe	*comparison*	*appeal*	*careful*
attempt	*define*	*appearance*	*clear*
conclusion	*discuss*	*description*	*intelligence*
emphasize	*explanation*	*decrease*	*important*
evaluate	*expression*	*improve*	*precise*
suggest	*failure*	*increase*	*relevant*

Now add five of your own nominalizations, verbs, and adjectives.

Exercise 3-4

Make up a few sentences using in each of them two or three of these verbs and adjectives. In some cases, you can change the adjective to an adverb. Then, if you can, rewrite those sentences, using the corresponding nominalizations to express the same idea. For example, picking *suggest, define,* and *precise,* you write:

> I **suggest** that we **define** the problem more **precisely.**

Then rewrite that sentence into its nominalized form:

> My **suggestion** is that our **definition** of the problem have greater **precision.**

It may seem odd to ask you to write a sentence less clear than one you've written. But only when you see how a sentence can be less clear than it is will you understand why it seems clear in the first place. And only when you understand how an unclear sentence can be clearer will you understand why it is unclear.

Exercise 3-5

Now do the reverse. Make up a few sentences using two or three nominalizations in each; then express the same idea using the corresponding verbs, adjectives, and adverbs. This is harder.

Exercise 3-6

Exchange some of the nominalized sentences that you made up with other students to see whether you can revise theirs and they can revise yours back into the originals.

Exercise 3-7

Revise any paragraph in Lesson One by substituting nominalizations for the important verbs. Then exchange your passage with others and try to revise their nominalized revision back into its original version.

FROM ANALYSIS TO REVISION

These two principles let us analyze and explain why we judge a sentence to be unclear, another direct. But just as important, these principles also suggest how we can revise it.

Three Steps toward Diagnosing and Revising

1. When you feel that your prose (or that of someone else) is abstract, complex, confusing, do two things.
   a. Find or construct the cast of characters.
   b. Find the actions those characters perform.

2. Then look for two characteristics:
   a. Actions and conditions that are not verbs and adjectives but rather abstract nouns.
   b. Central characters that are not the subjects of verbs.

3. If you find these two characteristics, do two things:
   1. Change the nominalizations into verbs and adjectives.
   2. Revise the sentence so that the subjects of those new verbs are the characters associated with the actions in those verbs.

Exercise 3-8

One of the paragraphs in the last few pages was thoroughly nominalized. Find and revise it.

Some Typical Patterns

A few patterns of nominalizations are easy to spot and revise.

1. When a nominalization follows a verb that has little specific meaning, change the nominalization to a verb and replace the empty verb with your new verb. In these cases, the subject is probably already a character:

   > The police *conducted* an **investigation** into the matter.

   > The police **investigated** the matter.

The committee *has* no **expectation** that it will adjourn.

The committee does not **expect** to adjourn.

2. When a nominalization follows *there is* or *there are,* change the nominalization to a verb and find a new subject.

> *There* is a **need** for further **study** of this program.
>
> *The engineering staff* **must study** this program further.
>
> *There was* **erosion** of the land from the floods.
>
> *The floods* **eroded** the land.

3. When the nominalization is the subject of an empty verb, change the nominalization to a verb and find a character to be the subject of that new verb:

> The **intention** of *the IRS is* to audit the records.
>
> *The IRS* **intends** to audit the records.
>
> *Our* **discussion** *concerned* a tax cut.
>
> *We* **discussed** a tax cut.

4. When nominalizations appear in a series, try turning the first one into a verb. Then either leave the second or turn it into a verb in a clause beginning with *how* or *why:*

> There was first a **review** *of* the **evolution** *of* the dorsal fin.
>
> First, she **reviewed** the **evolution** of the dorsal fin.
>
> First, she **reviewed** *how* the dorsal fin **evolved.**

5. When a nominalization appears in a subject, and a second nominalization in the COMPLEMENT of a linking verb or phrase, you have to revise more extensively. Usually, you have to create two new CLAUSES and link them with a word like *because, if, although,* and so on:

Subject:	Their **cessation of operations**
Connecting verb or phrase:	was the result of
Complement:	their market share **loss.**

To revise such sentences, do this:

(a) Change abstract nominalizations to verbs:
    cessation → *ceased, loss* → *lose.*

(b) Find subjects for those verbs: **they** *ceased,* **they** *lost.*

(c) Link the new clauses with a connecting word that expresses their logical connection. That connection will typically be some kind of causal relationship:

To express simple cause:	*because, since, when*
To express conditional cause:	*if, provided that, so long as*
To contradict expected causes:	*though, although, unless*

Schematically, we do this:

Their **cessation** of operations	→ They **ceased** operations
was the result of	→ **because**
their market share **loss**	→ they **lost** market share.

Exercise 3-9

These pairs contrast in nominal and verbal styles. Identify which is which. Circle nominalizations. Underline verbs.

1a. Some have argued that carbon dioxide in the atmosphere will almost certainly elevate global temperature.

1b. There has been speculation by educators as to the positive effect of a good family environment on educational achievement.

2a. Smoking during pregnancy may lead to fetal injury.

2b. When we nominalize many verbs, readers read less easily.

3a. AIDS researchers have identified the HIV virus but have failed to develop a vaccine that will immunize those at risk.

3b. Attempts by administrators at formulating principles for the definition of racial and ethnic abuse have not achieved success.

4a. Arguments by editorial writers about apathy among voters as a result of cynicism in regard to elected officials do not provide suggestions about dispelling it.

4b. Although many critics have <u>claimed</u> that when children <u>watch</u> television they <u>tend</u> to become less able readers, no one has yet <u>demonstrated</u> that to be true.

5a. The loss of the market to the Japanese by domestic auto makers could result in the unemployment of hundreds of thousands of workers and stagnation in the national economy.

5b. If educators could discover ways to use computer-assisted instruction, our schools could teach more complex subjects and students could learn faster.

6a. We <u>need to know</u> which areas of our national forests are being <u>logged</u> most extensively so that we can <u>save</u> virgin stands at greatest risk.

6b. There is a need for an analysis of the intensity of library use to provide a reliable projection of new resource requirements.

7a. Professional athletes often discover they are unprepared for life after stardom because their teams protect them from the problems that the rest of us adjust to every day.

7b. Many politicians have arrived at the realization that they lack understanding about the concerns of voters, because they have succeeded in convincing themselves that their constituents will give them their vote automatically and so they make few attempts to get an idea about their real worries.

8a. In this article, we examine how buyers influence advertising and how advertising agencies respond to those influences when they create a strategy that appeals to consumers.

8b. This study is an analysis of response to different rhetorical patterns and of judgments of textual well-formedness by readers in possession of prior knowledge of subject matter before reading.

Exercise 3-10

Now go back to the previous exercise and change the original verbal sentence in each pair into a nominalized sentence. Use the nominal version as a pattern. For example, if the nominalized sentence in the pair begins with *There*, begin the revised sentence with *there:*

1b. **There** has been speculation by educators as to the positive effect of a good family environment on educational achievement.

1a. Some have **argued** that carbon dioxide in the atmosphere will almost certainly elevate global temperature.

→1c. **There** have been **arguments** . . .

Exercise 3-11

Now do the reverse. Revise the original nominalized sentences into corresponding verbal sentences. Use the verbal version as a pattern. For example, if the verbal sentence in the pair begins with a *when,* begin the revised sentence with *when:*

2b. **When** we nominalize many verbs, readers read less easily.

2a. **Smoking** during pregnancy leads to fetal defects.

→2a. **When** pregnant women **smoke** . . .

Exercise 3-12

Revise these next sentences so that the nominalizations are verbs and the characters are the subjects of those verbs. In 1 to 5, characters are italicized and nominalizations are boldfaced.

1. *Lincoln's* **hope** was for the **preservation** of the Union without war, but the *South's* **attack** on Fort Sumter resulted in the **beginning** of the war.
2. **Attempts** were made on the part of *President Nixon's aides* to assert *his* **immunity** from a Supreme Court subpoena.
3. There were **predictions** by *members of the Administration* that the *nominee* would receive quick *committee* **approval.**
4. The *author's* **analysis** of our data omits any **citation** of **sources** that would provide **support** for *his* criticism of our argument.
5. *The health industry's* **inability** to exert cost **controls** could lead to the *public's* **decision** that *Congressional* **action** is needed.

In sentences 6 to 10, only the agents are boldfaced.

6. A **Papal** appeal was made to the **industrialized nations of the world** for assistance to **those in the Third World** who were experiencing starvation.

7. Explanations of the reasons for the decrease in **voter** participation were conducted by **independent investigators.**
8. The agreement by the **participants** on the program was based on the assumption that there was a promise of **federal** funds.
9. There was no independent **business-sector** analysis of the cause of the sudden increase in the trade deficit.
10. Agreement as to the need for revisions in the terms of the treaty was reached by **the two sides.**

In 11 to 15, only the nominalizations are boldfaced.

11. There was **uncertainty** in the White House about the Iraqi **intentions** in regard to **withdrawal** from Kuwait.
12. There must be thorough **preparation** of the specimen sections by the laboratory personnel.
13. Any **contradictions** among data in any result requires an **explanation** of the reasons for the **inconsistencies.**
14. The **rejection** of the proposal was a **disappointment** but not a **surprise** because of our **expectation** that a **decision** had already been made to delay any new initiatives.
15. Their **performance** of the play was done with great **enthusiasm** but their historical **accuracy** in **staging** was flawed.

SOME HAPPY CONSEQUENCES

We began with the two principles of characters as subjects and their actions as verbs, because they help us create more direct sentences. But when we observe those principles, we make other useful changes, as well:

1. You may have been told to avoid using too many PREPOSITIONAL PHRASES. It's not clear how many is "too many," but when you use nominalizations, you have to add prepositional phrases to keep the characters in the sentence. You eliminate most of the prepositional phrases when you use verbs. Compare:

> An evaluation **of** the program **by** us will encourage increases **in** efficiency **in** the servicing **of** clients.

> We will evaluate the program so that we can serve our clients more efficiently.

2. You may have been told to avoid abstractions, to write concretely. You write abstractly when you turn verbs into nouns and delete characters. But you write sentences that seem more concrete when you name characters in subjects and actions in verbs. Compare:

> There is an affirmative **decision** for program **termination.**
>
> *The Director* **has decided** to **terminate** the program.

3. You may have been told to order your ideas logically. When you nominalize verbs and string those nominalizations together in prepositional phrases, you can distort the logical sequence of your story. This next sequence of actions distorts the chronological sequence (actions are boldfaced, the numbers refer to the sequence in which the actions occur). Compare

> **Decisions**[4] in regard to **administration**[5] of medication despite **inability**[2] of irrational patients **appearing**[1] in Trauma Centers to provide legal **consent**[3] rest with physicians alone.
>
> When a patient **appears**[1] in a Trauma Center and **behaves**[2] so irrationally that he cannot legally **consent**[3] to treatment, only the physician can **decide**[4] whether to **administer**[5] medication.

When you use subjects to name characters and verbs to name their actions, you are more likely to match the logical grammar of your sentences to the chrono-logical sequence of your story.

4. You may have been told to clarify logical relationships. When you nominalize verbs, you often have to use diffuse connectors like *in regard to.* But when you use verbs, you can link the new sequences of clauses with logical SUBORDINATING CONJUNC- TIONS, with logical conjunctions like *because, although,* and *if.* Compare:

> The more effective presentation of needs by other agencies **resulted in** our failure in acquiring federal funds, **despite** intensive lobbying efforts on our part.
>
> **Although** we lobbied Congress intensively, we could not acquire federal funds **because** other agencies presented their needs more effectively.

In short, observe these first two principles and you benefit in many ways.

A PROBLEM AND ITS SOLUTION

At this point you can probably identify problems in someone else's writing, but you may have a harder time recognizing them in your own.

The Problem of Knowing Too Much

Most of us recognize this experience: I write something I think is clear, but when I get it back from a colleague or editor, I am told that my ideas are confusing, hard to understand. I wonder whether my critic is just being difficult, but I bite my tongue and try to fix what I am certain should have been clear to anyone who can read prose more complex than stories about My Dog Spot. And when I tell someone the same thing about his or her writing, I know that person is probably thinking the same thing about me. But almost always, I eventually realize that my readers were, in fact, right, that they recognized what was unclear better than I. How can I be right about other people's writing and so often wrong about my own?

The answer lies in this paradoxical fact: We can be wrong about the clarity of our own writing because we usually know more about our subject than do our readers, and we can be right about the clarity someone else's writing because we usually know less about its subject than does the writer.

This explains why we are so often our own worst editors: Who knows more about our subject than we do (or should)? In fact, as we re-read our own writing, we usually aren't reading; we're reminding ourselves of what we intended to mean when we wrote it. But since our readers lack our knowledge, they are likely to respond in ways that disconcert us. This also explains why two people can disagree about the quality of the same passage. Someone who understands its content is more likely to think the passage is well written than someone who knows less. Both can be right.

Ways to Sidestep Your Knowledge

Since we can never read as our readers do, we need to look at our own writing in ways that side-step our memory of what we intended to mean when we wrote. There are three ways to do this, in increasing order of difficulty and effectiveness.

1. The quickest way is to underline the first seven or eight words of every sentence. Try revising any passage that includes more than a few sentences with these two characteristics:

    a. You have to go more than seven or eight words into a sentence before you get past its subject and verb (ignore short introductory phrases like *As a result* and *At this time*).

    b. The subject of the sentence is not a character, but an abstraction, *particularly a nominalization part of a long subject,* as in:

    Our **analysis** of the results of the experiment still did not provide an explanation of why the failure occurred.

When you find a passage with many such sentences, revise them so that the central characters in your story appear as subjects and their actions as verbs, *even if you think the passage is already clear.*

When *we* **analyzed** the results of the experiment, it still did not provide an explanation for why the failure occurred.

2. A more demanding but more reliable method: Look at the subject of *every* verb, and then try to revise those subjects that are not characters but complex nominalizations. We can take the revision we started above one more step:

    When we analyzed the results of the experiment, it still did not provide an explanation for why **the failure** occurred.

    When we analyzed the results of the experiment, it still did not provide an explanation for why *it* **failed.**

3. The most demanding method is to start by looking for any nominalizations that you can turn into verbs, especially when the verbs you have already used are general verbs like *be, make, do, have, occur,* and so on. (In a few moments, we will describe nominalizations that you should leave nominalized.):

    When we analyzed the results of the experiment, it still did not provide **an explanation** for why it failed.

    When we analyzed the results of the experiment, we still could not **explain** why it failed.

You can locate passages most likely to need this kind of revision if you remember where in your drafting you were least confident, where you felt yourself struggling because your ideas seemed so complicated. That kind of uncertainty and confusion is most likely to reveal itself in confused and confusing abstraction.

USEFUL NOMINALIZATIONS

As strongly as I have urged you to avoid nominalizations, I will now seem to contradict myself by saying that, in fact, we cannot get along without them. Nominalizations can be useful, in many contexts necessary. The trick is to know which to revise into verbs, which to keep. Keep these:

1. The nominalization is a subject that refers to a previous sentence:

> **These arguments** all depend on a single unproven claim.

> **This decision** can lead to costly consequences.

These nominalizations link sentences into a more cohesive flow.

2. A succinct nominalization can replace an awkward "The fact that":

> **The fact that she denied what he accused her of** impressed the jury.

> **Her denial of his accusations** impressed the jury.

But then, why not,

> When she **denied** his accusations, she **impressed** the jury.

3. A nominalization can save a few words when it names what would be the object of the verb.

> I did not satisfy her **requests.**

> I did not satisfy **what she requested.**

This kind of nominalization also feels more concrete than the abstract nominalization. Contrast *request* above with this sense of *request,* one that is more of an action:

> Her **request** for assistance was a surprise.
>
> When she **requested** assistance, she surprised me.

4. We often use a nominalization at the end of the first sentence of a paragraph, after a *there is/are* construction, to introduce a topic that we intend to develop in sentences that follow:

> *There is* no **need,** then, for argument about the **existence,** the **inevitability,** and the **desirability** of **change** [in language]. *There is* **need,** however, for argument about the **existence** of such a thing as good English and correct English. Let us not hesitate to assert that "The pencil was laying on the table" and "He don't know nothing" are at present incorrect no matter how many know-nothings say them. Let us insist that . . . Let us demand that . . . Let us do these things not to satisfy "rules" or to gratify the whims of a pedagogue, but rather to express ourselves clearly, precisely, logically, and directly.
>
> —Theodore M. Bernstein, *The Careful Writer*

We might consider revising those first two sentences into this:

> While we need not debate whether language changes in ways that are inevitable and desirable, we do argue that there is such a thing as good and correct English.

Some critics claim that writers should always avoid *there is/are* because such phrases are static, wordy, and often overused. In fact, they are useful at the beginning of a paragraph to introduce its central idea, an idea often captured in a nominalization.

5. Some nominalizations refer to a concept so familiar that the concept itself is almost a character.

> Few problems have so divided us as **abortion on demand.**
>
> The Equal Rights **Amendment** was an issue in past **elections.**
>
> **Taxation** without **representation** was not the central concern of the American **Revolution.**

These nominalizations name familiar concepts: *abortion on demand, election, taxation, representation, Revolution.* We compress familiar concepts into nouns so that we need not repeatedly spell them out. Some nominalizations refer to ideas that we can express easily only in nominalizations: *freedom, death, love, life.* Without such abstract words, we would find it at least difficult to discuss subjects that have preoccupied us for millennia. We have to develop an eye for a nominalization that expresses one of these ideas and a nominalization that hides a significant action:

> There is a **demand** for an **end** to **taxation** on *entertainment.*

> We **demand** that the government **stop taxing** *entertainment.*

CLARITY, NOT SIMPLE-MINDEDNESS

To the degree that you can match your actions to your verbs, your readers will think that you write clearly. But to write clearly, you must not write sentences that sound as if they were written by an elementary school student. This was written by a student aspiring to academic sophistication:

> After Czar Alexander II's emancipation of Russian serfs in 1861, many newly freed peasants chose to live on communes for purposes of cooperation in agricultural production as well as for social stability. Despite some communes' attempts at economic and social equalization through the strategy of imposing low economic status on the peasants, which resulted in their reduction to near-poverty, a centuries-long history of social distinctions even among serfs prevented social equalization.

In his struggle to follow our principles, he revised that paragraph into sentences that sounded as if they were written by a precocious sixth grader:

> In 1861, Czar Alexander II emancipated the Russian serfs. Many of them chose to live on agricultural communes. There they thought they could cooperate with one another in agricultural production.

They could also create a stable social structure. The leaders of some of these communes tried to equalize the peasants economically and socially. As one strategy, they tried to impose on all a low economic status that reduced them to near-poverty. However, the communes failed to equalize them socially. This happened because even serfs had made social distinctions among themselves for centuries.

In Lessons Eight and Ten we will look at ways to revise a series of too-short, too-simple sentences into a style that is readable but still complex enough to communicate complex ideas. Applying those principles to his primer-style passage, the student revised once more:

After the Russian serfs were emancipated by Czar Alexander II in 1861, many chose to live on agricultural communes, hoping they could cooperate in working the land and establish a stable social structure. At first, those who led some of the communes tried to equalize the new peasants socially and economically by imposing on them all a low economic status, a strategy that reduced them to near-poverty. But the communes failed to equalize them socially because for centuries the serfs had observed social distinctions among themselves.

The first two sentences are long but clear, because the writer consistently aligned major characters with main subjects and their actions with verbs. Can we do this with every subject and every verb? Of course not. But to the degree that we can, our readers will think that we write clearly.

Exercise 3-13

Revise these sentences. At the end of each sentence is a hint.

1. The use of models in teaching prose style does not invariably result in improvements of clarity and directness. (although)
2. Precision in plotting the location of fragments of the vase enhances the possibility of accurate reconstruction. (when)
3. Any departures from the established procedures may cause delays and even termination of the program. (if)
4. A student's socialization into a field may lead to writing difficulties based on a lack of enough knowledge in regard to the con-

struction of arguments by those in the field. (When ..., xxxx, because....)

5. The successful implementation of a new curriculum depends on the cooperation of faculty with students in setting achievable goals within a reasonable time-frame. (In order to ..., ...)

6. Our evaluation of the outcomes of the programs placed emphasis on objective measures despite our recognition of the low level of rater agreement. (When ..., xxxx, even though....)

Exercise 3-14

On any page in Lesson One, find five nominalizations and decide whether they should be changed or remain as they are.

SUMMING UP
The System of Clarity

We can represent our principles systematically. As we read, we integrate two levels of structure. One level is its predictable grammatical sequence:

FIXED	Subject	Verb	Complement

The other level of structure is its story, a level of meaning whose elements have no fixed order, but do appear in one that we *expect:*

VARIABLE	Characters	Action	—

We can graphically represent the conjunction of these principles.

FIXED	Subject	Verb	Complement
VARIABLE	Characters	Action	—

Readers expect to see characters first, then their actions. But more specifically, they expect to see characters as subjects of verbs and they expect to see those verbs express important actions involving those characters. To the degree that we do not fulfill their expectations, to that degree we make them work harder.

All sentences have two levels of structure: A fixed level of grammar and a variable level of story. Think of that fixed level as the *geography* of a sentence and the variable level as containing its elements of meaning, variable elements that you can move through the fixed geography. But while you can move those elements of meaning to different places in a sentence, readers expect to see them in predictable places: They expect to see characters in subjects and actions in verbs. Those expectations give us our first two principles of style:

1. When appropriate, express actions and conditions in verbs:

    The **intention** of the committee is **improvement** of morale.

    The committee **intends** to **improve** morale.

2. When appropriate, make subjects of verbs the agents of actions.

    A decision on the part of **the Dean** in regard to the funding by **the Department** of the program must be made for there to be adequate **staff** preparation.

    If **the staff** is to prepare adequately, **the Dean** must decide whether **the Department** will fund the program.

Don't revise nominalizations that do the following:

1. Refer to a previous sentence:

    These arguments all depend on a single unproven claim.

    This decision can lead to costly consequences.

2. Sum up an awkward "The fact that":

    The fact that I strenuously objected impressed the jury.

    My strenuous objections impressed the jury.

3. Name what would be the object of its verbal form:

    I do not know her **intentions.**

    I do not know **what she intends.**

4. Refer to a familiar and often repeated concept:

> Few issues have so divided us as **abortion on demand.**
>
> The Equal Rights **Amendment** was an issue in past **elections.**

5. Occur after *there is/are* to introduce a topic that you intend to develop in the next few sentences:

> There are three ways to explain our **failures.** First, we ...

In the next Lesson, we revisit characters and subjects.

Lesson Four

Clarity 2: Characters

Style is the physiognomy of the mind.
ARTHUR SCHOPENHAUER

To me, style is just the outside of content, and content the
inside of style, like the outside and inside of the human body—
both go together, they can't be separated.
JEAN-LUC GODARD

There is no artifice as good and desirable as simplicity.
ST. FRANCIS DE SALES

Affected simplicity is refined imposture.
LA ROCHEFOUCAULD

THE CENTRALITY OF CHARACTERS

VERBS and ACTIONS are important: The specific actions in the verbs of (1a) make it clearer than (1b), with its dense pattern of NOMINALIZATIONS.

> 1a. I decided that she should investigate why they failed.

> 1b. I made a decision that she should conduct an investigation into the cause of their failure.

But CHARACTERS may be even more important, because your readers can tolerate nominalizations reasonably well, so long as they can see CHARACTERS in most of your SUBJECTS. Although (1b) is highly nominalized, it is clearer than (1c):

> 1c. A decision was made by me in favor of her conducting an investigation into the cause of their failure.

The subject of (1c) is an abstraction (*decision*), and its characters are buried in the OBJECT of a PREPOSITION (*by **me***) and in a modifier and POSSESSIVE PRONOUN (***their** failure*). So to the degree that you can put actions into verbs, good. But to the degree that you can put characters into subjects, better.

ROLES OF CHARACTERS

Characters can have different roles. The most important is that of AGENT, the source of an action or condition.

The group performed the play enthusiastically.

Some characters are secondary or remote agents:

Mayor Daley built Chicago into a giant among cities.

Some are figurative agents that stand in for the real agents:

> **The White House** today announced the President's schedule.
>
> **The business sector** is cooperating.

And in some sentences, subjects seem to name agents, but those subjects are really more like the instrument by which some hidden agent performs its action.

> **Studies** of coal production revealed these findings.
>
> **This evidence** proves my theory.

That is,

> When **they** *studied* coal production, **they** found these data.
>
> With this evidence **I** *prove* my theory.

In general, we judge prose to be *clearest* when agents of actions regularly appear as subjects of verbs. As we'll see, there are exceptions to this principle, but as a rough rule of thumb, it works.

Some characters, of course, are neither the agent nor the instrument of an action, but its receiver or goal. If so, those characters are usually not the subject of a verb, but its object.

> In Africa, AIDS has wiped out **whole villages.**

We can, of course, put the goal of an action into the subject of a PASSIVE verb:

> In Africa, **whole villages** have been wiped out by AIDS.

Later in this lesson and in the next, we'll look in more detail at active and passive verbs and at the special circumstances that cause us to put into a subject some character other than the agent of an action.

Subject and Object versus Agent and Goal

It's easy to confuse two grammatical terms—*subject* and *object*—with two other terms that refer to the roles those characters play in a story: *agent* and *goal.* The terms refer to different concepts.

— *Subject* and *object* refer to places in the grammatical structure of a sentence. Subjects are usually first; objects usually follow verbs:

   Carter$_{subject}$ defeated **Ford**$_{object}$ in 1976.

— *Agent* and *goal* refer to roles that *characters* play in a story. We can move characters in and out of the fixed grammatical positions of subjects and objects, while keeping their story roles intact. In the sentence about Carter and Ford, for example, the word *Carter* is the subject of a verb, but Carter himself is also the agent of the action, *defeat.* The word *Ford* is an object, but he is also the goal of an action, the entity on its receiving end. But we can move Ford into the subject position and Carter into an object, while keeping their roles the same. The simplest way is to use a passive verb:

   Ford$_{subject/goal}$ was defeated by **Carter**$_{object-of-preposition/agent}$.

Another, more clever way is to find a verb whose meaning lets us put the actual goal of an action into the grammatical subject of an active verb:

   Ford$_{subject/goal}$ lost to **Carter**$_{object-of-preposition/agent}$ in 1976.

   In Africa, whole villages have died from AIDS.

We risk confusion when we use the same term—*object*—to name both the position after a verb and the goal or receiver of an action.

FORMS OF CHARACTERS

Indefinite Characters

When we know the specific characters in our stories, we can name them. But when we want to make a general statement using indefinite characters, English offers few good choices. This sentence lacks characters:

2a. Multivariate strategies may be of more use in understanding the genetic factors which contribute to vulnerability to psychiatric disorder than strategies based on the assumption that the presence or absence of psychopathology is dependent on a major

> gene or than strategies in which a single biological variable is
> studied.

When we revise, do we use *one, we,* or name some generic "doer?"

> 2b If **one/we/researchers** are to understand genetic factors that
> make some patients vulnerable to psychiatric disorder, **one/we/
> they** should use multivariate strategies rather than strategies in
> which **one/we/they** assume that a major gene is responsible for
> psychopathology or strategies in which **one/we/they** study only a
> single biological variable.

English is a flexible language, but it has a chronic problem with
indefinite subjects. The general *one* is stiff, but *we* may be ambiguous
because it can refer just to the writer, to a group that includes the
writer but excludes the reader, to just reader and writer, or to everyone. And *they* may be ambiguous when the sentence has other plural
referents. As a consequence, many writers who want to avoid nominalizations but don't want to use these pronouns slip into passive
verbs (more about them later):

> 2c. To **understand** the genetic factors that make some patients vul-
> nerable to psychiatric disorders, multivariate strategies **should be
> used** rather than strategies in which it **is assumed** that a major
> gene causes psychopathology or strategies in which only a single
> biological variable **is studied.**

Abstract Characters

As we deal with increasingly complex and abstract matters, we almost
inevitably write abstract and complex prose, because we will tell
stories whose central characters are not flesh-and-blood people, but
abstract concepts. When our readers are not familiar with those
abstractions, they find it difficult to distinguish them from the other
abstractions around them.

If, for example, you are unfamiliar with "intention" as a distinct
philosophical concept, you may find it difficult under the best of circumstances to understand a story whose main characters are called
"Prospective Intention" and "Immediate Intention." And you will find
that story even more difficult to the degree that you have to cope with
more nominalizations than you should have to. Here is a story about

those two character-nominalizations, Prospective and Immediate Intention. To a reader not familiar with such philosophical stories, this passage will seem difficult because those characters (bold-faced) are embedded in a field of other nominalizations (italicized).

> The *argument* is this. The cognitive component of **intention** exhibits a high degree of *complexity.* **Intention** is temporally divisible into two: **prospective intention** and **immediate intention.** The cognitive *function* of prospective **intention** is the *representation* of a subject's similar past *actions,* his current situation, and his course of future *actions.* That is, the cognitive component of prospective **intention** is a *plan.* The cognitive *function* of immediate **intention** is the *monitoring* and *guidance* of ongoing bodily *movement.*
>
> —Myles Brand, *Intending and Acting*

When I revise peripheral nominalizations into verbs and introduce flesh-and-blood characters to accompany the abstract characters, the passage becomes clearer to someone unfamiliar with such stories:

> *I* argue this about **intention. Intention** has a complex cognitive component of two temporal kinds: **prospective intention** and **immediate intention. Prospective intention** lets us represent how *we* have acted in the past, how *we* act in the present and how *we* will act in the future. That is, *we* use the cognitive component of **prospective intention** to help *us* plan. **Immediate intention** lets us monitor and guide *our* bodies as *we* move them.

I have, of course, given the author a voice not his own, a presumptuousness he would have reason to reject. But have I made him say something he did not mean? Some argue that any change in form changes content, but I don't think so. In this case, only the author could say.

Obscured Characters

Readers also have problems when the flesh-and-blood characters that do appear are expressed in words that modify a nominalization or in the objects of prepositions such as *by, of, on the part of.*

> **The Federalists'** argument that the destabilization *of* **government** was the result *of* **popular democracy** was based on **their** belief in

the tendency *of* **factions** to further **their** self-interest at the expense of the common good.

In this clearer version, characters are consistently subjects:

> **The Federalists** argued that **popular democracy** destabilized **government,** because **they** believed that **factions** tended to further their self-interest at the expense of the common good.

Characters can also hide out in an ADJECTIVE:

> Medieval **theological** debates often addressed what to **modern** philosophical thought seems to be metaphysical triviality.

> Medieval **theologians** often debated issues that **philosophers** today might think were metaphysically trivial.

Missing but Understood Characters

Readers have the biggest problem when sentences lack characters altogether:

> A decision was made in favor of conducting an investigation into the failure.

Sentences like these typically appear in the context of other sentences that do name characters, so the writer typically assumes that the context is so clear that characters don't have to be made explicit. Such writers are sometimes right about that, but more often wrong.

Remote Characters

And in some cases, characters are so remote from the surface of a sentence that we have to do more than just find verbs hiding behind nominalizations. We have to reconstruct characters and actions out of what we think a writer "really" had in mind and then recast the entire sentence around them (actions are italicized, my invented characters boldfaced):

> There seems to be no apparent reason that would *account* for the *lack* of evidence.

You *have failed to give* me reasons why you *haven't been able to provide* evidence.

Exercise 4-1

Revise these next sentences so that each has a specific character as the subject of a specific verb. You will have to invent characters as subjects. Use *we, I,* or any other word that seems appropriate.

1. The existence of differences in interpretation about the meaning of the discovery of America has led to a re-assessment of Columbus's place in western history.
2. A solution to the UFO problem is impossible without a better understanding about the possibility of extra-terrestrial life.
3. Tracing the transitions in a book, or a well-written article will provide assistance in efforts at improving coherence in prose.
4. Decisions about forcibly administering medication in an emergency room setting despite the inability of an irrational patient to provide legal consent is an on-scene medical decision.
5. Resistance has been growing against building new mental health facilities in residential areas because of a distrust founded on the belief that the few examples of improper management are typical. There is a need for a modification of these perceptions.
6. With the decline in network television viewing in favor of cable and rental cassettes, awareness is growing at the networks of the changes in tastes and viewing habits, resulting in their need to do their programming accordingly.
7. Of concern is the increasing cost of protecting museum artifacts. Their mere display is a contributing factor to deterioration, to say nothing of the effects of their storage environment. The concept of conservation means that higher expenditures are necessary to ensure that skills and equipment will be available to ensure their preservation for future generations.
8. Recent assertions about failures to present information with accuracy and fairness is a correct description of journalism in the Middle East today. A comparison of press coverage from different countries of the same event reveals many inaccuracies in the reporting of politically biased newspapers. The omission of facts and the slanting of stories show the failure of journalism to carry

out its mission with the objectivity expected of it. As a result, lack of knowledge of the truth has resulted in a public opinion based more on emotion than on reason.

PASSIVES AND CHARACTERS: THE STANDARD ADVICE

Nominalizations make for hard reading. They force us to read extra words, to search out agents and actions and then re-assemble them into a coherent story. When characters are missing altogether, we have to reconstruct or even invent them. When writers fall into this kind of style because their cast of mind is distant, impersonal, aloof, they typically use another feature of style that encourages them to drop out even more characters: they choose the passive voice (not *tense*) instead of the active.

Like some other terms we've looked at, *active* and *passive* can be confusing, because we use them in two ways: We often call sentences passive that *feel* passive, usually because they are highly nominalized:

> The termination of the project was a consequence of an inability to achieve success in cost control monitoring.

But we also use passive to mean a grammatical construction. Here's the difference between passive as a term of feeling and passive as a term of grammar.

When we write in the active voice we typically name in the subject of our sentences the AGENT of an action, and name in the OBJECT of the verb the GOAL or receiver of that action:

$$\text{Active:} \quad \underset{\text{agent}}{\overset{\text{subject}}{\text{I}}} \quad \Rightarrow \quad \underset{\text{action}}{\overset{\text{verb}}{\text{lost}}} \quad \Rightarrow \quad \underset{\text{goal}}{\overset{\text{object}}{\text{the money}}}$$

In a sentence in the passive voice, the sequence is reversed: The subject expresses the goal of the action and the agent of the action appears optionally after the verb in a *by*-phrase. A form of *be* also precedes a PAST PARTICIPLE form of the verb:

	subject	(*be* + past participle)	prepositional phrase
Passive:	The money ⇐	was lost ⇐	[by me.]
	goal	action	agent

Critics of style relentlessly urge writers to avoid the passive, because a sentence with a passive verb has four potential problems:

— The passive requires an extra word, the form of *be.*
— The passive distorts what readers expect to find in the subject of a sentence—the agent of an action.
— The passive allows us to avoid assigning responsibility:

> The money was lost.

— The passive can result in sentences with complex subjects:

> **The complications arising from our recent decision to close our storage facility in Maryland and transfer its operations to Pennsylvania**_{subject} were also discussed.

And when we combine unnecessary passives with nominalizations, we create that kind of prose variously called *sociologicalese, educationese, legalese, bureaucratese*—all of the *-eses* of those who confuse authority and objectivity with polysyllabic abstraction and remote impersonality, a style in which no one exists to do anything. Contrast the impersonal passive with the active:

> A decrease in **restrictions** on **treatment** is **followed** by increased rate of **recovery.**

> When **we** *treat* patients less restrictively, **they** *recover* faster.

We can rely on the standard advice about choosing the active voice instead of the passive. But that's the easy generalization. In many cases, the passive is, in fact, the better choice.

CHOOSING BETWEEN ACTIVE AND PASSIVE

To choose active or passive, we have to answer five questions:

1. Must our readers know who is acting?
2. Do we *want* our readers to know who is acting?
3. Which would better help readers move from one sentence to the next?
4. Which would encourage readers to focus on a logically consistent string of subjects?
5. Which would focus our readers on the *right* string?

1. Must Your Reader Know Who Is Acting?

Often, we skip saying who is responsible for an action, because we don't know or our readers probably don't care:

> The President **was rumored** to have considered resigning.

> Those who **are found** guilty can **be fined.**

> Valuable records should always **be kept** in a fireproof safe.

In these, the passive is the natural choice. If we do not know who rumored, we cannot say. And since we all know who finds criminals guilty, who fines them, who should keep records in a safe, our readers wouldn't wonder. On this basis, the passive sentence (1a) would be more economical than its active version, (1b):

> (1a) Once this design *was developed* for our project, it *was* quickly *applied* to others.

> (1b) Once **those who worked on the design** *developed* it for our project, **others** could quickly *apply* it to theirs.

2. Do We *Want* Our Readers to Know Who Is Acting?

Of course, some writers deliberately avoid naming names when they don't want to assign responsibility for an action with bad consequences. In this next sentence, we might predict the passive, for reasons having to do less with style than with avoiding responsibility:

> Because the final safety inspection **was** not **monitored,** the brake assembly mechanism **was left** incorrectly aligned, a fact that **was**

known several months before it **was decided** to publicly reveal that information.

When someone writes "Mistakes were made," the writer probably knows who made the mistakes, and chances are good that it is that writer. In cases like this, readers might like to know who the agents are, but writers like to keep those agents out of sight. One way they do that is the passive voice. This kind of anonymity goes beyond clarity to the issue of ethics.

Since the passive is such an obvious device, crafty writers find other ways to obscure agency. In June, 1992, the California Attorney General's office accused the Sears Company of overcharging for automobile repairs. In response, Sears ran newspaper advertisements that included these two sentences:

> With over two million automotive customers serviced last year in California alone, mistakes may have occurred. However, Sears wants you to know that we would never intentionally violate the trust customers have shown in our company for 105 years.

The first sentence avoids mentioning Sears as the responsible party by asserting not that mistakes "were made" (implicitly by them) but that mistakes "occurred." The second sentence then explicitly names Sears in its subject as the responsible agent because that sentence refers to its good actions. If we revise the first sentence so that it explicitly refers to Sears and the second so that it hides Sears, we get an effect that the people in Sears' public relations department would gasp at:

> We at Sears serviced over two million automotive customers last year in California alone, so we may have made mistakes. However, you should know that no intentional violation of 105 years of trust occurred.

3. Does the Active or Passive Better Contribute to Flow?

When we read, we depend on the beginning of each sentence to locate us in a context of what we know before we follow the sentence to what we don't. But we find many sentences whose subjects confuse us by expressing new and therefore unexpected information. Such sentences are hard to read because their dislocated subjects break the flow from one sentence to the next.

In (2a), the subject of the second sentence (boldfaced) communicates new and complex information, while its object expresses a familiar concept from the previous sentence:

2a. Higher education must decide whether it will focus resources on improving education in the sciences alone or whether it will try to raise the level of education across the whole curriculum. [**The weight we give to two factors, industrial competitiveness and the value we attach to the liberal arts,**]$_{new\ information}$ will influence$_{active\ verb}$ [*this decision*]$_{old\ information}$.

That second sentence is in the active voice, but it would be more readable in the passive, because then the familiar information would be first and the new and unexpected information last:

2b. Higher education must decide whether it will focus resources on improving education in the sciences alone or whether it will try to raise the level of education across the whole curriculum. [*This decision*]$_{old\ information}$ will be influenced$_{passive\ verb}$ by [**the weight we give to two factors, industrial competitiveness and the value we attach to the liberal arts**]$_{new\ information}$.

Readers find long subjects difficult, especially subjects that express new information. You can often avoid this difficulty by switching subject and object with a passive verb, as in (2b).

4. Which Better Contributes to a Consistent Point of View?

The fourth consideration is more complex: It is whether the subjects in a sequence of sentences focus our readers' attention on a *consistent* sequence of concepts. Look at the subjects in this next paragraph about energy. In the first version, the subjects (boldfaced) of the verbs (italicized) seem to have been chosen almost at random:

> It *was found* that **data concerning resources allocated to the states** *were not obtained*. **This action** *is needed* so that **it** *can be determined* how **resources** *can be redirected* on a timely basis when conditions change. **Sufficient support** *must be provided* to the

Energy Secretary so that **data on fuel consumption** *may be gathered* on a regular basis.

In this next revision, the writer helps the reader get a consistent point of view by choosing active and passive verbs that will put a character into a subject:

We *found*$_{active}$ that **the Department of Energy** *did not obtain*$_{active}$ data about resources that **Federal offices** *were allocating*$_{active}$ to the states. **The Department** *needs*$_{active}$ these data so that **it** *can determine*$_{active}$ how to *redirect*$_{active}$ resources when **conditions** *change.* **The Energy Secretary** *must be provided*$_{passive}$ with support so that **his office** *can gather*$_{active}$ data on fuel consumption on a regular basis.

Now at the beginning of each sentence, each agent-subject anchors the reader in something familiar—the cast of characters. But note the passive in the last sentence:

The Energy Secretary **must be provided** with support . . .

That passive allowed the writer to keep the reader focused on a consistent point of view by keeping the main character in the sequence of subjects.

If in a series of passive sentences, you find yourself shifting from one unrelated subject to another, try rewriting those sentences in the active voice. But if you can make your sequence of subjects consistent with passive verbs, choose the passive.

5. Which Creates the Right Point of View?

Almost all stories have more than one character, and we can tell almost any story from any character's point of view:

Once upon a time, Little Red Riding Hood was walking . . .

Once upon a time, the Wolf was loitering in the woods . . .

Once upon a time, Grandma was getting hungry for lunch . . .

Once upon a time, the Woodsman was chopping down a tree . . .

We always have to choose whose story we want to tell. The writer of this next passage reports the end of World War II from the point of view of the Allies. In so doing, he used a series of active verbs (italicized) in order to tell their story:

> By March 1945, **the Allies** *had* essentially *defeated* the Axis nations; all that remained was a bloody climax. **American, French, and British forces** *had breached* German borders and *were bombing* both Germany and Japan around the clock. But **they** *had* not so *devastated* either country as to destroy its ability to resist.

Had the writer wanted the reader to understand history from the point of view of Germany and Japan, he could have used passive verbs to tell their story:

> By March 1945, **the Axis nations** *had been* essentially *defeated;* all that remained was a bloody climax. **German borders** *had been breached,* and **both Germany and Japan** *were being bombed* around the clock. **Neither country,** though, *had been so devastated* that **it** could not resist.

While the familiar advice about writing in the active voice is generally reliable, the passive has its uses: It can help you duck responsibility, but more important, it can help you move your readers from sentence to sentence easily and help you shape their point of view.

A Quick Diagnosis

On p. 46 we suggested some tests to predict how difficult your readers may find your writing. Those tests apply here too, but instead of checking simply for characters as subjects, check as well for the *consistency* of the sequence of your subjects. Skim through just the subjects of your CLAUSES, especially MAIN CLAUSES, to determine whether they constitute a coherent sequence. If they do not, try revising sentences whose subjects seem distinctly out of line with other subjects. We revisit this principle in Lesson Six.

Exercise 4-2

In the following, change as many active verbs as you can into passives, and passive into active. Which sentences improve? which not? (In the first five, the active verbs that can be made passive are italicized, the already passive verbs boldfaced.)

1. Independence **is gained** by those on welfare when skills **are taught** that the marketplace *values.*
2. In this textbook students **are trained** to perceive rhythm not as a series of individual notes but as a larger movement that *creates* a sense of musical architecture.
3. When fewer goods **are made** available to consumers while inflation *is raising* prices, the rate of inflation **will be accelerated** when consumers *hoard* goods that they most *need.*
4. The heat-resistant tiles on the space shuttle **had to be re-designed** and **replaced** because their surfaces **had been bombarded** by micrometeorites.
5. The different planes of the painting **are** immediately **noticed,** because their clashing colors **are set** against a background of subtle shades of grey that **are laid** on in thin layers that **cannot be noticed** unless the surface **is examined** closely.
6. Before Ann Richards was elected governor of Texas, she was attacked as a liberal Democrat with a background in which drugs may have been used, but her campaign was conducted in a way in which negative advertising was also used.
7. In this article, it is argued that the Vietnam War was fought to extend U.S. influence throughout Southeast Asia and was not ended until it was made clear that the United States could not defeat the Viet Cong and North Vietnam unless atomic weapons were used.
8. Science education cannot be improved to a level sufficient to ensure that American industry will be supplied with skilled workers and researchers until more money is provided to primary and secondary schools.
9. The tone in the first section of Bierce's "An Occurrence at Owl Creek Bridge" is presented in a dispassionate way. In the first paragraph, two sentinels are described in some detail, but the line, "It did not appear to be the duty of these two men to know what was occurring at the center of the bridge" takes all emotion away from them. In paragraph 2, a description is given of the surroundings and of the spectators but no feeling is betrayed because the language used is neutral and unemotional. This entire section is presented as devoid of emotion even though it is filled with details.

Exercise 4-3

Revise a paragraph in Lesson One so that all the active verbs are passive. Then exchange your paragraphs with someone and see if you can each rewrite your revisions back into the original.

THE "OBJECTIVE" PASSIVE

In one context, the passive voice has been given a special role: In the sciences, the passive allegedly protects scientific writing from the unscientific, subjective point of view. Here is an example:

> On the basis of their verbal intelligence, prior knowledge and essay scores, the essays **were analyzed** for hierarchical structure and **were evaluated** according to the richness of concepts. The subjects **were subdivided** into a high- or low-ability group. Half of each group **was** then randomly **assigned** to a treatment or a placebo group.

In fact, despite the widespread belief that we should avoid using *I* or *we* in academic writing, particularly in scientific writing, many highly regarded writers use *I* and *we* regularly. These next passages come from the openings of articles published in respected journals:

> This paper is concerned with two problems. How can **we** best handle, in a transformational grammar certain restrictions that ... To illustrate, **we** may cite ... **we** shall show ...

> Since the pituitary-adrenal axis is activated during the acute phase response, **we** have investigated the potential role ... Specifically, **we** have studied the effects of interleukin-1 ...

> Any study of tensions presupposes some acquaintance with certain findings of child psychology. **We** may begin by inquiring whether ... **we** should next proceed to investigate.

Here are the first few words from several consecutive sentences in an article from *Science,* a journal of considerable prestige:

> ... **we** want ... Survival gives ... **We** examine ... **We** compare ... **We** have used ... Each has been weighted ... **We** merely take

... They are subject ... **We** use ... Efron and Morris (3)
describe ... **We** observed ... **We** might find ... **We** know ...
Averages for a season ordinarily run ... Spread comes.... **We**
can shrink....

> —John P. Gilbert, Bucknam McPeek, and Frederick Mosteller,
> "Statistics and Ethics in Surgery and Anesthesia," *Science*

To be sure, some writers and editors resolutely avoid the first person
everywhere. But those who claim that good academic writing must
always be impersonally third person are wrong.

METADISCOURSE: WRITING ABOUT WRITING

When academic writers use the first person, however, they use it systematically. Look at the verbs in the passages above: *cite, show, begin
by inquiring, proceed to investigate, compare.* With those words,
writers refer not to their subject matter—statistics, ethics, grammar,
child psychology, but to their own acts of writing.

We **suggest** that these data are an artifact of observer bias.

This kind of self-referential language we call METADISCOURSE,
discourse about discourse. Metadiscourse is the language we use to
describe what we are doing as we think and write or to tell readers
what we want them to think as they read. We need some metadiscourse in everything we write because it helps us manage how our
readers follow and understand us. Some kinds:

— Rhetorical actions: *explain, show, argue, claim, deny, suggest,
   contrast, add, expand, summarize;*
— Parts of our discourse: *first, second, third; to begin, finally;*
— Logical connections: *therefore, however, consequently, if so;*
— Hedges to our beliefs: *It seems that, perhaps, I believe;*
— Guides for our readers: *Consider now, Recall, Imagine ...*

When academic writers use the first person, they typically use *I*
or *we* in introductions, where they announce their intentions: *We
claim that ..., We shall **show** ..., We **begin** by ...* If they use metadiscourse at the beginning, they are likely to use it again at the end,

when they summarize: *We have **suggested** ..., I have **shown** that ..., We have not **claimed**. ...*

On the other hand, academic and scholarly writers rarely use the first person to describe *particular* actions that they performed in their research. We are unlikely to find passages such as this:

> To determine if monokines directly elicited an adrenal steroidogenic response, *I **added*** monocyte-conditioned medium and purified preparations of ...

More likely is the passive verb of the original sentence and its technical subject:

> To determine if monokines directly elicited an adrenal steroidogenic response, *monocyte-conditioned medium and purified preparations ...* **were added** ...

But when the writer cast that sentence in the passive, he unselfconsciously dangled his modifier:

> To determine if ..., ... preparations were added ...

The implied subject of the infinitive verb *determine* is *I* or *we: I determine* or *we determine*. But that implied subject *I* or *we* differs from the explicit subject—*preparations.* That's when a modifier dangles: The implied subject of the introductory phrase differs from the explicit subject of the main clause. Writers of scientific prose use this pattern so often, however, that it has become standard usage. When editors with stern views about correct grammar reject both first person subjects and dangling modifiers, they put their authors into a predicament where they are damned if they do and damned if they don't. In truth, of course, the passive does not make prose more objective. It makes it only seem so.

As a small historical footnote, we might note that this impersonal "scientific" style is a modern development. In his "New Theory of Light and Colors" (1672), Sir Isaac Newton wrote this charming first-person account of an early experiment:

> I procured a triangular glass prism, to try therewith the celebrated phenomena of colors. And for that purpose, having darkened my laboratory, and made a small hole in my window

shade, to let in a convenient quantity of the sun's light, I placed
my prism at the entrance, that the light might be thereby
refracted to the opposite wall. It was at first a very pleasing
diversion to view the vivid and intense colors produced
thereby.

Exercise 4-4

Sentences (1) to (4) below are all passive, but two of them could be
active because those passive verbs are metadiscourse verbs that frequently take first person subjects. Change the verbs that should be
changed, but when you have finished doing that, go through each sentence again and revise into verbs any nominalizations that you think
are hiding important actions.

1. It <u>is concluded</u> that instability of the image <u>is caused</u> by a deteri-
    oration of the optical system.
2. The model has been subjected to statistical analysis.
3. An inability to export sufficient crude oil for hard currency needs
    is proposed here as the cause of the collapse of the Soviet econ-
    omy.
4. The assembly of extensive data is being considered, but no eval-
    uation has yet been made in regard to the potential of its
    reliability.

Sentences (5) to (8) are active, but two of their verbs should be passive because they are not metadiscourse verbs. Revise in other ways
that you think appropriate.

5. In Section IV, I <u>argue</u> that the indigenous culture engaged in over-
    cultivation of the land at the base of the mesa leading to its
    exhaustion as a viable food-producing area.
6. Our intention in this book is to help readers achieve an under-
    standing not only of the differences in grammar between Arabic
    and English, but also the differences in world view as reflected by
    Arabic vocabulary.
7. To make an evaluation of the changes in the flow-rate, I made a
    comparison of the original flow rate on the basis of figures I had
    compiled with figures that Jordan had collected in a study of the
    diversion patterns of slow-growth swamps.

8. We performed the tissue rejection study on the basis of methods developed with our discovery of increases in dermal sloughing as a result of cellular regeneration.

Exercise 4-5

Revise these passages. Change passives into actives only where doing so will improve the sentence. If necessary, invent a rhetorical situation to account for your choice of active or passive.

1. Your figures were reanalyzed to determine their accuracy. Results will be announced when it is judged appropriate.
2. Almost all home mortgage loans nowadays are made for 30 years. With the price of housing at inflated levels, those loans cannot be paid off in any shorter period of time.
3. The author's impassioned narrative style is abandoned and in its place a cautious treatment of theories of conspiracy is presented. But the moment the narrative line is picked up again, he invests his prose with the same vigor and force.
4. Many arguments were advanced against Darwinian evolution in the nineteenth century because basic assumptions about our place in the world were contradicted by it. No longer were humans defined as privileged creatures but rather as a product of natural forces.
5. For many years federal regulations concerning the use of wiretapping have been ignored. Only recently have tighter restrictions been imposed on the circumstances that warrant it.

In these sentences, change passives to actives and edit nominalizations into a more direct agent-action style. Invent agents where necessary.

6. It is my belief that the social significance of smoking receives its clearest explication through an analysis of peer interaction among adolescents. In particular, studies should be made of the manner in which relational interactive behavior is conditioned by social class.
7. These directives are written in a style of maximum simplicity as a result of an attempt at more effective communication with employees with limited reading skills who have been hired in accordance with guidelines that have been imposed.

8. The ability of the human brain to arrive at solutions of human problems has been undervalued, because studies have not been done that would be considered to have scientific reliability.

9. This is a slightly condensed version of a letter from the Chancellor of a major state university to parents of students. Why is the first part so impersonal? the second part more personal? Change the first part so that whoever performs the actions referred to are subjects of verbs. Then change the second part so that all the specific characters disappear. What is the difference? You will have to do more than simply revise a couple of passives into actives.

> As you probably have heard, the U of X campus has been the scene of a number of incidents of racial and sexual harassment over the last several weeks. The fact that similar incidents have occurred on campuses around the country does not make them any less offensive when they take place here. Of the 10 to 12 incidents that have been reported since early October, most have involved graffiti or spoken insults. In only two cases was any physical contact made, and in neither case was anyone injured.
>
> U of X is committed to providing its students with an environment where they can live, work, and study without fear of being taunted or harassed because of their race, gender, religion or ethnicity. I have made it clear that bigotry and intolerance will not be permitted and that U of X's commitment to diversity is unequivocal. We are also taking steps to improve security in campus housing. We at U of X are proud of this university's tradition of diversity . . .

NOUN + NOUN + NOUN

One more point of style can distort the coincidence that readers expect between the parts of an idea and parts of a sentence: the long COMPOUND NOUN phrase.

> **Early childhood thought disorder misdiagnosis** often occurs as a result of unfamiliarity with recent **research literature** describing such conditions. This paper is a review of seven recent studies in which are findings of particular relevance to **preteen hyperactivity**

diagnosis and to **treatment modalities** involving **medication maintenance level evaluation procedures.**

Some grammarians insist that we should never use one noun to modify another, but that would rule out such common phrases as *stone wall, student committee, space shuttle,* and a good many technical terms that technical writers need.

But we should reject a long series of nouns when they are ambiguous and especially when they include unnecessary nominalizations and appear just once or twice. (We will always debate what counts as "unnecessary," of course.) Whenever you find a string of nouns that you haven't seen before, try disassembling them. Start from the last and reverse their order, linking them with prepositional phrases. If one of the nouns is a nominalization, rewrite it into a full verb. Here is the first compound in the example passage revised:

1	2	3	4
early childhood	thought	disorder	misdiagnosis
$\Rightarrow$ misdiagnose	disordered	thought	in early childhood
4	3	2	1

Now we can see the ambiguity: What's early, the childhood, the disorder, or the diagnosis? Next we re-assemble them:

Physicians misdiagnose disordered thought in young children because they are unfamiliar with recent literature on the subject.

Exercise 4-6

Finish rewriting that passage about misdiagnosing disordered thought. Then turn the compound noun phrases in (1) to (4) into prepositional phrases.

1. The plant safety standards committee discussed recent air quality regulation announcements.
2. Diabetic patient blood pressure reduction may be brought about by renal depressor application.
3. The main goal of this article is to describe text comprehension processes and recall protocol production.
4. On the basis of these principles, we may now attempt to formulate narrative information extraction rules.

In these next sentences, unpack compound nouns and edit the indirect style by placing characters and actions in subjects and verbs. Invent characters where necessary.

5. This paper is an investigation into information processing behavior involved in computer human cognition simulation games.
6. Enforcement of guidelines for new automobile tire durability must be a Federal Trade Commission responsibility.
7. The Social Security program is a monthly income floor guarantee for individuals whose benefit package potential is based on a determination of lifelong contribution schedule.
8. Based on training needs assessment reviews and on office site visits, there was the identification of concepts and issues that can be used in our creation of an initial staff questionnaire instrument.
9. Corporate organization under state law supervision has resulted in federal government failures in regard to the effective implementation of pollution reduction measures.

THE PROFESSIONAL VOICE

Every group demands that its new members master a voice and vocabulary testifying that they have accepted the values of the group. The aspiring physicist or engineer or psychologist must learn not only to think like a professional, but also to sound like one. Too often, though, writers think that they sound professional only when they write in ways that are complex and abstract. Or they unknowingly fall into that style because they read so much of it. When they complicate substantive complexity with an unfriendly prose style, they make it difficult, often impossible, for the merely well-educated layperson to appreciate issues that might have significant consequences for society in general.

Some high-level scholarship, of course, cannot be made clear to any lay reader. But that is true less often than many scholars believe. Here is an excerpt from an article by Talcott Parsons, a social scientist who was as influential in shaping the way sociologists think about society as he was notorious for the opacity of his prose.

> Apart from theoretical conceptualization there would appear
> to be no method of selecting among the indefinite number of

varying kinds of factual observation which can be made about a
concrete phenomenon or field so that the various descriptive
statements about it articulate into a coherent whole, which constitutes an "adequate," a "determinate" description. Adequacy in
description is secured insofar as determinate and verifiable
answers can be given to all the scientifically important questions involved. What questions are important is largely
determined by the logical structure of the generalized conceptual scheme which, implicitly or explicitly, is employed.

If we revise this passage in all the ways we've described, we can make
it accessible to a moderately well-educated audience:

When scientists lack a theory, they cannot select from everything they
could say about a subject only that which they can fit into a coherent
whole, a whole that would be "adequate" or "determinate." Scientists
describe something "adequately" only when they can verify answers
to questions they think are important. They decide what questions are
important on the basis of the theories that they implicitly or explicitly
use.

Even that could be made more direct:

To describe something so that it fits into a whole, you need a theory.
You need a theory to ask questions because without one you can't
verify your answers. In fact, you need a theory to decide what to ask.

The simplest version omits Parson's nuances. But the ordinary mind
certainly loses those nuances as his excruciating style numbs all but
his most masochistically dedicated readers.

Whether we are readers or writers, teachers or editors, all of us
who read and write must understand three things about writing whose
style seems complex:

— such a style may precisely express complex ideas;
— such a style may gratuitously complicate already complex ideas;
— such a style may gratuitously complicate simple ideas.

Our task as readers is to discriminate among these kinds of complexity
so that we can know when a passage is gratuitously complex and, if
not condemn it, at least not blame ourselves for not understanding it.
As writers, our task is to recognize when we have committed that
gratuitous complexity and, if we have, to revise.

SUMMING UP

We can sum up these principles still using this scheme:

	Subject	Verb	Complement
FIXED			
VARIABLE	Characters	Action	

Use subjects to name characters and verbs to name their actions.

1. When you tell stories with abstract nominalizations as your main characters, use as few other nominalizations as you can:

    > A **nominalization** is a **transformation** of a verb into a noun, often resulting in the **displacement** of real characters from subjects by **actions.**

    > When a **nominalization** *transforms* a verb into a noun, **actions** often *displace* real characters from subjects.

2. Do not revise passives if the agent of an action is obvious:

    > The President **was re-elected** with 54 percent of the vote.

3. Do not revise passives into actives if the passive gives you a coherent sequence of subjects:

    > By March of 1945, **the Axis nations** had been essentially defeated; all that remained was a bloody, climax. **The German borders** had been breached, and **both Germany and Japan** were being bombed around the clock. **Neither country,** though, had been so devastated that **it** could not resist.

4. Feel free to revise passives into actives if the verbs are metadiscourse verbs:

    > Any study of tensions presupposes acquaintance with certain findings of child psychology. This study **may be initiated** by inquiring whether . . . Next should **be investigated** . . .

    > Any study of tensions presupposes acquaintance with certain findings of child psychology. **We** may begin by inquiring whether . . . **we** should next investigate. . . .

Lesson Five

Concision

Less is more.
ROBERT BROWNING

There is no artifice as good and desirable as simplicity.
ST. FRANCIS DE SALES

Loquacity and lying are cousins.
GERMAN PROVERB

To a Snail: If "compression is the first grace of style," you have it.
MARIANNE MOORE

If you require a practical rule of me, I will present you with this:
Whenever you feel an impulse to perpetrate a piece of exceptionally
fine writing, obey it—wholeheartedly—and delete it before sending
your manuscript to press. Murder your darlings.
ARTHUR QUILLER-COUCH

When a Discourse is to be bound down upon Paper, and subjected to
the calm leisurely Examination of nice Judgment, everything that is
needless gives Offense.
BENJAMIN FRANKLIN

Everything should be made as simple as possible, but not simpler.
ALBERT EINSTEIN

FIVE PRINCIPLES OF ECONOMY

You're a long way toward a readable style when you can control how your SUBJECTS and VERBS support the story you tell about your CHARACTERS and their ACTIONS. But even when you match your grammar to your story, your sentences may still seem wordy and graceless:

> In my personal opinion, it is necessary that we all not fail to listen to and think over in a very careful manner each and every suggestion that anyone offers to us.

The writer matched her agents and actions to her subjects and verbs, but used more words than her readers needed: Every opinion is personal, so cut *personal*. And since a statement like this is obviously opinion, cut *in my opinion*. *It is necessary* means *must*. *We* implies *all*. *Listen to and think over* means *consider*. *In a careful manner* means *carefully* and *very* adds nothing. *Each and every* is redundant, so we need only *each*. A suggestion is by definition offered to someone, so neither do we need *that anyone offers to us*. And since the negative *not fail* implies its positive, change the sentence to an affirmative. What's left is leaner:

> We must consider each suggestion carefully.

I pruned five kinds of wordiness that suggest five principles of economy:

1. Delete words that mean little or nothing: *very* and *all*.
2. Delete words that repeat other words: *every* in *each and every*.
3. Delete words whose meaning your reader can infer from other words: *that someone offers us* is from *suggestion*.
4. Replace a phrase with a word: *listen to and think over* ⇒ *consider*.
5. Change unnecessary negatives to affirmatives.

Unfortunately, these principles are easier for me to state than for you to follow, because the only reliable way you can identify and remedy wordiness is to slog through every sentence, word by word. That's hard work.

1. DELETE MEANINGLESS WORDS

Some modifiers are like verbal tics that we write as unconsciously as
we clear our throats:

kind of	really	basically	practically
actually	virtually	generally	certain
particular	individual	given	various

Productivity **actually** depends on **certain** factors that **basically**
involve psychology more than any **particular** technology.

Prune the meaningless modifiers, and we get something more concise:

Productivity depends more on psychology than on technology.

2. DELETE DOUBLED WORDS

English has a tradition of doubling words, a habit we acquired shortly
after English writers began to borrow from Latin and French. They
used both the native word and a borrowed synonym, because the borrowed word sounded more learned than the native one. Now we
double both native and borrowed words. Among the common pairs:

full and complete	true and accurate	hopes and desires
hope and trust	each and every	first and foremost
any and all	basic and fundamental	various and sundry

Whenever you use a pair of adjectives, consider whether your readers
need both.

3. DELETE WHAT READERS INFER

This is the most common redundancy, because readers infer meaning
in many ways. Here are a few:

Redundant Modifiers

In some cases, the meaning of a the main word implies the modifier: *completely finish, **past** history, **various** different, **each** individual.* Other examples:

basic fundamentals	**true** facts	**important** essentials
future plans	**sudden** crisis	**consensus** of opinion
personal beliefs	**terrible** tragedy	**end** result
final outcome	**free** gift	**initial** preparation

In every case, prune the modifier:

> Do not try to *anticipate* **in advance** those events that will **completely** *revolutionize* our society because **past** *history* shows that it is the **eventual** *outcome* of seemingly minor events that has **unexpectedly** *surprised* us most.

> Do not try to *anticipate revolutionary* events because *history* shows that the *outcome* of seemingly minor events *surprises* us most.

Redundant Categories

Every word implies the name of its category, so if a word is attached to the word for its category, you can usually cut the category word. We know time is a period, a membrane is an area, pink is a color, shiny is an appearance, so we don't have to write,

> During that **period** of *time,* the *membrane* **area** became *pink* in **color** and *shiny* in **appearance**.

We need only,

> During that *time,* the *membrane* became *pink and shiny.*

In some cases, when we eliminate the category, we have to change an ADJECTIVE into an ADVERB:

> The holes must be aligned in an *accurate* **manner.**

> The holes must be aligned *accurately.*

And sometimes, we can drop the name of the category, if we change an adjective modifying the category into a NOUN:

> The *educational* **process** and *athletic* **activities** are the responsibility of the *county* **government**.

> *The county* is responsible for *education* and *athletics.*

Here are some general nouns (boldfaced) often used redundantly:

large in **size**	of a *bright* **color**
round in **shape**	at an *early* **time**
honest in **character**	in a *confused* **state**
unusual in **nature**	*extreme* in **degree**
of a *strange* **type**	*curative* **process**
area of *mathematics*	**field** of *economics*

General Implications

This kind of wordiness is hard to spot because it can be so diffuse:

> Imagine a picture of someone engaged in the activity of trying to learn the rules for playing chess.

Imagine implies *picture; trying to learn* implies *engaged in an activity; chess* implies *playing.* A reader could infer it all from this:

> Imagine someone trying to learn the rules of chess.

Or consider this:

> When we write down our ideas, the audience that reads what we have to say will infer from our prose style something about the character we have.

We can write down only ideas; an audience is someone who reads what we have to say; we write only to them; our character is something we have. So in fewer words,

> Readers infer our character from our prose style.

Unnecessary Explanation

In technical writing addressed to an informed audience, writers assume a good deal of knowledge.

> The basic type of the verb stem results from simple rearrangement of the phonemic content of polysyllabic forms so that the initial CV of the first stem syllable is transposed with the first CV of the second stem syllable.

The writer didn't define *verb stem, phonemic content, stem syllable,* or *CV* because he assumed that a professional reader reading a professional journal would know. On the other hand, a student reading her first linguistics textbook would probably need a definition of *phonetic transcription:*

> To study language scientifically, we need some kind of phonetic transcription, a system to write a language so that visual symbols consistently represent segments of speech.

4. REPLACE A PHRASE WITH A WORD

This kind of redundancy is the most difficult to prune, because we need a large vocabulary and the wit to use it. For example,

> As you carefully read what you have written to improve your wording and catch small errors of spelling, punctuation, and so on, the thing to do before anything else is to try to see where sequences of subjects and verbs could replace the same ideas expressed in nouns rather than verbs.

That is,

> As you edit, first replace nominalizations with clauses.

I compressed five phrases into five words:

carefully read what you have written	$\Rightarrow$ edit
the thing to do before anything else	$\Rightarrow$ first
try to see where	$\Rightarrow$ find

sequences of subjects and verbs	$\Rightarrow$ clauses
ideas expressed in nouns rather than verbs	$\Rightarrow$ nominalizations

I can offer no general principles that will help you recognize phrases that you can revise into a word, much less give that word. I can only point out that we often can, and that we should be on the alert for opportunities to do so—which is to say, try.

Some common phrases you can watch for:

the reason for	
for the reason that	
due to the fact that	
owing to the fact that	because, since, why
in light of the fact that	
considering the fact that	
on the grounds that	

It is difficult to explain **the reason for** the delay in the completion of the investigation.

It is difficult to explain **why** . . .

In light of the fact that no profits were reported for years, the stock values remained largely **unchanged.**

Because no profits were reported . . .

despite the fact that	
regardless of the fact that	although, even though
notwithstanding the fact that	

Despite the fact that the results were checked, errors crept into the **findings.**

Even though the results . . .

in the event that	
if it should transpire/happen that	if
under circumstances in which	

In the event that the materials arrive after the scheduled date, contact the die shipping department immediately.

If the materials arrive . . .

on the occasion of
in a situation in which ⎱ when
under circumstances in which ⎰

In a situation in which a class is over-enrolled, you may request that the instructor reopen the class.

When a class is over-enrolled . . .

as regards
in reference to
with regard to ⎱ about
concerning the matter of ⎰
where . . . is concerned

I should now like to say a few words **concerning the matter of** money.

I should now like to say a few words **about** money.

it is crucial that
it is necessary that
there is a need/necessity for ⎱ must, should
it is important that ⎰
it is incumbent upon
cannot be avoided

There is a need for more careful inspection of all welds.

You **must** inspect all welds more **carefully.**

Inspect all welds more carefully.

It is important that the proposed North-South Thruway not displace significant numbers of residents.

The proposed North-South Thruway **must** not displace significant numbers of residents.

is able to
is in a position to
has the opportunity to ⎱ can
has the capacity for ⎰
has the ability to

We are in a position to make you a firm offer.

We **can** make you a firm offer.

it is possible that
there is a chance that   } may, might, can, could
it could happen that
the possibility exists for

It is possible that nothing will come of these preparations.

Nothing **may** come of these preparations.

prior to
in anticipation of
subsequent to   } before, when, as, after
following on
at the same time as
simultaneously with

Prior to the expiration of the apprenticeship period, it is incumbent upon you to make application for full membership.

Before your apprenticeship expires, apply for full membership.

increase in } more, less/fewer; better, worse
decrease in

There has been an **increase** in the number of universities offering adult education programs.

More universities are offering adult education programs.

We have noted a **decrease** in the quality of applicants.

We have noted that applicants are **less** qualified.

5. CHANGE NEGATIVES TO AFFIRMATIVES

When we write a negative sentence, we add a word, but more important, two negatives force readers to infer our meaning through a kind of algebraic computation. These two sentences mean about the same thing:

> Don't write in the negative. Write in the affirmative.

To be direct choose

> Write in the affirmative.

Do not translate a negative into an affirmative if you want to emphasize the negative (Is that such a sentence? I could have written, "Leave a negative sentence stand when . . .". But you can rewrite most negatives, some almost formulaically:

not different	→similar	not the same	→different
not many	→few	not often	→rarely
not remember	→forget	not old enough	→too young
not have	→lack	not allow	→prevent
not include	→omit	not admit	→deny
not consider	→ignore	not accept	→reject

When you combine negatives with passives and nominalizations, your readers will find your sentences unreadable:

> Disengagement of gears is not possible without locking the mechanism.

> Payments should not be forwarded if there has not been due notification of this office.

These sentences relate two events, one a precondition for the other. First we change nominalizations into verbs and passives into actives:

> You cannot disengage gears if you do not lock the mechanism.

> Do not forward payments if you have not notified this office.

Now we revise the negatives into affirmatives:

> To disengage gears, first lock the mechanism.

> Before you forward any payments, notify this office.

Which do we put first—the outcome or the condition? That depends on what we think our reader has in mind. In these sentences, the reader would have in mind the ideas of disengaging gears and forwarding payments. So we begin with what readers know and move to what they do not.

Some verbs, conjunctions, and propositions are implicitly negative:

Verbs: *preclude, prevent, lack, fail, doubt, reject, avoid; deny, refuse, exclude, contradict, prohibit, bar.*

Conjunctions and Prepositions: *except, unless, provided; without, against, lacking, absent, but for.*

As complex as multiple explicit negatives can be, we can baffle our readers if we combine them with implicitly negative verbs and conjunctions. Compare these:

> **Except** when applicants have **not** submitted applications **without** documentation, benefits will **not** be denied.

> You will receive benefits only if you submit your documents.

> To receive benefits, submit your documents.

Exercise 5-1

Prune the redundancy from these sentences.

1. Critics cannot avoid employing complex and abstract technical terms in order for them to successfully analyze literary texts and discuss them in a meaningful way.
2. Scientific research generally depends on precisely accurate data if it is to offer theories that will allow the world to advance into the future in a safe and cautious way.
3. In regard to prospects for desirable employment in teaching positions, the future of those engaged in studies at the graduate school level is at best uncertain.
4. Those various agencies and offices that provide aid and assistance to those who participate in our program activities have reversed themselves from the policy that they recently announced to return to the original policy established earlier.

5. It is true that in spite of the fact that the educational environment is a very significant and important facet to each and every one of our children in terms of his or her future development and growth, different groups do not support reasonable and fair tax assessments that are required for the purpose of providing an educational experience at a decent level of quality.

6. Most likely, a majority of all patients who appear at a public medical clinical facility do not expect special medical attention or treatment because their health problems and concerns often seem of a minor nature and can for the most part usually be adequately treated with minimal understanding and attention.

7. Notwithstanding the fact that all legal restrictions on the use of firearms are the subject of heated debate and argument, it is necessary that the general public continue carrying on discussions pro and con in regard to them.

8. Under circumstances in which individuals with financial resources to invest anticipate the possibility that the goods and services that they buy may continue to increase in price, those individuals will ordinarily put a majority of their discretionary financial resources into specific objects of artistic value and worth.

9. In the event that governors of the various states have the opportunity to gather and discuss matters of economic needs and problems in their respective states, it is possible that they will find a way to overcome the major problem they have of specifying exactly how to divide up and distribute Federal economic resources to their different states.

10. Those engaged in the profession of education and teaching have for a long time had an interest in gaining a better understanding about significant improvements in how individuals learn and commit to memory information from written textual material. The first problem is identifying common and different features among comparable passages of writing. The second addresses the difficult matter of assigning some kind of value to the quality and quantity of information that a reader does not forget after that person reads a passage.

Exercise 5-2

A paragraph in this Lesson is wordy. Find and revise it.

Exercise 5-3

What single words can you find for the negative phrases in these sentences? Each was in an earlier draft of this book and revised.

1. While the standard definition of a verb as an action word is not reliable, it is in fact not bad advice.
2. A second set of rules includes those whose observance we do not notice, and whose violation we do not notice either.
3. But we ought not accept the argument that we do not need the word *finalize*, or that it is ugly because of the *-ize*.
4. While it is not clear what counts as "too many" prepositions, it is clear that when you do not use abstract nouns, you do not need most of the prepositional phrases.
5. These choices among points of usage let those among us who wish to do so express our sense of linguistic decorum, a decorum that many of us believe testifies to our precision. It is an impulse we ought not scorn, so long as it is not ignorant or thoughtless.

Exercise 5-4

Where appropriate, change the following negatives to affirmatives. Do any additional editing you think useful.

1. There is no possibility in regard to a reduction in the federal deficit if reductions in federal spending are not introduced.
2. Do not discontinue medication unless symptoms of dizziness and nausea alleviate within 6 hours.
3. No one is prevented from participating in cost-sharing educational programs without a full hearing into the reasons for his or her not being accepted.
4. No agreement exists on the question of an open or closed universe, a dispute about which no resolution is likely as long as a computation of the total mass of the universe has not been done.
5. So long as taxpayers do not engage in widespread refusal to pay taxes, the government will have no difficulty in paying its debts.
6. No alternative exists in this country to the eventual development of tar sand, oil shale, and coal as sources of fuel, if we wish to stop being energy dependent on imported oil.

7. Not until a resolution between Catholics and Protestants in regard to papal authority supremacy is achieved will there be the start of a reconciliation between the two Christian religions.

8. Except when such expenses do not exceed $100 the Insured may not refuse to provide the Insurer with all relevant receipts, checks, or other evidence of costs.

9. It seems to me that in a look at the nature of advertising, it is not illogical to start out with a statement that will define the term. This will establish a common point of reference so that we will not be subjective in our approach to a subject matter that is not often the topic of unemotional discussion. There is no single definition or agreement for the word *advertising*, making the chances for possible objectivity not likely.

10. Regardless of the fact that we do not know with any degree of certainty whether or not there is the existence of life forms in the universe other than our own, evidence of a statistical nature makes it highly unlikely that life does not exist somewhere among the large number of probable planetary systems scattered throughout the length and the breadth of the universe as we know it.

A PARTICULAR KIND OF REDUNDANCY: METADISCOURSE

In Lesson Four, I described METADISCOURSE as the language we use to refer to elements in a rhetorical moment:

— to what we do as writers: *to sum up, candidly, I believe, therefore, however.*

— to what we want our readers to do: *note that, consider now, as you see.*

— to what we intend our text to do: *first, second, finally.*

We need metadiscourse in almost everything we write. But some writers use so much that it buries their ideas:

> The last point I would like to make is that in regard to men-women relationships, it is important to keep in mind that the greatest changes

> have probably occurred in the way men and women are working next to one another.

Only a few words in that sentence address men-women relationships:

> greatest changes have . . . occurred in the way men and women . . . work . . . next to one another.

The rest is metadiscourse:

> The last point I would like to make is that in regard to . . . it is important to keep in mind that . . . probably . . .

If we prune the metadiscourse, we tighten the sentence:

> The greatest changes in men-women relationships have occurred in the way that they work next to one another.

Once we see what the sentence says, we can make it more direct:

> Men and women have changed relationships most in the way they work together.

But in deciding how much metadiscourse to use, we need more than generalizations, because some successful writers use a lot; others equally successful, little. You can only read with an eye to how it is used by writers you think are clear and concise and do likewise.

Here are some of the common types that you can usually prune.

Metadiscourse that Announces Your Topic

These phrases tell your reader what you intend to write about:

> **This section introduces** another problem, that of noise pollution. **The first thing to say** about it is that noise pollution. . . .

You announce your topic more concisely without the metadiscourse:

> Another problem is noise pollution. It . . .

Look closely at any sentence opening with a metadiscourse subject and verb that just announce the topic of a whole document:

> **In this essay, I will discuss** Robert Frost's nature imagery in his
> early poems.

I usually write that kind of sentence when I am starting a first draft
with little idea where I am going. In effect, it says, "I have this topic
to write about and I hope that eventually I will think of something."
It is a kind of place-holder until I discover what to say about Frost's
nature imagery in his early poems. On the other hand, when that kind
of sentence appears in a journal article, it expresses not a hope, but a
promise.

When you find that kind of sentence in your own prose, try
rewriting it into a claim that needs no introduction. Then determine
whether what's left in fact says anything significant.

> **In this essay, I will discuss** Robert Frost's nature imagery in his
> early poems.

> Robert Frost used nature images in his early poems.

Unfortunately, you may find that you have little to say, a discovery that
is always distressing, but less so than hearing someone else say it.
When you see a sentence that banal, you know you have to think
harder.

Exercise 5-5

Here are sentences that announce a topic rather than state a thesis.
Delete the metadiscourse and rewrite what remains into a full statement. Then decide whether the full statement seems to make an
interesting and contestable claim. For example,

> In this study, I examine the history of Congressional legislation regard-
> ing the protection of children in the workplace.

First, delete the metadiscourse:

> the history of Congressional legislation regarding the protection of
> children in the workplace.

Then rewrite what is left into a full sentence:

> Congress has a history of legislating the protection of children in the workplace.

That appears to be a banal claim.

1. This essay will survey recent research in schemata theory as applied to the pedagogy of mathematical problem solving.
2. I will analyze Frost's use of imagery of seasons in his longer poems published at the end of his career.
3. This essay will explore the methodological differences between English and American histories of the War of 1812 that resulted in radically differing interpretations of the cause of the conflict.
4. This essay will discuss the traditional but self-contradictory values that once showed us how to be good mothers and wives.
5. We will consider scientific thinking and its historical roots in connection with the influence of Egypt on Greek thought.
6. In this study, I will analyze the mistaken assumption underlying Freud's interpretation of dreams.
7. This chapter discusses needle sharing among drug users.
8. The relationship between order of birth and academic success will be explored.
9. I intend to address the problem of the reasons for the failure and success of trade embargoes in this century.

Metadiscourse that Hedges and Intensifies

Each profession has its own idiom of caution and confidence. How successfully you walk the rhetorical line between seeming timid or smugly dogmatic depends a good deal on how you manage phrases like *a good deal*, a phrase that a few words ago allowed me to pull back from the more dogmatic statement:

> How successfully you walk the rhetorical line between timidity and aggressiveness depends on how you manage phrases like *a good deal.*

Hedges: Some readers think hedging is mealy mouthed, but we can use hedges as modest notes of civilized diffidence. They can say to one's colleagues, "I stand behind my claim, but I understand that it

can be only tentative." This next diffidently worded paragraph introduces the article that announced the most significant breakthrough in
the history of genetics, the discovery of the double helix of DNA. I
boldface hedges:

> We **wish to suggest a** structure for the salt of deoxyribose
> nucleic acid (D.N.A.). This structure has novel features which
> are of considerable biological interest. A structure for nucleic
> acid has already been proposed by Pauling and Corey. They
> kindly made their manuscript available to us in advance of pub-
> lication. Their model consists of three intertwined chains, with
> the phosphates near the fibre axis, and the bases on the outside.
> **In our opinion,** this structure is unsatisfactory for two reasons:
> (1) **We believe** that the material which gives the X-ray dia-
> grams is the salt, not the free acid.... (2) **Some** of the van der
> Walls distances **appear** to be too small.
>
>   J.D. Watson and F.H.C. Crick, "Molecular Structure of Nucleic
>   Acids," *Nature* (171) April 25, 1953, p. 737.

Remove the hedges and we get a more aggressive claim. I boldface
the stronger words.

> We **describe** here **the** structure for the salt of deoxyribose nucleic
> acid (D.N.A.). This structure has novel features which are of consider-
> able biological interest. A structure for nucleic acid has already been
> proposed by Pauling and Corey. They kindly made their manuscript
> available to us in advance of publication. Their model consists of three
> intertwined chains, with the phosphates near the fibre axis, and the
> bases on the outside. Their structure is unsatisfactory for two reasons:
> (1) The material which gives their X-ray diagrams is the salt, not the
> free acid.... (2) Their van der Walls distances **are** too small.

Some common hedges:

> usually, often, sometimes, almost, virtually, possibly, perhaps, appar-
> ently, seemingly, it would seem, it would appear.
>
> in some ways, to a certain extent, sort of, somewhat, more or less, for
> the most part, for all intents and purposes, in some respects, in my
> opinion at least.
>
> may, might, can, could, seem, appear, tend.

Unfortunately, some of us use hedges so often that they become verbal tics (see p. 90).

Intensifiers: An appropriate intensifier lets us emphasize what we believe—or would like our readers to think we believe. Confident writers use intensifiers less often than hedges because they do not want to sound smug. A few common ones:

> very, pretty, quite, rather, clearly, obviously, undoubtedly, certainly, of course, indeed, inevitably, invariably, always.

> key, central, crucial, basic, fundamental, major, cardinal, primary, principal, essential.

> as we know, as we can see, it is clear that, it is obvious that.

Words and phrases like these generally mean little more than "believe me." In some professions, there is a rule of thumb that anyone who opens a sentence with "It is clear that . . ." or "It is obvious that . . ." is about to claim something that is at least questionable. This is another case where a good ear serves better than a flat rule.

Metadiscourse that Attributes

Some writers announce that something has been anonymously *observed* to exist, is *found* to exist, is *seen, noticed, noted, etc.*

> High divorce rates **have been observed** to occur in areas that **have been determined** to have low population density.

> Patterns of drought and precipitation **have been found** to coincide with cycles of sunspot activity.

Try leaving out that something was noticed. Just say what is:

> High divorce rates **occur** in areas with low population density.

> Patterns of drought **coincide** with sunspot activity.

If you feel you have to hedge, drop in a *seems* or *apparently:*

> Patterns of drought **apparently** coincide with sunspot activity.

Metadiscourse that Highlights

There is one device of metadiscourse that serves to highlight phrases. Contrast that sentence with,

> One metadiscourse device serves to highlight phrases.

When you open a sentence with *there is/are/was/were,* you throw weight on the words that follow. Some teachers disparage this construction, but like the passive, it has its uses. One is to introduce an idea that the next few sentences will elaborate on (as in this paragraph). When you find that you have used this construction for any other purpose, try revising.

Other constructions call similar attention to a word or phrase:

> **In regard to** *a vigorous style,* the most important feature is a short, concrete subject followed by a forceful verb.

> **So far as** *China's industrial development* **is concerned,** it will be years before it will equal Japan's.

> **As to** *security,* that problem must be examined as well.

We use phrases and clauses such as *in regard to, where X is concerned, in the matter of, as for, as to, speaking of* to announce that we are moving on to a new idea. In any other context, try to maneuver that new idea into the body of the sentence with a short subject followed by a forceful verb.

> The most important feature of **a vigorous style** is a short, concrete subject followed by a forceful verb.

> **China's industrial development** will require years before it equals Japan's.

> **Security** must also be examined.

Exercise 5-6

In these, edit for both unnecessary metadiscourse and redundancy.

1. On the other hand, however, we can perhaps point out that it appears that there may always be TV programming that may appeal to what can be considered our most prurient and, therefore, lowest interests.

2. In this particular section, I intend to discuss my feelings about the possible need to dispense with the old approach to plea bargaining. I believe this is the case because of two basic reasons. The first reason that I am of the opinion that it is necessary to deal with plea bargaining is that there is a possibility that it may let hardened criminals not receive their just punishment. The second reason is the following: Plea bargaining virtually always appears to encourage a growing lack of respect for the judicial system.

3. Turning now to the next question to be discussed, there is in regard to the subject of wilderness area preservation activities one basic principle when attempting to formulate a way of approaching decisions as to those unspoiled areas that should be set aside and not developed for commercial exploitation or business purposes.

4. It is my belief that in regard to terrestrial-type snakes, the assumption can be made that in all probability there are none to speak of in those unmapped areas of the world that would be in excess of the size of those we already have knowledge of.

5. Depending on the particular view or position that one takes on this question before us, the family unit and other social institutions that exist in society take on a degree of importance that may be equal to or perhaps even exceeding the aforementioned educational system as a source of transmission of social values.

6. As we can see, I think that in regard to the current interest in life stages, it would appear that most investigators in the area have a tendency to take the position that the mid-life crisis is the most critical period or stage in a person's life development from a mental health point of view; that is to say, we are in a position to know that, for the most part, a large number of us seem to come to a decision at that time in our lives whether or not we are going to be on the winning or losing side of the game of life.

PRODUCTIVE REDUNDANCY

Learning by Writing

We signal membership in a community by what we say and how we say it. But a surer sign is in what we know to leave unsaid, because we know not only what our readers can infer, but what they take for granted as the common knowledge of our community. When we are outsiders to a community, we don't know what not to say. Here, for example, is the introduction to a paper written by someone who had just graduated from a good college, where he had been correctly judged to be a competent and mature writer (I know because I checked) but who was not writing his first paper in law school:

> It is my opinion that the ruling of the lower court concerning the case of *Haslem v. Lockwood* should be upheld, thereby denying the appeal of the plaintiff. The main point supporting my point of view on this case concerns the tenet of our court system which holds that in order to win his case, the plaintiff must prove that he was somehow wronged by the defendant. The burden of proof rests on the plaintiff. He must show enough evidence to convince the court that he is in the right.

To this person's legal writing teacher, everything after the first sentence was "filler," a tissue of self-evident truisms: Obviously if a court upholds a ruling, it denies the appeal; obviously a plaintiff can win only if he proves a defendant has wronged him; obviously a plaintiff has the burden of proof; obviously a plaintiff has to provide evidence. But at this point in his career, the writer was an outsider who had yet to assimilate that common knowledge, so he could not resist stating it.

The large-scale version of this problem is the complaint that a paper is all "summary" with no "analysis." Perhaps a writer who only summarizes does confuse summary with analysis or cannot analyze at all. But as we learn, we all belabor the obvious. In fact, when we articulate material we are trying to learn, we master it just so that we can leave it unsaid. It may be that before some of us—probably most of us—can analyze anything new and complex, we have to make it our own by articulating it in writing. And that often sounds like summary.

The difference between the experienced and inexperienced writer is that the experienced writer knows that summarizing is a good idea and does it deliberately, but also knows when to discard it. The inexperienced writer has to learn to use summary not as an end in itself, but in the service of analysis and argument.

Autobiographical Metadiscourse

Just as "belaboring the obvious" may signal a writer getting started in a field, so may some metadiscourse. When we are comfortable thinking through familiar problems, we can more easily suppress the narrative of that process. But when we are inexperienced in a subject, we often feel compelled to give a running commentary about what we thought and did:

> **I was concerned with** the structural integrity of the roof supports, so **I proceeded** to test the weight that the transverse beams would carry. **I have concluded** after numerous tests that the beams are sufficiently strong to carry the prescribed weight, but no more. **I think that it is important** that we notify every section that uses the facility of this finding.

If we eliminate the narrative devices and refocus attention on what the reader needs to know, we make the passage more pointed:

> We must notify every section using the storage facility not to exceed the prescribed kilogram-per-square-meter floor weight. Although tests establish the structural integrity of the transverse beams, they are strong enough to carry only the prescribed weights.

Look again at that paper by the first-year law student. Not only did he "belabor the obvious"; he made the machinery of his thinking too visible. (I boldface metadiscourse and italicize the self-evident):

> **It is my opinion that** the ruling of the lower court concerning *the case* of HASLEM V. LOCKWOOD should be upheld, *thereby denying the appeal of the plaintiff.* **The main point supporting my point of view on this case concerns** *the tenet of our court system which holds that in order to win his case, the plaintiff must prove that he was somehow wronged by the defendant. The burden of proof rests on the plaintiff. He must show enough evidence to convince the court that he is in the right.*

When we delete autobiographical narrative and commonplaces that knowledgeable readers assume, we are left with something leaner:

> *Haslem* should be affirmed because the plaintiff failed to meet his burden of proof.

It is easy to judge writing like the original as "wordy," or "empty," but we should hesitate before we assume that a writer has a problem with her intrinsic ability. She may have, but she may also be at that stage where she cannot yet recognize and delete the record of her thinking or resist expressing the obvious.

SUMMING UP

You will quite often find that you can get rid of a good deal of flab from your style of writing and generally reduce overall wordiness if you are able to eliminate the different kinds of abstraction that we analyzed and discussed earlier in Lessons Three and Four. But it is also often possible for you to transform your prose style into one that is less circumlocutory and more direct if you are also able to identify and then clear away the various different kinds of wordiness discussed in this Lesson. Unfortunately, I am not in a position at this time to provide you with any broad general principles that you can rely on that are as specific and concrete as those that I hope you will recall from Lessons Three and Four about making sure that the subjects of your sentences are the characters in the story you are telling your readers and that all, or at least most of your verbs in your sentences, are the particular actions in that story. The different kinds of vague and diffuse wordiness described in this Lesson are essentially similar to the gradual accumulation of specks and motes that individually may perhaps seem trivial and unimportant to a writer, but cumulatively blur to readers what otherwise would have seemed to them to have been a clear and concise passage. To make your writing really free from those accumulated little specks and motes, you have to be able to study your prose carefully, deleting a word here, compressing a phrase there. To succeed in this activity is a very labor intensive kind of work.

1. Redundant pairs

> If and when we can define and establish our final aims and goals, each and every member of our group will be ready and willing to offer aid and assistance.
>
> If we define our goals, every member will be ready to help.

2. Redundant modifiers

> In this world of today, official governmental red tape is seriously destroying initiative among individual businesses.
>
> Government red tape is destroying business initiative.

3. Redundant categories

> In the area of educational activities, tight financial conditions are forc-
> ing school board members to cut back in nonessential areas in a
> drastic manner.

> Tight finances are forcing school boards to cut nonessentials drasti-
> cally.

4. Meaningless modifiers

> Most students generally find some kind of summer work.

> Most students find summer work.

5. Obvious implications

> Energy used to power our industries and homes will in years to come
> be increasingly expensive in terms of dollars and cents.

> Energy will eventually cost more.

6. Excessive detail

> A microwave oven that you might buy in any department store uses
> less energy that is so expensive than a conventional oven that uses gas
> or electricity.

> Microwave ovens use less energy than conventional ones.

7. A phrase for a word

> A sail-powered craft that has turned on its side or completely over
> must remain buoyant enough so that it will bear the weight of those
> individuals who were aboard.

> A capsized sailboat must support its crew and passengers.

8. Excessive metadiscourse

> It is almost certainly the case that, for the most part, totalitarian sys-
> tems cannot allow a society to settle into what we would perceive to
> be stable modes of relationships.

> Totalitarianism cannot allow stable relationships.

9. Indirect negatives

There is no reason not to believe that engineering malfunctions in nuclear energy systems cannot always be anticipated.

Malfunctions in nuclear energy systems will occasionally surprise us.

Lesson Six

Cohesion and Coherence

The beginning is half of the whole.
PLATO

*That which the fool does in the end the wise man does in the
beginning.*
R.C. TRENCH

*If he would inform, he must advance regularly from Things
known to things unknown, distinctly without Confusion, and the
lower he begins the better. It is a common Fault in Writers, to
allow their Readers too much knowledge: They begin with that
which should be the Middle, and skipping backwards and
forwards, 'tis impossible for any one but he who is perfect in
the Subject before, to understand their Work, and such an one
has no Occasion to read it.*
BENJAMIN FRANKLIN

*"Begin at the beginning," the King said, gravely, "and go on till
you come to the end; then stop."*
LEWIS CARROLL

LOCAL COHESION AND GLOBAL COHERENCE

So far, we've looked at style as if we wrote individual sentences, independent of context or intention; as if we could map our experience of the world directly onto SUBJECTS and VERBS and thereby make our sentences clearly mirror the way CHARACTERS and ACTIONS behave "out there" in reality.

Now, in fact, when we do match characters to subjects and their actions to verbs, our readers do judge our sentences to be individually clear. But effective writing requires more than local clarity. Readers must also feel that they can move easily from one clear sentence to the next, that each sentence "coheres" with the ones before and after. Readers must also feel that a series of several sentences constituting a unified passage is not just a series of consecutively connected sentences, but a "coherent" whole. Even more than that, though, our readers should feel that the whole has a particular "shape," a shape that encourages them to understand our subject as we want them to. Explaining these experiences is the object of this lesson: What do readers mean when they say a passage not only "flows," but that a flowing passage "hangs together" into a coherent whole? We'll address the questions in that order.

COHESION: A SENSE OF FLOW

Compare these two passages:

1a. The means by which Asian companies have sought to compete with American products in market segments in the Western Pacific region will constitute the objective of the first phase of our study. The labor costs of our Asian competitors and their ability to introduce new products quickly are the main issues to be examined in detail. A plan that will demonstrate how American industry can restructure its operations so that it can better exploit unexpected market opportunities, particularly in the Pacific Rim, will be developed from this study.

1b. In the first phase of our study, we will examine market segments in the Western Pacific region to determine how Asian companies have competed with American products. The study will examine in detail labor costs and the ability of Asian competitors to introduce new products quickly. We will develop from this study a plan that will demonstrate how American industry can restructure its operations so that it can better exploit unexpected market opportunities, particularly in the Pacific Rim.

Most readers feel that (1b) is more readable than (1a), but they describe that response in words different from those they use to describe the nominalized and passive passages in Lessons Three and Four. Instead of calling (1a) "wordy" or "complex" or "impersonal," most readers say it is "disjointed," "unfocused," lacking "flow"; they describe (1b) as "flowing," "coherent," and "focused." This new language of response calls for a different vocabulary of analysis.

Something Old, Something New

In Lesson Four, we devoted a few pages (pp. 70–79) to qualifying that widely repeated advice: "Avoid PASSIVES." In general, choose not the passive verb in (a), but the ACTIVE verb (b):

a. A black hole **is created by** the collapse of a dead star into a point perhaps no larger than a marble.

b. The collapse of a dead star into a point perhaps no larger than a marble **creates** a black hole.

But we also saw that the passive had its uses. One is to duck responsibility, but a more important one is to create flow and cohesion. Consider this context for (a) and (b):

[1]Some astonishing questions about the nature of the universe have been raised by scientists exploring black holes in space.

2a/b _____

[3]So much matter compressed into so little volume changes the fabric of space around it in puzzling ways.

In that context, try first the passive sentence (a) and then active (b):

> [1]Some astonishing questions about the nature of the universe have been raised by scientists exploring black holes in space. [2a]A black hole is created by the collapse of a dead star into a point perhaps no larger than a marble. [3]So much matter compressed into so little volume changes the fabric of space around it in puzzling ways.

> [1]Some astonishing questions about the nature of the universe have been raised by scientists exploring black holes in space. [2b]The collapse of a dead star into a point perhaps no larger than a marble creates a black hole. [3]So much matter compressed into so little volume changes the fabric of space around it in puzzling ways.

Our sense of "flow" should tell us that this context calls not for the active verb, but for the passive. And the reason is clear. The last few words of sentence (1) introduce an important character—black holes:

> [1]Some astonishing questions about the nature of the universe have been raised by scientists exploring **black holes in space.**

But if the next sentence, (2), is in the active voice, the first concept the reader hits is collapsed stars and marbles, information that seems to come out of nowhere.

> [2b]The collapse of a dead star into a point perhaps no larger than a marble creates a **black hole.**

The information that we would recognize, *black hole,* doesn't appear until the end of that sentence.

We could move a reader from sentence (1) to (2) more easily if we began (2) with *a black hole,* something familiar that would let the reader connect the beginning of (2) to the last few words of (1). To make that shift, we can make *black hole* the SUBJECT of a passive verb:

> [1]. . . exploring *black holes in space.* [2a]*A black hole* **is created** by the collapse of a dead star into a point perhaps no larger than a marble. [3]So much matter compressed into so little volume changes the fabric of space . . .

Note too that we have now located at the end of sentence (2) words that we can easily recall when we begin sentence (3), thereby making sentences (2) and (3) cohere better:

> [1]exploring black holes in space. [2a]A black hole is created by the collapse of a dead star into **a point perhaps no larger than a marble.** [3]**So much matter compressed into so little volume** changes the fabric of space . . .

To be meaningful, a sentence must include information of two kinds: information that is old and information that is new. In every sentence, there has to be new information, as well as old. Each sentence has to have old and new information. New and old information has to be in each sentence. If you are baffled why I wrote the last three sentences, you should be. You understood them, but they were effectively meaningless because they offered you nothing new. They simply repeated the first sentence.

Functional Sentence Perspective, developed by Prague School linguists in the late 1930s, is the foundational theory for the study of cognitive processing of information expressed in introductory-Theme/completing-Rheme patterns. You were probably baffled by that sentence too, but in a different way: It consists almost entirely of new information; it offers you virtually no familiar information to help you link its new information to anything you've already learned about style. Here is the same new information, but presented so that each sentence opens with concepts that you recognize and only then introduces you to concepts that you do not.

> Those who study how we process the flow of old and new information in sentences base their work on a model of language developed in the 1930s by a group of linguists known as the Prague School, a model today called "Functional Sentence Perspective." In that model, sentences are divided not into subjects and predicates, but into introductory elements that communicate old information (Themes) and completing elements that communicate new information (Rhemes).

You may still find that passage difficult, but for a reason that is unavoidable: As long as you go on reading anything new, you will always have to deal with new words for new concepts. And as long as you go on writing, you will always have to think about the ways that you introduce concepts that may be old to you but are new to your readers.

That sense of continuing old-to-new creates in prose what we call "flow."

Creating that sense of flow is the problem—and the challenge—of English prose: With every sentence, we have to find the best trade-off between the principles that make individual sentences clear and the principles that give sentences that sense of a cohesive flow. *But in that compromise, we always give priority to those features of style that make discourse cohesive, those features that help the reader integrate individual sentences into a unified passage.*

The Principle of Cohesion: Old-to-New

We can now formulate two more principles of writing and revision:

— Begin sentences with ideas that your readers will readily recognize, ideas that you have just mentioned, referred to, or implied, or with concepts that you can assume they know.

Conversely:

— End sentences with information that your readers cannot anticipate or with information that is more difficult to understand: lists, technical words, complex conditions.

Those principles are easier to apply to the writing of others than to our own. In Lesson Three, I explained why (p. 53). We will always be our own worst editors because by the time we write a final draft, everything we write is old—to us. But to our readers, at least some of it must seem new (otherwise why read?). So even though we find it difficult to distinguish old information from new, we have to try, because we have to begin our sentences from our readers' point of view—with what they already know, either from the knowledge they bring to their reading or from the information that we provide in previous sentences.

Exercise 6-1

Revise this passage to improve its flow.

The Hart Queen is one of the best skis for beginning and intermediate skiers. A thin layer of tempered ash from the hardwood forests of

Kentucky makes up its inner core. Two innovations for strength and flexibility are built into its outer construction. Two sheets of ten-gauge steel reinforce a layer of ash for increased strength. A wrapping of fiberglass surrounds two steel sheets for increased flexibility. Most conventional bindings can be used with the Queen. The Salomon Double is the best binding, however. A cushion of foam and insulation firmly cradles the foot and ankle yet freedom of movement is still permitted.

COHERENCE: A SENSE OF FOCUS

Cohesion, however, is only the first step toward creating in your readers a sense of a whole. Your writing must also seem coherent, a quality different from cohesion. This next passage has cohesive "flow," because each sentence links to the one before and to the one after by the principle of old-new chaining:

> Saner, Wisconsin is the snow-mobile capital of the world. The buzzing of snowmobile engines fills the air, and their tank-like tracks criss-cross the snow. The snow reminds me of Mom's mashed potatoes, covered with furrows I would draw with my fork. Mom's mashed potatoes usually made me sick, that's why I was playing with them. I like to make a hole in the middle of the potatoes and fill it with melted butter. This behavior has been the subject of long chats between me and my analyst.

While this passage may flow cohesively from one sentence to the next, it feels incoherent because each sentence shifts to a new topic. The first begins with Saner, Wisconsin, the next with the buzzing of snowmobiles, the next with snow, the next with Mom's mashed potatoes, the next with the writer, the last with behavior. As a consequence, those sentences do not focus our attention on a consistent set of central concepts. (The passage was created by six different writers, five of whom each sequentially added one sentence to a single preceding sentence.)

To understand coherence, we have to understand not just how we link pairs of individual sentences, but how sequences of sentences merge into a unified passage.

The Difficult Craft of Opening Sentences Well

It's hard to begin a sentence well because in its first few words we often have to juggle three or four elements that delay readers from getting to its point.

1. To connect a sentence to the preceding one, we use transitional metadiscourse, such as *and, but, therefore, as a result:*

   And therefore . . .

2. To help readers evaluate what follows, we use expressions such as *fortunately, perhaps, allegedly, it is important to note, for the most part, under these circumstances, politically speaking.*

   And, therefore, **it is important to note that, politically speaking,** . . .

3. We indicate time and place: *then, later, in May, in Europe.*

   And therefore, it is important to note that, politically speaking, **in the Eastern states in recent years** . . .

4. And most important (note the evaluation), we announce at the beginning of a sentence its TOPIC—the concept in that sentence that we intend to say something "about." We ordinarily name the "topic" of a sentence in its subject:

   And, therefore, it is important to note that, politically speaking, in the Eastern states in recent years, **sources of acid rain** have been a matter of much concern.

That sentence is not centrally "about" the idea of politics, or Eastern states, or recent years, but about its topic, *sources of acid rain.*

Because we have so much to think about when we start a sentence, we can overload its beginning, as I did that one about acid rain, with what seems like endless throat-clearing. And when we do that in sentence after sentence, our prose will seem unfocused. Your style will seem clear to the degree that you reduce or even eliminate the first three of the elements that can open a sentence so that you clearly focus on the fourth, on its topic.

Topics are important to the way we read individual sentences, not just because they focus our attention on what a single sentence is about, but because they influence how we interpret a whole passage. Through a series of sentences, we look at the sequence of their topics to understand what a passage is globally about. To understand how that happens, we have to look at this concept of topics more closely.

Subjects, Topics, and Grammar

For 500 years, English teachers have defined *subject* in two ways:

— The subject of a sentence is the "doer" of the action.
— The subject of a sentence is "what the sentence is about."

In Lessons Three and Four, we saw why we could not rely on that first definition for sentences like this:

Analysis of the data led to **our** discovery of a flaw.

The "doer" is not in the SIMPLE SUBJECT, *analysis,* but in *our.* Revised:

When **we** analyzed the data, **we** discovered a flaw.

But if that definition about "doers" does not hold for all sentences, we saw that it suggests some good advice: In prose that we judge to be clear, subjects usually are "doers;" that is, CHARACTERS who are also agents.

Also flawed but useful is that second schoolbook definition: A subject is what a sentence is "about." In this sense, "about" does not mean gist or summary, but the first explicit main idea that we read in a sentence. That main idea is usually in a NOUN and is usually the subject. This next sentence is "about" its topic, *international terrorism,* a phrase that also happens to be its subject.

International terrorism is no longer the threat it once was.

Subjects, Topics, and Psychology

But sometimes subjects are not topics. In these next sentences, the subjects (italicized) do not announce what these sentences are "about." These sentences are instead about the boldfaced words, words that are the topics of these sentences.

1. *It* is possible for **these claims** to be misunderstood.

The subject of (1) is *it,* but the sentence is "about" its topic, *these claims,* the object of *for.*

2. As to **these claims,** *I* believe we should be cautious.

The subject of (2) is *I,* but the sentence is "about" its topic, *these claims,* the object of *to.*

3. **Any other reasons for these claims** *we* do not know.

The subject of (3) is *we,* but the sentence is "about" its topic, *Any other reasons for these claims,* the object of *know.*

4. *It*'s likely that **these claims** will be rejected.

The subject of (4) is *it,* but the sentence is "about" its topic, *these claims,* the subject of a SUBORDINATE CLAUSE.

So when we use the term "topic" to mean what a sentence is "about," we mean its *psychological subject.* The topic of a sentence is *usually* also its grammatical subject, but not always. If the topic is not the subject, it will be among the first few words of a sentence *explicitly on the page.* Think of "topic" as a term that refers to the psychological geography of a sentence: A topic is always among the first few words of a sentence, the words that say "Reader, here is the specific concept that this sentence is going to be about."

A Principle of Coherence: Consistent Strings of Topics

Topics are important because readers look to the topics in a series of sentences to understand not just what the individual sentences are about, *but what a whole passage is about.* Predictably, this principle of reading suggests a principle of coherent writing.

> To make a series of individual sentences into a coherent passage, focus your topics on a limited number of concepts so that you do not scatter your readers' sense of what a passage is globally "about" through many unrelated ideas.

Compare the coherence of these substantively identical passages:

1a. In this paragraph, **boldface** indicates sentence topics. **The particular ideas toward the beginning of sentences** define what a passage is centrally "about" for a reader, so **a sense of coherence** crucially depends on topics. **Moving through a paragraph from a cumulatively coherent point of view** is made possible by a sequence of topics that seem to constitute this coherent sequence of topicalized ideas. **A seeming absence of context for each sentence** is one consequence of making random shifts in topics. **Feelings of dislocation, disorientation, and lack of focus** will occur when **that** happens.

1b.   In this paragraph, **I** have boldfaced topics. **Topics** are crucial for a reader because **they** focus attention on particular ideas toward the beginning of sentences and thereby notify readers what a whole passage is "about." If **a sequence of topics** seems coherent, then **readers** will feel they are moving through a paragraph from a cumulatively coherent point of view. But if through that paragraph **topics** shift randomly, then **the reader** has to begin each sentence out of context, from no coherent point of view. When **that** happens, **the reader** will feel dislocated, disoriented, out of focus.

Most readers feel the first is "disjointed" or "disorganized." The second "flows," it seems "focused." To understand why we respond that way, read straight through just the string of topics in both passages. In the first, the topics are inconsistent. In the second, the topics are consistent because they focus on some variation of just two concepts: *topics* and *reader.*

Do not take this advice to mean that you should restrict your topics to just one or two different words. The point is to see your strings of topics as your readers will. If you are certain that they can see how those topics constitute a coherent set, then use as many different ones as you need. On the other hand, if your readers cannot see how even just three topics constitute a coherent set, then just those three could confuse them. The point is to focus your readers' attention on a set of topics that *they* feel is coherent.

THE SYSTEM OF SYSTEMS

These principles about old and new and about a consistent topic string reinforce the points we made about characters and actions:

	Subject	Verb	Comp
FIXED			
VARIABLE	Characters	Action	—

When you design sentences so that your subjects consistently name central characters—real or abstract, you begin your sentences from a point of view that readers will feel is consistent. Just as important, readers will also begin sentences with information that seems familiar, because no elements in a story become more familiar than its characters. So to that pair of principles about characters as subjects and verbs as actions, we add these (I'll fill in the empty box in the next lesson.):

	Topic	
FIXED		
VARIABLE	Old Information	New Information
FIXED	Subject	Verb
VARIABLE	Characters	Action

1. Make most of your topics subjects.

2. Locate in the topics of your sentences old information that the reader carries forward from previous sentences, and locate new information toward the ends of your sentences.

3. Through a series of sentences that you want to constitute a coherent passage, focus on a restricted set of topics.

Exercise 6-2

Revise these passages to give them consistent topic strings. First determine the characters, then their actions. Then start each sentence with a character, and let the sentence take you where it wants to go. In (1), I boldface words that could be consistent subject/topics.

1. **Vegetation** covers the earth, except for those areas continuously covered with ice or utterly scorched by continual heat. Richly fertilized plains and river valleys are places where **plants** grow most richly, but also at the edge of perpetual snow in high mountains. The ocean and its edges as well as in and around lakes and swamps are densely **vegetated.** The cracks of busy city sidewalks

have **plants** in them as well as in seemingly barren cliffs. Before man existed the earth was covered with **vegetation,** and the earth will have **vegetation** long after evolutionary history swallows us up.

2. The power to create and communicate a new message to fit a new experience is not a competence animals have in their natural states. Their genetic code limits the number and kind of messages that they can communicate. Information about distance, direction, source, and richness of pollen in flowers constitutes the only information that can be communicated by bees. A limited repertoire of messages delivered in the same way, for generation after generation, is characteristic of animals of the same species, in all significant respects.

3. The importance of language skills in children's problem solving ability was stressed by Jones (1985) in his paper on children's thinking. Improvement in nonverbal problem solving occurred as a result of improvements in language skills. The use of previously acquired language habits for problem articulation and activation of knowledge previously learned through language was the cause of better performance. Therefore, systematic practice in the verbal formulation of nonlinguistic problems prior to attempts at their solution might be an avenue for exploration in the enhancement of problem solving in general.

Exercise 6-3

Distort the topic strings in any paragraph you have read so far. Then exchange your revision with someone and try to revise that person's revision back to the original.

SOME DEVICES FOR KEEPING TOPICS VISIBLE

We can now appreciate why we have to begin sentences briskly. Readers have to be able to pick up the topic of a sentence quickly, but more important than that, they have to recognize in a string of topics those concepts that unify individual sentences into a coherent passage. English offers us several ways to switch such elements to the opening of a sentence.

Passives Again

As we saw with the "black holes in space" example (p. 116), you can use the passive to replace a long subject full of new information with a short one that expresses familiar information. In that way, you locate the reader in the context of something familiar before moving on to something new (I boldface what is familiar and italicize what is new):

> During the first years of our nation, *a series of brilliant and virtuous presidents committed to democracy yet confident in their own worth* conducted **its administration.**

> During the first years of our nation, **its administration** was conducted by *a series of brilliant and virtuous presidents committed to democracy yet confident in their own worth.*

> *Astronomers, physicists, and others familiar with the problem of quasars* have confirmed **these observations.**

> **These observations** have been confirmed by *astronomers, physicists, and others familiar with the problem of quasars.*

These sentences illustrate the main reason the passive exists in the language—to improve cohesion and emphasis.

Subject-Complement Switching

Sometimes, we simply flip the subject and COMPLEMENT around the verb, especially when what follows the linking verb *be* refers to something mentioned earlier:

> *The source of the American attitude toward rural dialects* is **more interesting** [than something just mentioned].

> **More interesting** [than something just mentioned] is *the source of the American attitude toward rural dialects.*

We can make a similar switch around a few other verbs:

> *The failure of the administration to halt the rising costs of hospital care* lies **at the heart of the problem.**

> **At the heart of the problem** lies *the failure of the administration to halt the rising costs of hospital care.*

> *Some complex issues* run **through these questions.**

> **Through these questions** run *some complex issues.*

Minimal Metadiscourse

This next passage appeared in a curriculum review that was thought quite good—by the few willing to struggle through it. But it went largely unread because its style was so thick with metadiscourse that few of us could get past the first few pages. I have italicized metadiscourse and bold-faced the appropriate character/topic—programs.

> *We think it useful to provide some relatively detailed illustration of* the varied ways "corporate curricular personalities" organize themselves in **programs.** *We choose to feature as a central device in our presentation what are called* "introductory," "survey," or "foundational" courses. *It is important, however, to recognize* the diversity of what occurs in **programs** after the different initial survey courses. *But what is also suggested is that if one talks about* a **program** *simply in terms of* the intellectual strategies or techniques engaged in, when these *are understood in a general way, it becomes* difficult to distinguish many **programs** from others.

If we get rid of the metadiscourse and make the central character—programs—the topic, we get a substantially more readable passage:

> We illustrate how kinds of curricula organize themselves into programs, particularly through their "introductory," "survey," or "foundational" courses. After these introductory courses, **programs** offer diverse curricula, but **they** seem alike because **they** employ similar intellectual strategies.

At this point, some of you may be recalling advice about avoiding monotony—"avoid beginning sentences with the same subjects."
In general, bad advice.
Your prose will seem monotonous for reasons more serious than repeated topics. It will seem monotonous if you write one short sentence after another, or if you string one long sentence after another,

or if you pack most of your sentences with nominalizations and passives. You avoid monotony by so thoroughly engaging your readers with the force of your ideas that they lose touch with the surface of your sentences and let themselves be carried along by the current of your thinking. Readers are less bored by repeated subjects than are writers.

Two Qualifications

Having asserted that general principle, I must qualify it in two ways. First, to be sure, we can pursue the same topic so relentlessly that a passage becomes mind-numbingly repetitive. The writer of this next passage mistook advice about consistent topics not as a diagnostic principle, but as a rigid rule:

> "Moral climate" is created when an objectivized moral standard for treating people is accepted by others. Moral climate results from norms of behavior which are accepted by society whereby if people conform they are socially approved of, or if they don't they are shunned. In this light, moral climate acts as a reason to refrain from saying or doing things that the community does not support. A moral climate encourages individuals to conform to a moral standard and apply that standard to their own circumstances.
>
> The moral climate in Germany in 1933 encouraged individuals to accept Jews as a threat by creating a moral climate where antisemitism was the norm. The moral climate was established by Hitler in his words and actions. This moral climate was evident in the laws that he had passed against the Jews, and in his speeches against the Jews "contaminating" the German race. Such a moral climate influenced the behavior of Germans. As a result, the moral climate of antisemitism put pressure on Germans to follow these norms.

If you find that through several consecutive sentences you have used *exactly* the same words for the same topic in the same position, you may have created a topic string that is too consistent. If so, revise: Use pronouns, move the topic into a prepositional phrase, paraphrase the topic. Be cautious though: most writers change topics too often.

And a second qualification: The simplest and clearest topic is a short noun phrase that appears early in a sentence, usually as its subject. But what a passage is "about" is not as the property of a single word. That sense of aboutness can be communicated in verbs and adjectives as well. This paragraph is out of focus; it doesn't flow because its sentences do not open from any consistent point of view:

> In recent years, many strides in identifying Alzheimer's disease have been made in psychiatric medicine. Not too long ago, **senility in an older patient who seemed to be losing touch with reality** was often confused with Alzheimer's. In the past few years, however, **blood chemistry and genetic clues** have become tools to diagnose this condition. There is, however, **the risk of human tragedy of another kind** as a result of the increasing accuracy of these procedures: Long before the appearance of any of its overt symptoms, **physicians may be able to predict Alzheimer's.** At that point, **an otherwise apparently healthy person** could be devastated by such an early and accurate diagnosis.

In this next revised paragraph, I open sentences with concepts that paraphrase the central concept of this passage—*identifying Alzheimer's disease,* but notice how I express this central topic in ways other than in just subjects:

> In recent years, psychiatric medicine has made considerable strides in identifying Alzheimer's disease. Not too long ago, when **a physician examined an older patient who seemed out of touch with reality,** she had to guess whether that person had Alzheimer's or was senile, an entirely different syndrome. In the past few years, however, **new and more reliable tests** have focused on blood chemistry and genetic clues. In **the accuracy of these new tests,** however, lies the risk of human tragedy of another kind: **Physicians may be able to predict Alzheimer's** long before its overt appearance, but **such an early and accurate diagnosis** could devastate an otherwise apparently healthy person.

In this revised passage, I expressed what the passage was about in subject noun phrases: *the accuracy of these new tests,* and *such an early and accurate diagnosis.* But I also expressed the topic in the object of a preposition: *in the accuracy of these new tests,* and in whole clauses: *a physician examined an older patient who seemed out of touch with reality, physicians may be able to predict Alzheimer's.*

The general point is this: Consistently locate what you think a whole passage is "about" early in your sentences, in their topic positions. That usually means in a noun in a subject. But you can also distribute that old information through subjects and verbs.

Organic vs. Factitious Coherence

I've described here what some call "organic coherence." Texts seem organically coherent when readers move through individual sentences and from one to the next but do not notice how consistently the information in each sentence carries them from old to new and how the string of topics focuses their attention on just a few central concepts. The reader feels the passage hangs together not because of its artful style, but because its structure, content, and logic seem by their very nature intrinsically consistent and coherent. Sometimes, though, we try to impose a factitious coherence on an intrinsically incoherent passage by lacing it with conjunctions like *thus, therefore, however,* and so on, regardless of whether its logic reflects the connections that those conjunctions signal. Here is one such passage. The writer starts almost every sentence with a word that he hoped would make each sentence seem to connect with the one before.

> Because the press is a source of interaction between the President and the people, how the press portrays him can influence his popularity. Therefore, the press should report on the President objectively. However, both reporters and the President are human, subject not only to error but to favoritism. Furthermore, people act differently in public than they do in private. Hence, it is important to know the whole person, his environment, upbringing, and education in order to understand his behavior. Indeed, from the correspondence with his family, we can learn much about Harry S Truman, our thirty-third President. Nevertheless, while the letters may be uncensored, certain ones may have been withheld. Consequently, to understand him, it is important to read other information about him.

Words like *furthermore, hence, but,* and so on help readers see connections among your ideas, but when you find yourself using them more than once or twice a paragraph, look closely. You may need them, but if the logic of your ideas is coherent, you probably don't. More crucially, you may be trying to impose coherence on a passage that is intrinsicially incoherent.

A Quick Diagnosis

Here is a quick way to determine how you have managed the beginnings of your sentences: Break your text into its smallest passages. Then in each passage underline the first six or seven words of every sentence and read the underlined phrases and clauses straight through, as if they were a list. If any of them seems to introduce an idea that clearly falls outside the general sequence of topics or if few of them capture what your good sense tells you the whole passage is generally "about," try revising them. And if those first few words regularly include connectors like *therefore, consequently, moreover,* and so on, try deleting all of them. If what's left cannot stand on its own, then the whole passage probably needs more than tinkering at its style. However, give the benefit of the doubt to connectors like *however, but, nevertheless, on the other hand.* You must always warn readers when you are about to contradict something that you have just said.

Exercise 6-4

Revise these three passages so that they have more consistent topic strings. Before you begin, decide who the main character should be, and then make that main character the subject of as many sentences as you can. In the first example, I have boldfaced topics so that you can see how inconsistent they are.

1. **Some potential threats** exist in the modern mass communications media, though there are many significant advantages. If **a powerful minority** should happen to control it, **public opinion** could be manipulated through biased reporting. And while **a wide knowledge of public affairs** is a great advantage that results from national coverage, **divisiveness and factionalism** can be accentuated by connecting otherwise isolated, local conflicts into a single larger conflict as a result of showing that **conflicts about the same issues** are occurring in different places. It will always be true, of course, that **human nature** produces differences of opinion, but **the threat of faction and division** may be reinforced when **national coverage** publicizes uninformed opinions. According to some, **education** can suppress faction when **the true nature of conflicts** reaches the

public through the media, but **history** has shown that as **much coverage** is given to people who encourage conflict as to people who try to remove conflict.

2. Some sort of palace revolt or popular revolution plagued seven out of eight reigns of the Romanov line after Peter the Great. In 1722, achievement by merit was made the basis of succession when the principle of heredity was terminated by Peter. This resulted in many tsars not appointing a successor before dying, including Peter. Ivan VI was less than two months old when appointed by Czarina Anna, but Elizabeth, daughter of Peter the Great, defeated Anna and ascended to the throne in 1741. Succession not dependent upon authority resulted in the boyars' regularly disputing who was to become sovereign. Male primogeniture became the law in 1797 when Paul I codified the law of succession. But conspirators strangled him, one of whom was probably his son, Alexander I.

3. Many issues other than science faced Truman when he was considering the Oppenheimer committee's recommendation to stop the hydrogen bomb project. A Sino-Soviet bloc had been proclaimed by Russia and China, so the Cold War was becoming an issue. Support for Truman's foreign policy was shrinking among Republican leaders in Congress. And the first Russian atom bomb test made the public demand a strong response from him. Truman's conclusion that he could not afford letting the public think that Russia had been allowed to be first in developing the most powerful weapon yet was inevitable. In retrospect, the risk in the Oppenheimer recommendation was worth taking according to some historians, but the political issues that Truman had to face were too powerful to ignore.

Exercise 6-5

Revise the "moral climate" passage. First, cut redundancy. Then revise topics so that the passage does not repeat the same topic in the same position in every sentence. You can replace some topics with *it*. You can also combine some sentences:

> Hitler contributed to the moral climate in Germany in the 1930s when he . . .

SHAPING SUBJECTS, TOPICS, AGENTS

You may have noticed that I have not used the words "good" and "bad" to describe writing that seems more or less clear. I have called some passages "unclear," "disjointed," "out of focus," and I have matched them with passages that seem "clear," "flowing," and "focused," but not "good" and "bad." I have avoided those words because sometimes we want to be unclear: We don't know what we're talking about, and we don't want anyone else to know that. Or we do know what we're talking about, and we don't want anyone else to know what we know. On those occasions, we write unclearly deliberately, and if what we write gets the job done, then we say the writing is "good."

But "good" has two meanings. Assassins can be "good" at their jobs but not be "good" people. In the same way, writing can be "good" if it gets a job done, but if the job is ethically questionable, then the writing may be bad just because it is so good.

Here is the text of a letter from a natural gas utility notifying its customers that it was raising their rates (I boldface sentence topics):

> **The Illinois Commerce Commission** has authorized a restructuring of our rates together with an increase in Service Charge revenues effective with service rendered on and after November 12, 1990. **This** is the first increase in rates for Peoples Gas in over six years. **The restructuring of rates** is consistent with the policy of The Public Utilities Act that rates for service to various classes of utility customers be based upon the cost of providing that service. **The new rates** move revenues from every class of customer closer to the cost actually incurred to provide gas service. **This bill** covers a period in which proration of Service Charges is occurring. **Proration** means that part of the bill is based on the former Service Charges, which are identified on your bill as "Old Rate," and part of the bill is based on newly authorized Service charges, which are identified on your bill as "New Rate."

That notice is not immediately clear, even to an educated reader. In effect, it says simply "Starting this month, you have to pay us more for the natural gas we sell to you." The writer mentions one character,

Peoples Gas, only once, in the third person, and not as a topic/agent/ subject:

> ... increase in rates for **Peoples Gas** in over six years.

And it mentions the reader only three times, again in the third person, and again not as a topic/agent/subject:

> ... for services to various classes of **utility customers**

> ... move revenues from every class of **customer** closer ...

> ... **your** bill ...

Had the gas company wanted to make itself the agent/topics of its sentences, it would have written the notice more like this:

> The Illinois Commerce Commission has authorized us to restructure rates and increase what **we** charge you for service after November 12, 1990. **We** have not increased the rate you pay for our gas in over six years. Under the Public Utilities Act, however, **we** can ...

Exercise 6-6

Go on revising this notice, using *we* as a topic/agent/subject wherever you can. Then revise it a second time so that the topic/agent/subject is *you.* For example,

> As the Illinois Commerce Commission has authorized, **you** will have to pay us higher Service Charges after November 12, 1990. **You** have not had to pay higher rates in ...

Why would the company resist sending either revised version? What ethical issues does the original raise? In what sense is this "good" writing?

In 1985, the Government Accounting Office sponsored a study that inquired into why fewer than half the automobile owners who received recall letters complied. That study found that many car owners did not bring their cars in because they could not understand the letters or were not particularly moved by them. I actually received the following. It illustrates how writers can meet legal obligations and ignore ethical ones.

> [1]A defect which involves the possible failure of a frame support plate may exist on your vehicle. [2]This plate (front suspension pivot bar support plate) connects a portion of the front suspension to the vehicle frame, and [3]its failure could affect vehicle directional control, particularly during heavy brake application. [4]In addition, your vehicle may require adjustment service to the hood secondary catch system. [5]The secondary catch may be misaligned so that the hood may not be adequately restrained to prevent hood fly-up in the event the primary latch is inadvertently left unengaged. [6]Sudden hood fly-up beyond the secondary catch while driving could impair driver visibility. [7]In certain circumstances, occurrence of either of the above conditions could result in vehicle crash without prior warning.

Look at the topics of the sentences:

[1]a defect	[2]this plate	[3]its failure
[4]your vehicle	[5]the secondary catch	
[6]sudden hood fly-up	[7]occurrence of . . . conditions.	

The writers did not try to tell a story about me the driver, much less about themselves as manufacturers. The topics of this story, its main characters, are car parts and events. The author—probably a committee-—nominalized verbs that might make me anxious and made most other verbs passive. Then they deleted most references to me and all references to themselves.

Exercise 6-7

Revise that recall letter so that you topicalize *you* as often as you can. Certainly one of the sentences will read,

> If **you** brake hard and the plate fails, **you** will. . . .

Why would the company have been reluctant to send out that version? What ethical issues are involved here? Are they different from those in the gas company notice? Is the original "good" writing?

DESIGNING TOPICS FOR SPECIAL EFFECTS

In everything I have said so far about clarity and directness, I may have seemed to be laying down inviolable rules: Make every subject a character, every verb an action. I did not intend that, of course. I was offering instead principles of interpretation, guidelines for diagnosis, prediction, and revision.

But the automobile recall letter suggests that you can't pick any character to serve as the subject/topic of your sentences. Almost every story has several characters, so you have to choose *which* characters to topicalize, even whether to topicalize flesh-and-blood characters at all (look again at the story about Prospective and Immediate Intention (p. 67)). You can create subtly different effects by finding verbs that let you shift into the subject/topic position different characters to serve different purposes. Children learn how quickly. Even four-year-olds understand the difference between,

> I bumped into Tom, dropped my glass, and spilled the juice.

> Tom and me bumped, the glass dropped and the juice spilled.

Neither sentence is more or less "true." But second assigns responsibility in a way different from the first. As we get older, we learn how to manage our stories in more subtle ways:

> **You** make me lonely when **you** don't tell me what **you** think.

> **I** feel lonely when **we** don't share our thoughts.

We can best appreciate nuances of topics when we see how skilled writers manipulate them to achieve important ends.

When Thomas Jefferson wrote the Declaration of Independence, he knew that he had to write it carefully because the world would read it as our justification for throwing off British rule. Note in the first two paragraphs how Jefferson seems to have *designed* most of the sentences so that they do not open with the colonists acting as willful agents, asserting their own actions, but rather with words that topicalize events, rights, duties, needs—concepts that make the colonists seem to be the objects of more actions than they initiate, concepts

that compel the colonists to act on behalf of higher forces. I boldface
what I think are the main topics of clauses:

> When in **the Course of human events,** it becomes necessary
> for one people to dissolve the political bands which have con-
> nected them with another, and to assume among the powers of
> the earth, the separate and equal station to which the Laws of
> Nature and of Nature's God entitle them, **a decent respect to
> the opinions of mankind** requires that they should declare
> the causes which impel them to the separation.
>
> **We** hold these truths to be self-evident, that **all men** are
> created equal, that **they** are endowed by their Creator with cer-
> tain unalienable Rights, that among **these [rights]** are Life,
> Liberty and the pursuit of Happiness. That to secure **these
> rights,** Governments are instituted among Men, deriving their
> just powers from the consent of the governed. That whenever
> **any Form of Government** becomes destructive of these ends,
> it is **the Right of the People** to alter or to abolish it, and to
> institute new Government, laying its foundation on such princi-
> ples and organizing its powers in such form, as to them shall
> seem most likely to affect their Safety and Happiness. **Pru-
> dence,** indeed, will dictate that **Governments long
> established** should not be changed for light and transient
> causes. . . .

Contrast that with a different version, one in which the colonists
are consistently made freely acting topic/agents of every action:

> **We** have decided that **we** should dissolve the political bands that have
> connected us with Britain and assume among the powers of the earth
> the separate and equal station that **we** claim through the Laws of
> Nature and of Nature's God. Since **we** decently respect the opinions of
> mankind, **we** declare why **we** do so. **These truths** are self-evident—
> **we** are all equal in our creation, **we** derive from God certain Rights
> that **we** intend to keep. **We** include among those rights . . . [Revise the
> rest of the introduction in the same way.]

My revision topicalizes the colonists, making them seem to act simply
because they will themselves to. But at first Jefferson wanted to avoid
assigning to the colonists responsibility for the profoundly violent
political act of the American Revolution, so he created characters, topics out of higher Forces, out of abstract principles of rights and
obligations.

But after Jefferson established the principles that forced the colonists to act, he then switched his topic/subjects to King George, making him an agent who seemed to act out of his own malign will:

> **He** has refused his Assent to Laws . . .
>
> **He** has forbidden his Governors to pass Laws . . .
>
> **He** has refused to pass other Laws . . .
>
> **He** has called together . . .

Someone who believed in the divine right of kings could have made George the constrained object of demands from some Higher Order:

> **Duty to His Divine responsibilities** *demanded* that . . .
>
> **Prudence** *required* His opposition to Laws . . .
>
> **Necessity** *obligated* his Dissolution of Representative Houses . . .

When Jefferson finished his bill of particulars, he was ready to move to his third set of subjects/topics/agents and draw the inevitable conclusion (the capitalization in the last paragraph is Jefferson's):

> In every stage of these Oppressions **We** have Petitioned for Redress in the most humble terms: **Our repeated Petitions** have been answered only by repeated injury. **A Prince,** whose character is thus marked by every act which may define a Tyrant, is unfit to be the ruler of a free people.
>
> Nor have **We** been wanting in attention to our British brethren. **We** have warned them from time to time of attempts by their legislature to extend an unwarrantable jurisdiction over us. **We** have reminded them of the circumstances of our emigration and settlement here. **We** have appealed to their native justice and magnanimity, and **we** have conjured them by the ties of our common kindred to disavow these usurpations, which would inevitably interrupt our connections and correspondence. **They** too have been deaf to the voice of justice and of consanguinity. **We** must, therefore, acquiesce in the necessity, which denounces our Separation, and hold them, as **we** hold the rest of mankind, Enemies in War, in Peace Friends.
>
> **We,** THEREFORE, the Representatives of the UNITED STATES OF AMERICA, in General Congress, Assembled, appealing to the Supreme judge of the world for the rectitude of our

intentions, do, in the Name, and by Authority of the good People of these Colonies, solemnly publish and declare, That **these United Colonies** are, and of Right ought to be FREE AND INDEPENDENT STATES; that **they** are Absolved from all Allegiance to the British Crown, and **that all political connection between them and the State of Great Britain,** is and ought to be totally dissolved; and that as **Free and Independent States, they** have full Power to levy War, conclude Peace, contract Alliances, establish Commerce, and to do all other Acts and Things which Independent States may of right do. And for the support of this Declaration, with a firm reliance on the protection of Divine Providence, **we** mutually pledge to each other our Lives, our Fortunes and our sacred Honor.

Did Jefferson "intend" this sequence of topic/subject/agents, beginning with abstractions, moving to *he,* and concluding with *we?* Who knows? But once we see a pattern, we have to interpret it in the service of a point. In this case by topicalizing higher actions and abstract forces, Jefferson established that higher powers forced our forebears to act when they were oppressed by evil forces. Then by topicalizing King George, Jefferson established him as the malign agent of evil actions. Having established those first two principles in the first two parts, he was ready in the third to topicalize colonists as topic/agent/subjects justified in acting on the basis of their own will.

The lesson to be drawn (both politically and stylistically, perhaps) is that local principles must always yield to higher ones. The problem is to recognize when we should subordinate one topic or one principle to another.

Exercise 6-8

This passage tells the story of women in a classroom.

> [W]omen are more interested than are the men in talking in class to support friends, and in spirited shared discussion; they also feel more at ease with teachers who do not impose their views on others. Women are seemingly more concerned than are the men with the teaching-learning process and attend more to the personal experiences of other students ... [Women] consider the openness and supportiveness of the instructor the salient factor in determining whether they feel comfortable about talking in class and give more importance than do men to

the teacher's attempts to insure that class members feel good about each other.

from Cheris Kramarae and Paula A. Treichler "Power Relationships in the Classroom," *Gender in the Classroom: Power and Pedagogy,* ed. Susan L. Gabriel and Isaiah Smithson. University of Illinois Press: Urbana 1990. p. 54

Revise it so that it says "the same thing" but tells the story of men. That is, you might begin,

Men are less interested than women . . .

What is the consequence? How does this change the story?

Exercise 6-9

At the beginning of this passage from his essay, "Stranger in the Village," James Baldwin makes the cathedral at Chartres the topic and metaphorical agency. Here is his first sentence:

The cathedral at Chartres, I have said, *says* something to the people of this village which **it** *cannot say* to me, but it is important to understand that **this cathedral** *says* something to me which **it** *cannot say* to them.

But in the second sentence, he switches the topic/subjects to the villagers and to himself:

Perhaps **they** *are struck* by the power of the spires, the glory of the windows; but **they** *have known* God, after all, longer than **I** *have known* him, and in a different way, and **I** *am terrified* . . .

Revise this passage so that you change the sequence of topics in a variety of ways. Here is one new version:

I have said that **I** hear something from the cathedral at Chartres that **the people** of this village do not hear, but it is important to understand that . . .

How do they differ? What are the consequences?

The cathedral at Chartres, I have said, says something to the people of this village which it cannot say to me, but it is important to understand that this cathedral says something to me which it cannot say to them. Perhaps they are struck by the power of the spires, the glory of the windows; but they have known God, after all, longer than I have known him, and in a different way, and I am terrified by the slippery bottomless well to be found in the crypt, down which heretics were hurled to death, and by the obscene, inescapable gargoyles jutting out of the stone and seeming to say that God and the devil can never be divorced. I doubt that the villagers think of the devil when they face a cathedral because they have never been identified with the devil. But I must accept the status which myth, if nothing else, gives me in the West before I can hope to change the myth.

Exercise 6-10

Revise Lincoln's Gettysburg Address so that the topics are not human characters, but abstractions. The first sentence might be, "Four score and seven years ago, **this continent** was the place where **a new nation** was brought forth by our fathers . . ." How do the new topics change the impact of the speech?

S U M M I N G   U P

When you locate your characters in subjects and your actions in verbs, you make your style readable. But try as well to locate old information toward the beginning of your sentences and new information toward the ends. Use your subjects to express topics, and through a series of sentences, do not vary your topics randomly. To the degree that through a series of sentences you can maintain a consistent point of view, to that degree those sentences will constitute a unified passage of prose.

FIXED	Topic	
VARIABLE	Old Information	New Information
FIXED	Subject	Verb
VARIABLE	Characters	Action

1. Open your sentences with what you have already mentioned or with knowledge that you can assume you and your reader share.

> The number of wounded and dead in the Civil War exceeded that in **all the other wars in American history.** One of the reasons for the lingering animosity between North and South today is **the memory of this terrible carnage.**

> **Of all the wars in American history,** none has exceeded the Civil War in the number of wounded and dead. **The memory of this terrible carnage** is one of the reasons for the animosity between North and South today.

2. Through a series of sentences that you want your readers to understand as a coherent, focused passage, keep your topics short and reasonably consistent:

> **How Asian companies that have sought to compete with American products in six market segments in the Western Pacific region** will constitute the objective of the first phase of this study. **The labor costs of the Asian competitors and their ability to introduce new products quickly** are the main issues that we will examine in detail in each section. **A plan that will show how American industry can restructure its facilities so that it can better exploit unexpected opportunities, particularly in the Pacific Rim market,** will be developed from this study.

> In the first phase of this study, **we** will examine six market segments in the Western Pacific region to determine how **Asian companies** have competed with American products. In each section, **the study** will examine in detail labor costs and their ability to introduce new products quickly. **We** will develop from this study a plan that will show American industry how to restructure its facilities so that **it** can better exploit unexpected opportunities, particularly in the Pacific Rim market.

3. Choose topics that control your reader's point of view. Your success will depend on how you can use verbs to make one or another of your characters a seeming agent. Which of these would better serve the needs of a patient suing a physician is obvious:

> **A patient** whose reactions go unmonitored may claim physician liability. In this case, **a patient** took Cloromax as prescribed, resulting in renal failure. **The manufacturer's literature** indicated that the

patient should be observed and should immediately report any sign of infection.

If **a physician** does not monitor his patient's reactions, **he** may be held liable. In this case, **the physician** prescribed Cloromax, which caused the patient to experience renal failure. **The physician** had been cautioned by the manufacturer's literature that **he** should observe the patient and instruct the patient to report any sign of infection.

Lesson Seven

Emphasis

The end of a matter is better than its beginning.
ECCLESIASTES 7:8

All's well that ends well.
WILLIAM SHAKESPEARE

Beginning and end shake hands with each other.
GERMAN PROVERB.

In the end is my beginning.
T. S. ELIOT

When you begin a sentence well, you're more than half way toward ending it well. If you consistently organize your SUBJECT/TOPICS around a few central characters or concepts and quickly close your subjects with precise VERBS, you will have opened your sentences with clear, short subjects that consistently locate your reader in familiar territory. When you choose that subject wisely, you also shape your readers' understanding in a way that achieves your end. Once you get all that straight, you will almost by default locate your most complex, most important new ideas where they belong—close to the ends of your sentences.

ENDING WELL

But however naturally your most important ideas may find their way there, you ought to spend some time thinking about those last few words. The first few words of every sentence control clarity and focus; your last few control emphasis and strength. Compare these.

> A charge of gross violation of academic responsibility is required for a Board of Trustees to dismiss a tenured faculty member for cause, and an elaborate hearing procedure with a prior statement of charges is provided for before a tenured faculty member may be dismissed for cause, in most States.

> In most States, before a Board of Trustees may dismiss a tenured faculty member for cause, it must charge him with a gross violation of academic responsibility and provide him with a statement of charges and an elaborate hearing procedure.

The first trails off; the second builds to a climax.

Because one of the elements that open a sentence is so important, we gave it a technical name: *topic.* The end of a sentence plays a role almost as important, so we will name it as well. When you utter a sentence, your voice naturally rises and falls. When you approach its end, you ordinarily raise the pitch on one of those last few words and stress it more strongly than you do the others:

$$\acute{o}\text{-}$$
more strongly than you do the
-thers.

We'll call this climactic part of a sentence its *stress*. The words that you locate under that final stress and just before it, you emphasize, and whatever you emphasize, your readers will take to be most significant.

MANAGING ENDINGS

If you don't get the right words under the stress in your first draft, you have to revise. First identify the rhetorically most important words: words that express surprising information, words that carry the greatest emotional weight, technical terms that a reader might not recognize, especially words expressing ideas that you intend to develop in the next several sentences. If they are not already at or close to the ends of your sentences, do the following.

Trim the End

In some cases, you can just lop off unnecessary words until you get to the information you want to stress.

> Sociobiologists make the provocative claim that our genes determine our social behavior **in the way we act in situations we find around us every day.**

Since *social behavior* means the way we act, we can just drop everything after *behavior:*

> Sociobiologists make the provocative claim that our genes determine our social behavior.

Shift Less Important Ideas to the Front of a Sentence

You can also move phrases to the left, away from the end of a sentence, to emphasize what you leave exposed:

> The data that are offered to establish the existence of ESP do not make believers of us **for the most part.**

> **For the most part,** the data that are offered to establish the existence of ESP do not make us believers.

Particularly avoid ending with anticlimactic METADISCOURSE.

> Opportunities are particularly rich at the graduate level, **it must be remembered.**

> **It must be remembered** that opportunities at the graduate level are particularly rich.

Shift More Important Ideas toward the End of the Sentence

Moving information to the right, toward the end of a sentence is a more common way we manage stress. And that sentence illustrates a missed opportunity to do so. This would have been more emphatic:

> A more common way we manage stress is by moving information to the right, toward the end of a sentence.

In fact, this is the converse of moving old information to the left, to the beginning of a sentence. A sentence that introduces a paragraph is frequently in an *X is Y* form. One part, X, usually older information, glances back at what has gone before; the other, Y, announces something new. As we have seen, the older information should come first, the newer last. When it doesn't, we switch subject and COMPLEMENT (new information is boldfaced, old italicized):

> **Questions relating to the ethics of withdrawing intravenous fluid** are *more important* [than something else].

> *More important* [than something else] are **questions relating to the ethics of withdrawing intravenous fluid.**

The switch not only puts at the beginning of its sentence references to the preceding sentences, *more important,* but it also stresses at the end information that the next several sentences will probably develop.

> ... **the ethics of withdrawing intravenous fluid.** For example, should **fluids be withdrawn** when ...

In fact, this kind of cohesion is a major function of stress.

STRESS: BRIDGING COHESION AND COHERENCE

In the last Lesson, we spent a good deal of time working through principles of cohesion and coherence. You may have found the difference between them a bit abstruse, but now that we see how stress works, we can see why it's useful to understand how cohesion and coherence differ and how we use stress to help create both.

When we make pairs of sentences cohesive, we repeat information that appears in the stress of one sentence at the beginning of the next:

> [1]One of the best skis for beginning and intermediate skiers is **the Hart Queen.** [2]**It** has an inner core that consists of a thin layer of tempered ash from the hardwood forest of Kentucky.

To make a passage coherent, we begin a string of consistent topics, in this case references to the ski and its parts:

> [2]**It** *has an inner core* that consists of a thin layer of tempered ash from the hardwood forest of Kentucky.

> [3]**Its** *outer construction* features two innovations for strength and flexibility.

To shift topics, the writer can pick up on the information in the stress of any sentence and begin a new topic string.

> [1]One of the best skis for beginning and intermediate skiers is **the Hart Queen.** [2]**It** has an inner core that consists of a thin layer of tempered ash from the hardwood forest of Kentucky. [3]**Its** outer construction features two innovations for **strength and flexibility.** [4]To increase **its**

strength, the layer of ash is molded with two sheets of ten-gauge steel, ⁵and to increase **its flexibility,** the two sheets of steel are wrapped with fiberglass.

At this point, the writer could in sentence (6) return to *Hart Queen* as a topic,

⁶While **the Queen** can be used with most conventional bindings, . . .

But she might do that only to set up in the stress of this sentence new topics for sentences (7) and (8):

⁶While **the Queen** can be used with most conventional bindings, the best binding is *the Salomon Double.* ⁷It firmly cradles the foot and ankle in a reinforced cushion of foam and insulation, yet **it** allows complete freedom of movement.

That is how we create passages of cohesive and coherent prose. We use the end of one sentence to introduce a new topic that the next few or many sentences will repeat. But in the stress of any one of those next sentences, we might introduce a new bit of information that we intend to use as a new series of topics in the sentences following it. And when we are finished with that sequence of sentences we can return to the first topic or move on to yet a different one.

Exercise 7-1

We can use the stress of a sentence to introduce not only new characters, but new key concepts, as well. Here are three opening sentences and the rest of a paragraph. Which one better sets up the ideas in that following paragraph? In this case, the reader would be familiar with the characters—Russian rulers. What we have to introduce are the new concepts to be associated with those rulers. The last few words of a sentence that opens a paragraph should stress the key concepts that the rest of the paragraph develops.

1. The next century the situation changed, because disputes over succession to the throne caused some sort of palace revolt or popular revolution in seven out of eight reigns of the Romanov line after Peter the Great.

2. The next century the situation changed, because after Peter the Great seven out of eight reigns of the Romanov line were plagued by turmoil over disputed succession to the throne.

3. **Because turmoil over disputed succession to the throne plagued seven out of eight reigns of the Romanov line after Peter the Great, the situation changed in the next century.**

The problems began in 1722, when Peter the Great passed a law of succession that terminated the principle of heredity and required the sovereign to appoint a successor. But because many Tsars, including Peter, died before they named successors, those who aspired to rule had no authority by appointment, and so their succession was often disputed by the boyars, lower level aristocrats. There was turmoil even when successors were appointed. In 1740, Ivan VI was adopted by Czarina Anna Ivanovna and named as her successor at age two months, but his succession was challenged by Elizabeth, daughter of Peter the Great. In 1741, she defeated Anna and ascended to the throne herself. In 1797 Paul tried to eliminate these disputes by codifying a new law: primogeniture in the male line. But turmoil continued. Paul was strangled by conspirators, one of whom was probably his son, Alexander I.

I know that much of this must sound mechanical, formal, constraining and that some writers think that if we all observed these principles, our readers would feel that all writing would sound the same. But passages of prose are alike in the same way that people are alike. All of us have the same general inner structures, but we appear to one another in a vast range of outer forms. Prose is the same. It all has the same general inner structure, but when we flesh it out with words, it all seems different. And no less important, these patterns play a key role in how we read. They are crucial to a reader's sense of cohesion and coherence.

SOME SYNTACTIC DEVICES

There are a few special devices that throw syntactic weight to the end of a sentence.

There

I wrote the sentence above without realizing that I had illustrated this first device. I could have written,

> A few syntactic devices throw weight to the end of a sentence.

But that would open the sentence with new information. When you open a sentence with *there,* you push toward the end of that sentence ideas that you can develop in the next sentences. You may remember someone telling you not to begin sentences with *there.* And it is true: If you begin too many sentences with *There is* or *There are,* your prose will lack movement or energy. But like passives, *there-* constructions have a function: to stress those ideas that you intend to develop in the next few sentences.

Passives One More Time

An important function of the passive is to shift to the end of a sentence information that you intend to develop in subsequent sentences:

> Sociobiologists make the provocative claim that **our genes** *determine* our social behavior.

> Sociobiologists make the provocative claim that our social behavior *is determined* by **our genes.**

The first leads us to expect that the passage will go on to discuss social behavior; the second leads us to expect something about genes.

What-Shift

A *what*-sentence throws special emphasis on the words that follow a linking verb. Compare these:

> We need *a monetary policy that will end wild fluctuations in money supply, unemployment, and inflation.*

> **What** we need **is** *a monetary policy that will end wild fluctuations in money supply, unemployment, and inflation.*

The cost of this emphasis is two words, so use this device sparingly.

It-shift 1

By using *it* as a subject, you can shift an introductory clause that would have been the subject to a position after the verb:

> *That domestic oil prices must eventually rise to the level set by OPEC* once seemed inevitable.

> **It** once seemed inevitable *that domestic oil prices must eventually rise to the level set by OPEC.*

It-shift 2

In this pattern, you simultaneously select and emphasize a topic and throw added weight on the stress. Compare:

> In 1933 this country experienced a depression that almost wrecked our democratic system of government.

> **It was** *in 1933* **that** this country experienced a depression that almost wrecked our democratic system of government.

> Sociobiologists make the provocative claim that our genes determine our social behavior.

> Sociobiologists make the provocative claim that **it is** *our genes* **that** determine our social behavior.

When All Else Fails

If you are stuck with a sentence that ends flatly because you must repeat a word or a phrase from a previous sentence, use a pronoun:

> When the rate of inflation dropped in 1983, large numbers of investors fled the bond market and invested in **stocks.** However, many of those particularly interested in the high tech market did not carefully investigate **those stocks.**

> When the rate of inflation dropped in 1983, large numbers of investors fled the bond market and invested in **stocks.** However, many of those particularly interested in the high tech market did not carefully investigate **them.**

By substituting the pronoun for the lightly stressed repeated word, you throw emphasis on the word just before the pronoun.

Exercise 7-2

Revise these sentences so that the concepts that deserve emphasis appear at the end. In the first five, I have boldfaced elements that I think should be stressed. Then eliminate wordiness, unnecessary nominalization, etc.

1. **The judiciary's tendency to rewrite the Constitution** is the biggest danger in the republic, in my opinion, at least.
2. **A new judicial philosophy that could affect our society well into the twenty-first century** may emerge from these studies.
3. There are **limited** opportunities for teachers to work with individual students in large American colleges and universities.
4. As used in the industry, "turnkey" means **responsibility for the satisfactory performance of a piece of equipment in addition to the manufacture and installation** of that equipment, according to everyone who understands the matter.
5. **Several upper and lower eyelid reconstruction evaluation studies** are presented with the aforementioned summary discussions for your general information.
6. Overbuilding of suburban housing developments has led to the existence of extensive and widespread flooding and economic disaster in parts of our country in recent years, it is now clear.
7. The teacher who makes an assignment of a long final term paper at the end of the semester and who then gives only a grade at the end and nothing else such as a critical comment is a common complaint among people who take college courses.
8. Renting textbooks for basic required courses rather than buying them—such as mathematics, foreign languages, and English— whose textbooks do not experience change from year to year is possible and feasible, however, economically speaking.
9. The outcome of the war was changed as a result of an event that occurred at about this same point in time, on the other hand.
10. Guidelines set forth in the MLA style sheet and the NCTE guidelines for the non-sexist use of language should be adhered to by speakers and writers, to the best of their ability.

Exercise 7-3

Revise these passages so that their sentences begin with appropriate topics and end with appropriate emphasis.

1. The story of King Lear and his daughters was a popular one during the reign of Queen Elizabeth. At least a dozen available books offered the story to anyone wishing to read it, by the time Elizabeth died. The characters were undeveloped in most of these stories, however, making the story a simple narrative that stated obvious morals. When he began work on *Lear,* one of his great tragedies, Shakespeare must have had several versions of this story available to him. He turned the characters into credible human beings with complex motives, however, even though they were based on the stock figures of legend.

2. Whether the date an operation intends to close down might be part of management's "duty to disclose" during contract bargaining is the issue here, it would appear. The minimization of conflict is the central rationale for the duty that management has to bargain in good faith. In order to allow the union to put forth proposals on behalf of its members, companies are obligated to disclose major changes in an operation during bargaining, though the case law is scanty on this matter.

3. Athens' catastrophic Sicilian Invasion is the most important event in Thucydides' *History of the Peloponnesian War.* Three-quarters of the history is devoted to setting up the invasion because of this. Through the step-by-step decline in Athenian society that Thucydides describes we can see how Thucydides chose to anticipate the Sicilian Invasion. What need was there to anticipate the invasion? The inevitability that we associate with the tragic drama is the basic reason.

This next passage will seem difficult, because it deals with a subject probably distant from your experience. But even if you don't understand the words, you can still make it more readable.

4. Mucosal and vascular permeability altered by a toxin elaborated by the vibrio is a current hypothesis to explain this kind of severe condition. Changes in small capillaries located near the basal surface of the epithelial cells, and the appearance of numerous

microvesicles in the cytoplasm of the mucosal cells is evidence in favor of this hypothesis. Hydrodynamic transport of fluid into the interstitial tissue and then through the mucosa into the lumen of the gut is believed to depend on altered capillary permeability.

Revise this next passage so that the most important data appear consistently at the ends of their sentences.

5. Changes in revenues are as follows. An increase to $56,792 from $32,934, a net increase of approximately 73%, was realized July 1–August 31 in the Ohio and Kentucky areas. In the Indiana and Illinois areas there was in the same period a 10% increase of $15,370, from $153,281 to $168,651. However, a decrease to $190,580 from $200,102, or 5%, occurred in the Wisconsin and Minnesota regions in almost the same period of time.

Exercise 7-4

In Lesson Six, you were asked to revise a few passages according to the old/new principle (pp. 125–126, 132–133). Look at your revisions again from the point of view of these two principles of cohesion and coherence. Look particularly at the opening sentences of those passages and if necessary revise them.

THE NUANCES OF EMPHASIS

Technical Terms

Whenever you write technical prose, your audience is likely to include some readers who will not understand all your terminology, so for them you must define your terms. But when you first introduce those terms, you must locate them in the stress of your sentences.

Exercise 7-5

In these next two passages, underline each term that you do not understand. Once you have underlined its first occurrence, don't underline it again in that passage. As you read the second passage, assume you are reading it for the first time. Then generalize: Where in the passages do the technical terms occur? How does that difference affect how easily you read the two? What other devices did I use to revise the first into the second?

1a. The effects of <u>calcium blockers</u> in the control of cardiac irregularity can be seen through an understanding of the role of calcium in the activation of muscle groups. The <u>regulatory proteins</u> <u>actin, myosin, tropomyosin, and troponin</u> make up the <u>sarcomere,</u> the basic unit of muscle contraction. The thick filament is made up of <u>ATPase</u>, an energy producing protein myosin, while actin, tropomyosin, and troponin make up the thin filament.

1b. When muscles contract, they need calcium. We must therefore understand how calcium influences muscle contraction in order to understand how cardiac irregularity is controlled by drugs called calcium blockers. The basic unit of muscle contraction is the sarcomere. It has two filaments, one thin and one thick, consisting of proteins that regulate contraction. Muscles contract when two of these proteins interact: One is in the thin filament: actin. The other is in the thick filament: it is myosin, an energy producing or ATPase protein.

Both passages have the same technical terms, the same complex information, but for the novice in muscle chemistry, (1b) is more readable than (1a). The versions differ in two ways.

1. I made information that was implicit in (1a) explicit in (1b):

1a. . . . and troponin make up the sarcomere, the basic unit of muscle contraction. The thick filament is made up of . . .

1b. The basic unit of muscle contraction is the sarcomere. It has two filaments . . .

I also converted information that was indirectly stated in an adjective in (1a) into direct statements with full subjects and verbs in (1b):

regulatory proteins → proteins that regulate.

2. I also moved technical terms to the ends of their sentences:

> 2a. The regulatory proteins actin, myosin, tropomyosin, and troponin make up the **sarcomere,** the basic unit of muscle contraction.

> 2b. The basic unit of muscle contraction is **the sarcomere.**

So in addition to everything else we've discussed, here is another key to communicating complex information: When you introduce your audience to a technical term, design the sentence it first appears in so that the term appears at the end of that sentence, in its stress, *never at the beginning, in its topic.* Writers introduce terms in this way in even the most specialized and professional writing. This is from *The New England Journal of Medicine:*

> We previously described [note the first person metadiscourse] a method for generating lymphocytes with antitumor reactivity. The incubation of peripheral-blood lymphocytes with a lympho-kine, interleukin-2, generates lymphoid cells that can lyse fresh, noncultured, natural-killer-cellresistant tumor cells but not normal cells. *We term these cells* [more first person metadiscourse that moves the technical term to the stress] **lymphokine-activated killer (LAK) cells.**

Rhetorical Emphasis

When we manage stress carefully, we can also control how strongly we assert our claims. Compare how the sentences in these passages end. One is by W. Averell Harriman, a Democratic critic of a Republican administration; the other is my revision.

> 2a. The Administration has blurred the issue of verification—so central to arms control. Irresponsible charges, innuendo and leaks have submerged serious problems with Soviet compliance. The objective, instead, should be not to exploit these concerns in order to further poison our relations, repudiate existing agreements, or, worse still, terminate arms control altogether, but to clarify questionable Soviet behavior and insist on compliance.

> 2b. The issue of verification—so central to arms control—has been blurred by the Administration. Serious problems with Soviet compliance have been submerged in irresponsible

charges, innuendo and leaks. The objective, instead, should
be to clarify questionable Soviet behavior and insist on
compliance—not to exploit these concerns in order to further poison our relations, repudiate existing agreements, or,
worse still, terminate arms control altogether.

Harriman wrote (2b), the one that stresses *blurred by the Administration; irresponsible charges, innuendo and leaks, poison our
relations; . . . terminate arms control altogether.* In so doing, he came
down hard not on the then-Soviet Union, but on the Republican
administration.

In some cases, a writer can manipulate the stress of sentences in
ways that encourage readers to respond not to what *is* surprising, but
to what the writer wants readers to *feel* is surprising. In this next
passage, Joan Didion located in the stresses of her sentences information that, in contrast to what is in the rest of her sentences,
seems mundane, unsurprising, apparently contradicting our principles. Before you read the whole passage, read just the boldfaced
words:

We put "Lay Lady Lay" on the record player, and "Suzanne." We
went down to Melrose Avenue to see the Flying Burritos. There
was a jasmine vine grown over the verandah of the big house on
Franklin Avenue, and in the evenings the smell of jasmine came
in through all the open doors and windows. I made bouillabaisse for people who did not eat meat. I imagined that my own
life was simple and sweet, and sometimes it was, but there were
odd things **going on around town.** There were **rumors.**
There were **stories.** Everything was unmentionable but nothing
was **unimaginable.** This mystical flirtation with the idea of
"sin"—this sense that it was possible to go "too far," and that
many people were doing it—was very much **with us in Los
Angeles in 1968 and 1969.** A demented and seductive vortical
tension was building **in the community.** The jitters were **setting in.** I recall a time when the dogs barked **every night** and
the moon was **always full.** On August 9, 1969, I was sitting in
the shallow end of my sister-in-law's swimming pool in Beverly
Hills when she received a telephone call from a friend who had
just heard about the murders **at Sharon Tate Polanski's house
on Cielo Drive.** The phone rang many times **during the next
hour.** These early reports were **garbled** and **contradictory.**
One caller would say **hoods,** the next would say **chains.** There

were twenty dead, no twelve, ten, **eighteen.** Black masses were
imagined and bad trips **blamed.** I remember all of the day's mis-
information very **clearly,** and I also remember this, and I wish I
did not: *I remember that **no one was surprised.***

—Joan Didion, "The White Album"

With few exceptions, Didion stresses at the ends of her sentences mundane information—places, dates, times. We might expect
an ordinarily competent writer to stress information that would shock
and surprise us. Here is that passage revised according to our principles. It is less interesting. First read just the boldfaced words.

The record player played "Lay Lady Lay" and "Suzanne." We went
down to Melrose Avenue to see the Flying Burritos. At the big house
on Franklin Avenue there was a jasmine vine grown over the verandah
and in the evenings the smell of jasmine came in through all the open
doors and windows. I made bouillabaisse for people who did not eat
meat. I imagined that my own life was simple and sweet, and sometimes it was, but going around town were some things that seemed
odd. There were **stories.** There were **rumors.** Everything was
unmentionable but nothing was **unimaginable.** In Los Angeles in
1968 and 1969, we all had this sense that it was possible to go "too
far," and that many people were **doing it.** It was a mystical flirtation
with the idea of **"sin."** Our community was building a vortical tension, a tension that was **seductive and demented.** We were getting
the jitters. I recall a time the moon was **always full** and the dogs
barked every night. On August 9, 1969, as I was sitting in the shallow end of my sister-in-law's swimming pool in Beverly Hills, she
received a telephone call from a friend who had just heard that over
on Cielo drive, at Roman Polanski's house, Sharon Tate and others **had
been murdered.** During the next hour the phone **rang many times.**
These early reports were **garbled and contradictory.** One caller
would say **hoods,** the next would say **chains.** There were ten, no
twelve, eighteen, **twenty dead.** People blamed bad trips and imagined
black masses. I remember very clearly all of the day's **misinforma-
tion,** and I also remember this, and I wish I did not: *I remember that
it surprised* **no one.**

Didion was writing about everyone's casual acceptance that evil
existed, that what in ordinary times would shock anyone did not surprise her friends, because to them evil was so familiar. To reflect that
familiarity, she constructs her sentences to introduce evil in their least
emphatic place, not at the ends, but in their middles. What she thinks

is surprising is not evil, but its accidental circumstances, so she stresses that mundane information at the ends of her sentences.

Exercise 7-6

Look again at the automobile recall letter in Lesson Six (p. 136). Where in those sentences are the words referring to alarming facts? beginning? middle? end? Why were they placed there?

SUMMING UP
The Whole System of Clarity

By now, we begin to appreciate the extraordinary complexity of an ordinary English sentence. A sentence is more than its subject, verb, and object, more than the sum of its parts. It is a system of systems whose parts we can fit together in delicate ways to achieve delicate ends—if we know how. We can match, mismatch, or metaphorically manipulate the grammatical units and their meanings:

FIXED	Topic		Stress
VARIABLE	Old Information	New Information	
FIXED	Subject	Verb	Complement
VARIABLE	Characters	Actions	—

We don't want to march every one of our sentences lockstep across the page in this character/topic/subject-action order. But when for no good reason our sentences depart from this pattern, when we consistently hide agency, nominalize active verbs, and end sentences on unimportant information, our prose will seem not just hard to read, but weak and incoherent.

When we step back from the details of subjects, agents, passives, nominalizations, topic and stress, when we can hear our prose as others will, we should hear something beyond clarity and coherence. We should hear a voice. The voice that our readers hear contributes substantially to the character that they think we project. Some teachers of writing want to make voice a moral choice between a false voice and a voice "authentic." But we all speak in many voices, no one of which is more or less authentic. When we are being authoritative and aloof, then that's the voice we choose to project because that's what we're being. When we want to be businesslike and direct, then we should be able to choose that voice. Our problem is to choose the voice that we want our readers to hear. That's no more false than choosing how we dress, how we behave, how we live. Some among us have learned to make those choices naturally, without thought or instruction.

The rest of us have to work at it.

Lesson Eight

Controlling Sprawl

The structure of every sentence is a lesson in logic.
J.S. MILL

Sentences in their variety run from simplicity to complexity, a
progression not necessarily reflected in length: a long sentence may be
extremely simple in construction—indeed must be simple if it is to
convey its sense easily.
SIR HERBERT READ

A long complicated sentence should force itself upon you, make you
know yourself knowing it.
GERTRUDE STEIN

Long sentences in a short composition are like large rooms in
a little house.
WILLIAM SHENSTONE

Too much of a good thing is worse than none at all.
ENGLISH PROVERB

You never know what is enough until you know what is
more than enough.
WILLIAM BLAKE

T he ability to write a clear sentence is a singular achievement. But if our clear sentences never went beyond twenty words, we'd be like a pianist who could use only the middle octave: We could pick out a few clear and simple tunes, but not much more. We have to know how to write short concise sentences. But we also must know how to write a long sentence that is as clear as a series of short ones. In fact, sometimes we have to write a long sentence to synthesize our ideas into a single coherent conceptual structure.

TWO KINDS OF LENGTH

Compare these:

    1a. Pursuing varied strategies is of more use in understanding genetic factors contributing to vulnerability to psychiatric disorders than a single strategy based on an assumption that psychopathology is dependent on a major gene or a strategy based on the study of only a single biological variable.

That sentence is difficult partly because it is long, but more importantly, because it is full of NOMINALIZATIONS and empty of CHARACTERS. We can make it clearer if we revise it around VERBS:

    1b. To understand the genetic factors that make people vulnerable to psychiatric disorders, we should pursue varied strategies, which is better than a single strategy that assumes that psychopathology depends on a major gene or that studies only a single biological variable.

While that sentence is a bit easier to understand, perhaps, it still seems ungainly, sprawling. We could cut it into shorter sentences:

    1c. To understand the genetic factors that make people vulnerable to psychiatric disorders, we should use multivariate strategies. We should not use a strategy that assumes that psychopathology depends on a major gene. Nor should we use a strategy in which we study only a single biological variable.

But now (1c) fragments a complex concept into a series of disconnected assertions. We must re-combine those short sentences:

1d. To understand the genetic factors that make people vulnerable to psychiatric disorders, we should use a variety of strategies, not just one that assumes that psychopathology depends on a major gene or that studies only a single biological variable.

That is almost as long as (1a) and (1b), but it is not difficult to understand, and it does not sprawl. So it is not mere number of words that causes sprawl, but the lack of internal architecture. The nature of that internal architecture is the object of this Lesson.

DIAGNOSING AND CONTROLLING SPRAWL

It's easy to diagnose sprawl in someone else's writing. We get lost in the middle of sentences, we long for a sentence to end. But since most of us are less good about diagnosing problems in our own writing, we need a way to diagnose sprawl that sidesteps our understanding. One simple way is to put a slash mark after every PUNCTUATED SENTENCE. Then pick out those sentences that run for more than three typed lines. Read them aloud, slowly, pausing where it feels natural to do so. If you feel you are about to run out of breath before you come to a pause, you have identified sentences that you may want to revise.

There are four ways to revise a long sentence. The simplest and least demanding is to divide it into shorter ones. But that may create the choppy disconnectedness of (1c). Other ways are more complicated, but they produce more satisfying results:

1. Condense RELATIVE CLAUSES into PHRASES.
2. Construct sentences with internal patterns of COORDINATION.
3. Create three kinds of modifiers that you probably have never studied before: RESUMPTIVE, SUMMATIVE, and FREE.

1. MANAGING RELATIVE CLAUSES

A string of relative clauses is invariably limp and graceless:

> Of the areas of science **that** are important not just to the future of knowledge but to life on this planet, few are more promising than genetic engineering, **which** is a new way of manipulating the elemental structures and units of life itself, **which** are the genes and chromosomes **that** direct our cells how to reproduce and become the parts **that** create the shape of all life.

You can always remedy a limp sentence like this by simply cutting it in two.

> Of all the areas of science that are important not just to the future of knowledge but to life on this planet, few are more promising than genetic engineering, which is a new way of manipulating the elemental structures and units of life itself. **These units** are the genes and chromosomes that direct our cells how to reproduce and become the parts that create the shape of all life.

But you can also tidy up longer sentences if in relative clauses you can delete a few of the *who/that/which* + *is/are/was,* etc.

> Of all the areas of science […] important not just to the future of knowledge but to life on this planet, few are more promising than genetic engineering, […] a new way of manipulating the elemental structures and units of life itself. **These units** are the genes and chromosomes **that** direct our cells how to reproduce and become the parts **that** create the shape of all life.

> Work **that is** not done on time must be submitted on a date **which will be** set by those **who are** responsible for scheduling.

> Work […] not done on time must be submitted on a date […] set by those […] responsible for scheduling.

Occasionally when you drop *that/which/who,* you may have to rewrite the following verb into a different form.

> Organized labor has lost the political power it once used to support programs **that benefitted** rank-and-file workers.

Organized labor has lost the political power it once used to support programs [...] **benefitting** rank-and-file workers.

The day is coming when we will all have numbers **that will identify** every transaction so that the IRS can monitor all areas of our lives **that involve** economic activity.

The day is coming when we will all have numbers [...] **identifying** every transaction so that the IRS can monitor all areas of our lives [...] **involving** economic activity.

Watch for long subjects that contain a relative clause:

[A doctor **who has been a medical consultant for a company and who helped the company develop medical policies**]$_{subject}$ must testify in trials involving malpractice.

You can often turn a long relative clause like this into an introductory adverbial clause beginning with *if* or *when:*

If a doctor has been a medical consultant for a company and helped the company develop medical policies, he or she must testify in trials involving malpractice.

But move the clause to the end of its sentence if it is long, complicated, and contains information that the next sentences develop:

A doctor is required to testify in trials involving malpractice **if he or she has been a medical consultant for a company and helped the company develop medical policies. Those policies ...**

2. MANAGING COORDINATION

Compare these. The original is first; my revision is the second:

For the aspiring artist, the minor, the unfinished, or even the botched work, may be a[n] instructive model for how things should—and should not be done. For the amateur spectator, such works are the daily fare which provide good, honest nourishment—and which can lead to appreciation of more refined, or deeper pleasures.

from Eva Hoffman, "Minor Art Offers Special Pleasures."

The aspiring artist may find that even a minor unfinished work which was botched may be an instructive model for how things should be done, while for the amateur spectator, such works are the daily fare which provide good, honest entertainment leading to an appreciation of deeper pleasures that may also be more refined.

My revision sprawls through a string of tacked-on clauses.

The aspiring artist may find that even a minor, unfinished work

> **which** was botched may be an instructive model for how things should be done,
>> while for the amateur spectator, such works are the daily fare
>>> **which** provide good, honest entertainment
>>>> **that** lead to appreciation of deeper pleasures
>>>>> **that** may also be more refined.

Her original passage has a series of balanced coordinations that give this short passage a shape:

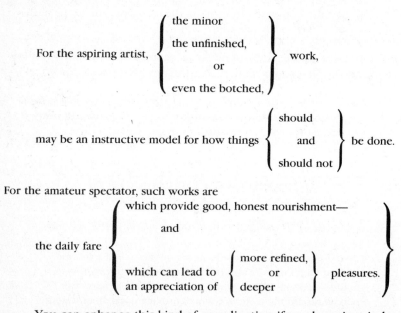

You can enhance this kind of coordination if you keep in mind a few simple principles.

Coordinate Grammatically Parallel Elements

A common rule of rhetoric and grammar is that we should coordinate elements only of the same grammatical structure: clause and clause, PREDICATE and predicate, PREPOSITIONAL PHRASE and prepositional phrase, etc. When you coordinate parts that have different grammatical structures, you may create an offensive lack of PARALLELISM. Most careful writers would avoid this:

These advertisements persuade us $\begin{cases} \textbf{that the corporation supports} \\ \text{environmentalism} \\ \\ \textbf{but not} \\ \\ \textbf{to buy} \text{ its frivolous products.} \end{cases}$

Corrected:

persuade us $\begin{cases} \textbf{that the corporation supports environmentalism} \\ \textbf{but not} \\ \textbf{that we should buy} \text{ its frivolous products.} \end{cases}$

This also would be considered nonparallel:

The committee recommends $\begin{cases} \textbf{revising the curriculum} \text{ to reflect} \\ \text{trends in local employment} \\ \\ \textbf{and} \\ \\ \textbf{that the division be reorganized} \\ \textbf{to} \text{ reflect the new curriculum.} \end{cases}$

Corrected:

...recommends $\begin{cases} \textbf{that the curriculum be revised} \text{ to reflect} \ldots \\ \text{and} \\ \textbf{that the division be reorganized} \text{ to reflect} \ldots \end{cases}$

But some nonparallel coordinations often occur in well-written prose. Many competent writers often coordinate a noun phrase with a *how*-clause.

Every attempt will be made to delineate {
the problems of education among under-developed nations

and

how coordinated efforts can address them in economical ways
}

Or an ADJECTIVE or adverb with a prepositional phrase:

The proposal appears to have been written {
intelligently, carefully,

and

with the full cooper-ation of all the involved agencies.
}

Some careful teachers insist on rewriting these into perfectly parallel form, but this kind of "faulty" parallelism is overlooked by most careful readers.

Coordinate Rhetorically Parallel Elements

Coordination works best when the elements that you coordinate balance not only in grammar, but in thought. This seems "off":

> Many voters believe fervently that elected officials are guilty of abusing their privileges **and** are calling for term limitations **and** believe that the power of incumbency is too great to overcome to make fair elections possible.

While the elements may be coordinate grammatically, they aren't coordinate in thought. They are a linear sequence of causes and effects:

> Many voters believe **so** fervently that elected officials are guilty of abusing their privileges **that** they are calling for term limitations, **because** they believe that the power of incumbency is too great to make fair elections possible.

Unfortunately, I can offer no sure way to identify when elements are coordinate in grammar but not in content. You just have to be thoughtful. That's little help.

Keep Grammatical Connections Visible

What bothers readers more than faulty parallelism is a coordination so long that they lose track of its internal connections:

> Every teacher ought to remember that students are vulnerable, inse-
> cure and uncertain about those everyday, ego-bruising moments that
> adults no longer concern themselves with, and that they do not
> understand that one day they will become as confident and as secure
> as the adults that bruise them.

There is a momentary flicker of hesitation about where to connect

> ... and that they do not understand that one day they ...

It is enough to interrupt the flow of the sentence.

To revise a sentence like this, try to make the first half of the coordination shorter so that the second half of the coordination begins closer to the point where the coordination began:

> Every teacher ought to remember that students are vulnerable to
> those ego-bruising moments that adults have learned to cope with and
> that those students do not understand that one day ...

If you can't do that, try repeating a word that will remind the reader where the second half of the coordination begins:

> Every teacher ought **to remember** that students are vulnerable to
> those ego-bruising moments that adults have learned to cope with, **to**
> **remember** that those students do not understand that one day ...

And, of course, you can always begin a new sentence:

> ... adults no longer concern themselves with. Every teacher should
> remember that students do not understand ...

You can clarify and strengthen the elements of the coordination if you judiciously use CORRELATIVE CONJUNCTIONS such as *both X and Y, not only X but also Y, neither X nor Y.* Compare:

> An historical study of any profound social change must recognize the economic basis of the change and its political climate and its demographic foundations.

> An historical study of any profound social change must recognize **not only** the economic basis of the change **but both** its political climate **and** its demographic foundations, as well.

Exercise 8-1

The best way to learn how to manage coordination is by imitating it. Try imitating any of the passages laid out above. For example, here is a sentence from p. 168.

For the aspiring artist

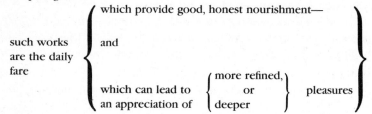

You might write,

> For the serious student, trips to the library are quiet times that provide an opportunity to be alone and to think through problems that may be too complex or too painful to think about in a noisy and crowded dormitory.

---

3. RESUMPTIVE, SUMMATIVE, AND FREE MODIFIERS

You've probably never hear of these terms before, but since mature writers often use these kinds of modifiers, we need terms to describe a sentence like the one that you are now reading, a sentence that I could have ended seven words ago, but that I extended to show how resumptive modifiers work.

Resumptive Modifiers

A resumptive modifier lets you extend the length of a sentence but avoids a sprawling series of relative clauses. Read these aloud:

> But since mature writers often use these kinds of modifiers, we need terms to describe a sentence like the one you are now reading, a sentence that I could have ended seven words ago, but that I extended to show how resumptive modifiers work.

> But since mature writers often use these kinds of modifiers, we need terms to describe a sentence like the one that you are now reading that I could have ended seven words ago but that I extended to show how a sentence sprawls without them.

The first sentence lets you take a breath after *now reading*, then repeats the phrase and continues. That second sentence just runs on and on.

To create the resumptive modifier, I did this:

1. When I felt I had gone on too long, I paused with a comma:

> But since mature writers often use these kinds of modifiers, we need these terms to describe a sentence like the one you are now reading,

2. Then I found an important word close to the end of that clause, *sentence,* and repeated it:

> But since mature writers often use these kinds of modifiers, we need these terms to describe *a sentence* like the one you are now reading,
> **a sentence . . .**

3. Then to that repeated word, *sentence,* I added a relative clause, modifying what went before.

> But since mature writers often use these kinds of modifiers, we need these terms to describe a sentence like the one you are now reading,
> *a sentence* **that I could have ended seven words ago, but that I extended to show how resumptive modifiers work.**

You can pause and resume with adjectives as well:

> It was American writers who first used a vernacular that was both
> **true** and **lyrical,**
> > **true** to the rhythms of the working man's speech, **lyrical** in its
> > celebration of his labor.

And with verbs:

> All of us who value our independence should **resist** the trivialization
> of necessary regulation,
> > **resist** the bureaucratic obsession toward administrative tidiness
> > and its compulsion to arrange things not for our convenience
> > but for the convenience of those who regulate our affairs.

Summative Modifiers

This kind of modifier lets you both extend a sentence and avoid
the kind of sprawl that sometimes occurs when you tack on a
which-clause referring to everything that preceded, as in this ungainly
sentence:

> Changes in economic and social conditions have caused European
> population growth to drop almost to zero, **which in years to come
> will have profound social implications.**

But a summative modifier doesn't repeat a word. It depends on your
finding a word that sums up everything that has gone before:

> Changes in economic and social conditions have caused European
> population growth to drop almost to zero,
> > **a demographic event** that in years to come will have profound
> > social implications.

To create a summative modifier, do this:

1. End a segment of a sentence with a comma,

> Changes in social conditions have caused European population growth
> to drop almost to zero,

2. Find a noun that sums up the substance of the preceding clause,

> Changes in social conditions have caused European population growth to drop almost to zero,
> > **a demographic event . . .**

3. Continue with a relative clause:

> Changes in social conditions have caused European population growth to drop almost to zero,
> > *a demographic event* **that in years to come will have profound social implications.**

Free Modifiers

Like the other two, a free modifier can appear at the end of a clause, but instead of repeating a key word or summing up what went before, it modifies or comments on the subject of the closest verb.

> Free modifiers resemble resumptive and summative modifiers, **letting** [i.e., the modifier lets] you extend the line of a sentence while avoiding a train of phases and clauses.

Compare these two:

> Socrates, who questioned the foundations of political behavior, forced his fellow citizens to examine the duty they owed to the laws of their gods and to the laws of their state and encouraged young people to question the authority of their elders while he maintained that he was trying in his poor way only to puzzle out the truth as best he could.

> Socrates questioned the foundations of political behavior,
> > **forcing** his fellow citizens to examine the duty they owed to the laws of their gods and to the laws of their state,
> > **encouraging** young people to question the authority of their elders,
> > **maintaining** all the while that he was trying in his poor way only to puzzle out the truth as best he could.

Free modifiers most often begin with an -*ing* PRESENT PARTICIPLE, but they can also begin with a PAST PARTICIPLE form of the verb:

> Leonardo da Vinci was a man of powerful intellect,
> { **driven** by an insatiable curiosity and   }
> { **haunted** by a vision of artistic perfection. }

A free modifier can also begin with an adjective:

> In 1939, we began to assist the British against Germany,
> **aware** that we faced another world war.

We call these modifiers free because they can both conclude and introduce a sentence:

> Driven by an insatiable curiosity, Leonardo da Vinci was . . .
>
> Aware that we faced another world war, in 1939 we began . . .

You have to be certain that the free modifier implies the subject of the clause it attaches to. If not, you have a DANGLING MODIFIER.

> The results of the tests underwent the most extensive reviews in the history of our laboratory, **hoping to find some cause of the flaw that threatened the entire project.**

The modifier, *hoping to find . . . ,* dangles because its implicit subject, *somebody who hopes,* differs from the subject of the clause it attaches to: *the results of recent tests.* Results cannot hope.

Exercise 8-2

In these sentences, create resumptive, summative, and free modifiers. In the first five, start the resumptive modifier with the word in italics. Then use the word in parentheses to create another sentence with a summative modifier. Then on your own create some sentences with free modifiers. For example:

> Within ten years, we could meet our *energy needs* with solar power.
> (a possibility)

Resumptive:

> Within ten years, we could meet our *energy needs* with solar power, **needs that will grow as our population grows.**

Summative:

> Within ten years, we could meet our energy needs with solar power, ***a possibility* that few anticipated ten years ago.**

Free:

> Within ten years, we could meet our energy needs with solar power, **freeing ourselves of dependence on foreign oil.**

But before you begin adding resumptive and summative modifiers, edit these sentences for redundancy, wordiness, nominalizations, etc.

1. Many different school systems are making a return back to old-fashioned traditional *education* in the basics. (a change)
2. Within the period of the last few years or so, automobile manufacturers have been trying to meet new and more stringent-type mileage *requirements.* (a challenge)
3. The reasons for the cause of our aging are a *puzzle* that has perplexed humanity for millennia. (a mystery)
4. The majority of the young people in the modern world of today cannot even begin to achieve an understanding or grasp of the *insecurity* that a large number of older people had experience of during the period known as the Great Depression. (a failure)
5. The successful accomplishment of test-tube fertilization of embryos raised many *issues* of an ethical nature that continue to trouble both scientists and laypeople. (an event)
6. Many who lived during the period of the Victorian era were appalled when Darwin put forth the suggestion that their ancestry might have included creatures such as apes.

In these next sentences, prune the redundancy and the abstraction and then create coordinate modifiers of your own devising. For example, here is a coordinate resumptive modifier built into (5) above:

> . . . ethical *issues* that are troubling both scientists and laypeople, *issues* that will yield easily to neither historical religious principles nor contemporary legal theory.

7. The general concept of systematic skepticism is in effect a kind of denial that there can ever be any kind of certain knowledge of reality screened and influenced by human perception.

8. The originating point when the field of scientific inquiry began to develop is to be found in the individual and personal observations of naive primitive peoples about the natural things that seem to them to occur in a regular way.

9. In the period known to scholars and historians as the Renaissance, increases in affluence and stability in the area of political affairs had the consequence of allowing streams of thought of different kinds to merge and flow together.

MOVEMENT AND MOMENTUM

To write one long sentence as clear as a series of short ones, you have to let your readers take a breath at appropriate places; you can also echo one part of a sentence against another with coordinated and parallel elements. But most important, you cannot interrupt its flow.

Maintaining the Largest Grammatical Connections

If a sentence is to flow easily, we must maintain its two most important grammatical links—subject >< verb and verb >< object. When we prevent our readers from completing those links quickly and surely, they will feel that our sentences hesitate:

1a. A semantic theory, if it is to represent in real-time processing terms on-line cognitive behavior, must propose more neurally plausible psychological processes than those described here.

1b. If a semantic theory is to represent on-line cognitive behavior in real-time terms, it must propose psychological processes that are more neurally plausible than those described here.

Both sentences make you pause, but in (1a) that long *if*-clause after the subject, *if it is to represent . . . cognitive behavior,* forces you to hold your breath until you reach the verb, *must propose.* Even as you read that interrupting *if*-clause, you had to suspend the sense after its verb, *represent,* because another, shorter interruption, *in real-time processing terms,* kept you from getting to its object, *on-line cognitive behavior.* The interruptions look like this:

<pre>
A semantic theory →   ←must propose
       if it is to represent→   ←on-line cognitive behavior
              in real-time processing terms
</pre>

And then the *more* at the end is split from its second member, *than those described here:*

<pre>
more→   ←than those described here
      neurally plausible psychological processes
</pre>

On the other hand, the revised sentence (1b) lets you take a breath half way through. But more important, you are able to connect uninterrupted subjects with their verbs and verbs with their objects:

<pre>
         If a semantic theory → ← is to represent
               is to represent → ← on-line cognitive behavior
    on-line cognitive behavior → ← in real time processing terms,
                           it → ← must propose psychological
                                     processes
       more neurally plausible → ← than those suggested here.
</pre>

If you interrupt the connections between the subject and verb or verb and object, you force your reader to hesitate. It's true that you may briefly interrupt those links with short modifiers.

> Scientists the world over > **deliberately** < write in a style that is aloof, impersonal, and objective.

But longer phrases and clauses fit less comfortably:

> Scientists the world over, > **because they deliberately write in a style that is aloof, impersonal, and objective,** < have difficulty communicating with lay people.

If you find a long phrase or clause interrupting the subject >< verb or verb >< object link, move that phrase or clause to the beginning of its sentence or to its end. But think first about what comes next. These two sentences create different expectations about what will follow:

> **Because scientists the world over deliberately write in a style that is aloof, impersonal, and objective,** they have difficulty communicating with lay people.

> Scientists the world over have difficulty communicating with lay people **because they deliberately write in a style that is aloof, impersonal, and objective.**

The first suggests that the next few sentences will address the difficulty scientists have communicating. The second suggests that the next sentences will address their impersonal style.

Maintaining the Smallest Grammatical Connections

To avoid even small hitches in the rhythm of a sentence, look for adjectives that you have split off from the phrases that modify them. We often put an adjective before the noun it modifies, but split off the phrase that modifies that adjective and put it after that noun. The boldfaced words and phrases belong together.

> The accountant has given **as accurate** *a projection* **as any that could be provided.**

> We are facing **a more serious** *decision* **than what you described earlier.**

> A **close** *relationship* **to the one just discovered** is the degree to which **similar** *genetic material* **to that of related species** can be modified by **different** *DNA chains* **from the ones first selected by Adams and Walsh.**

> **Another** *course of action* **than the present one** is necessary to accumulate **sufficient** *capital* **to complete such** *projects* **as those you have described.**

In each case, we have split an adjective from its modifying phrase by putting the adjective before a noun and its modifying phrase after:

as accurate	a projection	**as any that . . .**
a more serious	decision	**than what**
a close	relationship	**to the one**

similar	genetic material	**to that of related**
different	DNA chains	**from the ones**
another	course of action	**than the present one**
sufficient	capital	**to complete**
such	projects	**as those you . . .**

We maintain a smoother rhythm if we put the adjective *after* the noun, so that we can directly connect the adjective to the phrase that modifies it:

> The accountant has given a projection **as accurate** → ← **as** any that could have been provided.

> We are facing a decision **more serious** → ← **than** what you described earlier.

> A relationship **close** → ← **to** the one just discovered is the degree to which genetic material **similar** → ← **to** that of related species can be modified by DNA chains **different** → ← **from** the ones first selected by Adams and Walsh.

> A course of action **other** → ← **than** the present one is necessary to accumulate capital **sufficient** → ← **to** complete projects **such** → ← **as** those you describe.

Some adjectives that we frequently split off from their modifiers:

more . . . than	less . . . than	other . . . than
as . . . as	similar . . . to	equal . . . to
identical . . . to	different . . . from	such . . . as
separate . . . from	distant. . . from	related . . . to
close . . . to	next . . . to	difficult . . . to

Exercise 8-3

These sentences contain unfortunate interruptions. First, revise to eliminate wordiness and correct the interruption. Then devise summative, resumptive, and free modifiers. Then create a coordinate member to balance the modifier you've added. See how long a sentence you can write before it collapses.

1. The construction of the Interstate Highway System, owing to the fact that Congress, on the occasion when it originally voted funds

for it, did not anticipate the cost of inflation, has run into serious financial problems.

2. Such conduct or behavior, for whatever reasons proffered, is rarely not at least to some degree prejudicial to good order and discipline.

3. TV game shows, due to the fact that they have an appeal to the basic cupidity in us all, are just about the most popular shows that appear on TV.

4. The merit selection of those who serve as judges, given the low quality and character of elected officials, is an idea whose time came long ago.

5. The field of physics, working with certain devices that can actually accelerate particles to a speed almost as fast as the speed of light, is exploring the ultimate nature and makeup of matter.

6. The continued and unabated emission of carbon dioxide gas into the atmospheric environment, unless there is a marked reduction prior to the end of the century, will eventually result in a change in the climate of the world as we know it today.

7. Insistence that there is no proof by scientific means of a certain causal link between the activity of smoking and various disease entities such as cardiac heart diseases and malignant growths, despite the fact that there is a strong statistical correlation between smoking behavior and disease entities, continues to be the official stated position and policy of the cigarette companies.

Exercise 8-4

These sentences contain awkwardly disjoined adjective phrases. Revise them to reunite the phrases and to make the style more direct. The separated phrases in (1) and (2) are bold-faced.

1. An **identical** ecological impact statement **to that submitted the previous year** indicates that it will again contain **difficult** data **to evaluate.**

2. Under the circumstances in which **similar** EKG readings are obtained **to those obtained earlier, other** conditions **than cardiac disease** must come under suspicion. To determine those conditions, the diagnostician must follow the **same** procedures **as those outlined above** and must be closely adhered to on the

expectation that **as effective** results **as those outlined there** can be achieved in such cases.

3. As a result of the reorganization of the marketing research division, more rapid information processing than that which has been possible in the past should allow more reliable identification of different market segments from those that have been traditionally aimed at. This will be relatively easy information to process as a result of the fact that there has already been accumulated such demographic data as the average financial income, expenditure patterns, etc., for many different markets. As a result of all this, greater efficiency than that which we achieved in our earlier operation last year may be a reasonable expectation.

POTENTIAL PROBLEMS WITH LONGER SENTENCES

When you add modifiers, readers may lose track of the grammatical connections between the modifier and the modified.

Dangling Modifiers

Modifiers can dangle at both ends of a sentence. Again, a modifier "dangles" when its implied subject differs from the explicit subject of the clause it attaches to. In this sentence, the implied subject of *contain* differs from the explicit subject of its main clause, *the area.*

> **In order to contain the epidemic,** *the area* was sealed off.

Constructions like these amuse more often than they confuse. But since they cause some readers to hesitate, avoid them. Either rewrite the introductory phrase so that it has an explicit subject:

> In order for **us** to contain the fire, the area was sealed off.

Or make the subject of the main clause agree with the implied subject of the introductory phrase:

> In order to contain the fire, **we** sealed off the area.

Some dangling modifiers we generally ignore. Few of us notice when the implied subject of the modifier is different from the explicit subject of the main clause when either is METADISCOURSE:

> *In order* [for someone] *to start the motor,* **it** is essential that the retroflex cam connecting rod be disengaged.

Misplaced Modifiers

A second problem with modifiers is that sometimes they seem to modify either of two things or the wrong thing. An ambiguous modifier can refer forward or back:

> Overextending oneself in strenuous physical activity **too frequently** results in a variety of physical ailments.
>
> We failed **entirely** to understand the problem.

In each of these, we make the modifier unambiguous:

> Overextending oneself **too frequently** in strenuous exercise . . .
>
> Overextending oneself in physical exercise results **too frequently** in a variety of physical ailments.
>
> We **entirely** failed to understand the problem.
>
> We failed to **entirely** understand the problem.

(Of course, some might now criticize the split infinitive. (See p. 24))
    An ambiguous modifier at the end of a clause can modify either a neighboring or a more distant phrase:

> Scientists have learned that their observations are as subjective as those in any other field **in recent years.**

We can move the modifier to a less ambiguous position:

> **In recent years,** scientists have learned that . . .
>
> Scientists have learned that **in recent years** their . . .

Ambiguous Pronoun Reference

Ambiguous pronoun reference can especially afflict a long sentence with many nouns and pronouns. If there is any chance a pronoun will confuse your reader, repeat the noun. If you can distinguish nouns by singular and plural, you can use singular and plural pronouns. Compare:

> **Physicians** must never forget that **their patients** are vitally concerned about **their** treatment and **their** prognosis, but that **they** are often unwilling to ask for fear of what **they** will say.

> **A physician** must never forget that **her patients** are vitally concerned about **their** treatment and **their** prognosis, but that **they** are often unwilling to ask for fear of what **she** will say.

Exercise 8-5

These sentences suffer from a variety of problem modifiers. Correct and revise the sentences in any other ways you see fit.

1. Having no previous familiarity with it, the metal deposit detection device did not function as expected.
2. With every expectation of success, new efforts to resolve the differences that have resulted in interference with communication in a short time are necessary.
3. Realizing that the undergraduate curriculum must be completely reevaluated in the next few weeks, proposals have suddenly appeared on the agenda that had received earlier discussion.
4. After making an audit of all internal operations in the summer of 1988, a second audit examined the record of foreign affiliates that had not been previously audited by their local headquarters.

These devices can help you shape a long sentence, but not even the best syntax can save it, if its content is silly or incoherent. This next sentence appeared one Sunday in *The New York Times* travel section.

> [In the preceding sentence, the writer had introduced the professional women of Amsterdam's red-light district.] They are so unself-conscious about their profession that by day they can

be seen standing naked in doorways, chatting with their neighbors in the shadow of the Oudekerstoren Church, which offers
Saturday carillon concerts at 4 P.M. and a panoramic view of the
city from its tower in summer.

This syntactically well-formed sentence opens with a coherent clause:

They are so unself-conscious about their profession that by day they
can be seen standing naked in doorways,

It continues with a free modifier:

chatting with their neighbors in the shadow of the Ouderkerstoren
Church . . .

It then concludes with a relative clause that contains a coherently
coordinated pair of direct objects:

$$\text{which offers} \begin{cases} \text{Saturday carillon concerts at 4 P.M.} \\ \quad\quad\quad\text{and} \\ \text{a panoramic view of the city from its tower in} \\ \text{the summer.} \end{cases}$$

But the progression of the ideas is at best goofy (or sly evidence of a
zany sense of humor). With no controlling idea, coherent syntax provides only external decoration. To support that decoration you need
internal substance.

SUMMING UP

1. Avoid rhythmically unbroken sentences consisting of one clause
   tacked onto another tacked onto another. Use these devices:
   a. Coordination

   Besides the fact that no civilization has experienced such rapid
   alterations in the condition of daily life, the life of the mind has
   changed greatly too.

   No civilization has experienced such rapid alterations **in the
   condition of daily life** *or* **in the life of the mind.**

b. Resumptive modifiers

> Our discovery that the earth was not at the center of the uni-
> verse reshaped our understanding not only of where we are but
> of who we are, **which was changed again by Darwin, and
> again by Freud, and again by Einstein.**

> Our discovery that the earth was not the center of the universe
> reshaped **our understanding** not only of where we are but of
> who we are, **an understanding** that was changed again by Dar-
> win, and again by Freud, and again by Einstein.

c. Summative modifiers

> Some people have maintained that the way to anticipate energy
> crises is to build a synthetic fuel industry, **which is** *rejected by
> environmentalists who argue that we can achieve the same
> result by investments in mass transportation and insulation.*

> Some people have maintained that the way to anticipate energy
> crises is to build a synthetic fuel industry, **a position** *rejected
> by environmentalists who argue that we can achieve the same
> result by investments in mass transportation and insulation.*

d. Free modifiers

> Global warming has become one of the central political issues
> of the 20th century, **which raises questions that affect the
> standard of living in every Western nation.**

> Global warming has become one of the central political issues
> of the 20th century, **raising questions that affect the stan-
> dard of living in every Western nation.**

2. To maintain the momentum in a long sentence, don't break links
between subject and verb or verb and object.

> **The Protagoras,** > *despite its questionable logic and rather superfi-
> cial philosophical content,* < **remains** one of Plato's most
> dramatically appealing dialogues.

> *Despite its questionable logic and rather superficial philosophical
> content,* **the Protagoras** > < **remains** one of Plato's most dramati-
> cally appealing dialogues.

On the other hand, if the object is long and the interrupting phrase is short, put the modifier between the verb and object.

> Few politicians are willing to admit > < that the electorate regards them essentially as parasites **even to themselves.**

> Few politicians are willing to admit > **even to themselves** < that the electorate regards them essentially as parasites.

3. Watch for modifiers that may seem to modify something other than what you intended:

> Re-examining the issues that had been earlier discussed, a new perspective on them arose among the committee.

> Re-examining the issues that had been earlier discussed, the committee took a new perspective on them.

Lesson Nine

Punctuation

I know there are some Persons who affect to despise it, and treat this whole Subject with the utmost Contempt, as a Trifle far below their Notice, and a Formality unworthy of their Regard: They do not hold it difficult, but despicable; and neglect it, as being above it. Yet many learned Men have been highly sensible to its Use; and some ingenious and elegant Writers have condescended to point their Works with Care; and very eminent Scholars have not disdained to teach the Method of doing it with Propriety.
JAMES BURROW

In music, the punctuation is absolutely strict; the bars and rests are absolutely defined. But our prose cannot be quite strict, because we have to relate it to the audience. In other words we are continually changing the score.
SIR RALPH RICHARDSON

One who uses many periods is a philosopher; many interrogations, a student; many exclamations, a fanatic.
J. L. BASFORD

There are some punctuations that are interesting and there are some that are not.
GERTRUDE STEIN

For most of us, punctuation is about as aesthetically challenging as straightening up a closet: We engage with it just long enough to get things straight. Yet deployed carefully, commas, colons, and semicolons can make your sentences not only clear, but even a bit stylish. It takes more than punctuation to turn a monotone into the Hallelujah Chorus, but a little care can produce gratifying results.

I begin with the least you have to know about punctuation, then explore its fine points. I'll address the matter not by the kind of mark, but as a functional problem: How do we punctuate the beginning of a sentence, its middle, and its end? I'll begin at the end, because most readers take how we punctuate the ends of sentences to indicate the level of our basic literacy.

PUNCTUATED AND GRAMMATICAL SENTENCES

We first have to distinguish two kinds of sentences; the one you are reading, for example, is one long sentence, but it is long because I have chosen to punctuate what might have been a series of shorter sentences as one PUNCTUATED SENTENCE: a sentence that begins with a capital letter and ends with a period; that semicolon, for example, could have been a period—and that dash could have been one as well.

I can write a different kind of sentence that is as almost as long as that one, but one that I could not break up into shorter punctuated sentences merely by replacing a period with a comma, a semicolon, or a dash, because it is a sentence made up of several SUBORDINATE CLAUSES, all of them depending on one MAIN CLAUSE—a sentence such as the one you have almost finished reading.

Independent and Subordinate Clauses

Both of those sentences are single punctuated sentences: Both begin with a capital letter and end with a period. But the first sentence consists of a series of GRAMMATICAL SENTENCES, of a series of short INDEPENDENT CLAUSES. I could transform those independent clauses into separate punctuated sentences by replacing commas, semi-colons, and dashes with periods. First the original, with bold-faced punctuation to show where I might have put a period; then a re-punctuated revision, changed only enough to make sense:

1a. We first have to distinguish two kinds of sentences; the one you are reading, for example, is one long sentence, but it is long because I have chosen to punctuate what might have been a series of shorter sentences as one long punctuated sentence: a sentence that begins with a capital letter and ends with a period; that semicolon, for example, could have been a period—and that dash could have been one as well.

1b. We first have to distinguish two kinds of sentences. The one you are reading, for example, is a short sentence. But it is short because I have chosen to punctuate what might have been one long punctuated sentence as a series of shorter sentences: a sentence that begins with a capital letter and ends with a period. That period, for example, could have been a semi-colon. And that period could have been a dash.

On the other hand, my second long sentence consisted of just one independent main clause:

2a. I can write a different kind of sentence . . .

And it is followed by a series of DEPENDENT subordinate clauses:

. . . [that is almost as long as that one]₁, but one [that I could not ɔreak up into shorter punctuated sentences merely by replacing a period with a comma, a semicolon, or a dash]₂, [because it is a sentence made up of several subordinate clauses, all of them depending on one main clause]₃,—a sentence such as the one [you have almost finished reading]₄.

To revise that long grammatical sentence into a series of shorter grammatical sentences, I have to do more than drop in periods; I have to revise its grammatical structure. Here is a version that is incorrect, because it is a series of FRAGMENTS (with the exception of the first sentence, which is correctly punctuated):

2b. I can write a different kind of sentence. That is just as long as that one. But one that I could not break up into shorter punctuated

> sentences. Merely by replacing a period with a comma, a semi-colon, or a dash. Because it is a sentence made up of several subordinate parts. All of them depending on one main clause. Sentences such as the one you are now reading.

This is correctly revised.

> 2c. I could write a different kind of sentence that is just as long as that one. But I could not just break it up into shorter punctuated sentences. I could not replace a period with a comma, a semi-colon, or a dash, because it is a long grammatical sentence made up of several subordinate parts. All of them depend on one main clause. It is not like these sentences.

Here's the point: There are different kinds of long punctuated sentences. Some are long because we put lots of short grammatical sentences between a capital letter and period; others are long because they consist of many subordinate clauses. Unless we recognize how sentences grow too long (or remain too short), we don't know how best to punctuate them.

Simple, Compound, Complex

We can create a single punctuated sentence by linking two or more independent clauses with semicolons or with COORDINATING CONJUNCTIONS such as *and, but, yet, for, so, or,* or *nor.* Traditionally, we call that kind of sentence *compound.* On the other hand, if a single grammatical sentence consists of a single independent clause, we call it *simple.* If it has an independent clause and at least one subordinate clause, we call it *complex.*

> Simple: The source of knowledge always puzzled Socrates.

> Complex: [Although there are many good dictionaries,] the greatest of them is the *Oxford English Dictionary.*

The problem with that terminology is that a grammatically simple sentence may *feel* more complex than a grammatically complex sentence (I italicize the SUBJECTs and boldface the verbs):

> Grammatically simple: *Our review of the test* **resulted** in a recommendation for its termination because of its negative enrollment affect.

> Grammatically complex: When *we* **reviewed** the test, *we* **recom-**
> **mended** that *it* **be terminated** because *it*
> **reduced** enrollment.

To most readers, the grammatically simple sentence feels stylistically
more complex than the grammatically complex sentence. So these
terms simple and complex can refer to how a sentence makes us feel
or to a point of technical grammar. We should keep them distinct.

PUNCTUATING INDEPENDENT CLAUSES

To punctuate the end of a sentence, you have to know when you have
reached the end of a *grammatical* sentence with nothing left over. At
that point, you can stop with a period, as in the sentence you just
read, this one, and the next. Never run one grammatical sentence into
the next without punctuation or a conjunction:

> In 1957 and again in 1960, Congress passed civil rights laws that
> remedied problems of registration and voting both had significant
> political consequences throughout the South.

But if that is wrong, you have several choices to make it right.

Semicolons Alone

You can use a semicolon to indicate that your first independent clause
is closely linked to a second independent clause.

> In 1957 and again in 1960, Congress passed civil rights laws that
> remedied problems of registration and voting; both had significant
> political consequences throughout the South.

There is a common occasion on which even well-educated writers
incorrectly use a comma instead of a semi-colon: it is at the end of
one grammatical sentence when the next one begins with *however:*

> Taxpayers have been generally willing to support public education
> through a variety of taxes, **however,** they are beginning to resist
> because taxes have been rising so steeply.

That requires a period or a semicolon:

> Taxpayers have been generally willing to support public education through a variety of taxes; **however**, they are beginning to resist because taxes have been rising so steeply.

Writers use a comma there incorrectly because they often see *however* inside a grammatical sentence, where it is correctly surrounded by commas:

> Taxpayers have been generally willing to support public education through a variety of taxes. They are beginning to resist, **however,** because taxes have been rising so steeply.

Whenever you put a comma before a *however,* double-check. If you have to backtrack several words before you come to a period, you probably need a semicolon or a period right before the *however.*

Semicolon + Coordinating Conjunction

Writers do not often end one grammatical sentence with a semicolon and begin the next one with a coordinating conjunction:

> In the 1950s religion came to be viewed as a bulwark against communism; **so** it was not long after that that atheism was felt to be a threat to national security.

> American intellectuals always followed the lead of European Marxists; **but** American academic culture has only recently proven to be hospitable to marxist analysis.

More commonly, they use a comma. But the semicolon is correct if the two grammatical sentences are fairly long with internal commas:

> Problem solving, one of the most active areas of research in cognitive psychology, has made great strides in the last decade, particularly in regard to the problem-solving behavior of experts and novices; **so** it is no surprise that trainers in large corporations have followed that research with great interest.

Of course, we could also replace that semicolon with a period.

Comma + Coordinating Conjunction

You can end a grammatical sentence with a comma when (1) the next clause is also a grammatical sentence and (2) that next clause begins with a coordinating conjunction: *and, but, yet, for, so, or, nor.*

> In the 1950s religion came to be viewed as a bulwark against communism, **so** it was not long after that that atheism was felt to be a threat to national security.

> American intellectuals have always followed the lead of European Marxists, **but** American academic culture has only recently proven to be hospitable to marxist analysis.

[handwritten: must use a comma b/f c.j. & independent clause]

Three Special Forms of End-Punctuation

1. Comma Alone: If two clauses are short, closely linked, and balanced, you can link two grammatical sentences with just a comma: Be sure, though, that neither has any internal commas.

   > Football appeals to our love of violence, baseball satisfies our more measured tastes. *[handwritten: comma splice]*

   > Women have always been underpaid, they are now doing something about it.

   Though some writers of the best prose use just a comma to separate (and join) two short grammatical sentences, many teachers consider it incorrect, so check with your audience before you experiment.

2. Conjunction Alone: Nor is it uncommon to join two short clauses with the conjunction alone, omitting the comma:

   > Oscar Wilde brazenly violated one of the fundamental laws of British *[handwritten: ⭐]* society, **and** we all know what happened to him.

   Again, some frown on this pattern, so be cautious about using it.

3. Period + Coordinating Conjunction: Some writers think it an error to begin a sentence with a coordinating conjunction:

   > We cannot rely on a large army to ensure political stability. **But** we cannot reduce our forces suddenly.

You can begin a punctuated sentence with a coordinating conjunction when you want to call attention to it.

Special Cases: Colon and Dash

A mark of punctuation that adds a touch of elegance is the colon: At the end of a grammatical sentence, it is shorthand for *to illustrate, for example, that is, let me expand on what I just said, therefore:*

, must be
   a complet sentence

Only one question remains: What if we lose money?

> Dance is not widely supported: no company operates at a profit, and there are few outside major cities.

> Computer scientists like to compare their hardware to the human brain: They wax eloquent on its speed and flexibility.

A colon lets you balance one clause against another a bit more elegantly than with a comma or semicolon:

> Civil disobedience is the public conscience of a democracy: mass enthusiasm is the public consensus of a tyranny.

In some contexts a dash serves as a less formal colon—it has a casual immediacy that suggests an afterthought:

> Stonehenge is a wonder of the ancient world—only a genius could have conceived of it.

Try that with a colon: you'll sense the difference.

Do not capitalize the first word after a colon if that word does not begin a grammatical sentence. But if what follows is a grammatical sentence, capitalize the first word or not, depending on how emphatic you want to make that clause. Don't capitalize after a dash.

Avoid putting a colon between a verb and its COMPLEMENT. Not this:

> Effective genetic counseling requires: **a thorough** knowledge of statistical genetics, an awareness of choices open to parents, and psychological competence to deal with emotional trauma.

Complete the clause before you begin a list:

> Effective genetic counseling requires the following preparation: a thorough knowledge of statistical genetics, an awareness of. . . .

Eight Ways of Punctuating a Sentence

In short, you can separate grammatical sentences in eight ways:

1. period alone:	I win. You lose
2. period + coordination conjunction:	I win. **And** you lose.
3. semicolon alone:	I win; you lose.
4. semi-colon + coordinating conjunction:	I win, **and** you lose.
5. comma + coordinating conjunction	I win; **and** you lose.
6. conjunction alone:	I win **and** you lose.
7. colon or dash:	I win—you lose.
8. comma alone:	I win, you lose.

In that order, these ways of separating grammatical sentences bring them closer together. Since this kind of punctuation requires that you understand not only grammar but content, be certain you understand how closely linked the ideas in the clauses really are.

PUNCTUATING BEGINNINGS

You have no problems with punctuation when you begin a sentence directly with a subject, as with this sentence. However, as with this sentence, when you find that you have begun a sentence with modifying PHRASES, and clauses, especially when they are numerous and have internal punctuation, and you have to decide how to separate out those introductory elements, the best solution is to revise:

> When you find that you have begun a sentence with several modifying phrases and clauses with internal punctuation, try revising.

You can follow a few absolute rules, but more often you have to exercise good judgment.

The Absolute Rules

1. Never put a semicolon at the end of an introductory element, no matter how long and complicated. Never this:

   When the Administration first learned that Iraq had invaded Kuwait and as a consequence threatened American interests in Saudi Arabia; it reacted quickly and decisively.

   Use a comma there.
2. Do not use a comma after a subordinating conjunction. Not this:

   Although, the practice of punctuation not complicated, it is rarely mastered.

The Generally Reliable Rules

1. Resist a comma after coordinating conjunctions *and, but, yet, for, so, or, no.* Not this:

   But, we cannot know whether life on other planets realizes that we're here and simply prefers to ignore us.

Some writers who punctuate heavily will put a comma after *and, but, yet, for, so, or, nor* if an introductory word or phrase follows:

   Yet, **during this period,** prices continued to rise.

That is a matter of taste.

2. Put a comma after introductory words or phrases that comment on the whole of the following sentence. This includes elements such as *however, nevertheless, regardless, instead, moreover,* etc.

   Fortunately, psychological studies indicate that these groups are no more neurotic or disturbed than others.

   But if you find yourself introducing sentence after sentence with words and phrases like these, consider revising. A comma after a word or two slows the pace of a sentence when it should be picking up speed. Too many such sentences not only retard the flow of the passage; they may indicate that you are trying to create logical connections that don't really exist. (See p. 131.)

We typically but not invariably omit a comma after these four introductory words: *now, therefore, thus, hence:*

> **Now** it is clear that many will not support this position. **Thus** the only alternative is to choose some other action.

3. Always separate an introductory word, phrase, or clause—no matter how short—if a reader might misunderstand:

> Before a lawyer begins her argument should be as clear as she can make it.

4. You don't need punctuation if you open a sentence with a short introductory phrase and directly follow it with a subject:

> **Once again [   ]** we find similar responses to such stimuli.

> **In 1945 [   ]** few servicemen anticipated the dramatic social changes that had transformed American society.

It is not wrong to put a comma after those short introductory phrases, but writers today use less punctuation than did earlier ones.

When you introduce a sentence with a subordinate clause, there are other considerations. How long is it and how closely does its meaning relate to the meaning of the main clause? You can omit the comma after an introductory subordinate clause when the clause is short, its subject is the same as the subject of the main clause, and its meaning closely depends on the meaning of the main clause:

> When Hitler realized that he had lost the war he resolved to destroy every city through which his army would retreat.

Keep the comma if the subjects of the clauses differ and the ideas contrast. Compare:

> Since **we** accepted the IRS' data **we** dropped further appeals.

> Although **the IRS** overruled us, **we** will follow our original procedures.

Punctuating Long Subjects

The best policy is to avoid long subjects altogether by revising them before the question of punctuating them arises at all (see p. 121). But if you cannot avoid a long subject because you feel you have to open with a list of items, you can help your readers if at the end of that subject you insert a colon or a dash and summarize the list with a short summative subject that restates the list in a word or two. Compare:

> *The President, the Vice-President, the Secretaries of the Executive Departments, Senators, members of the House of Representatives, and Supreme Court Justices,* take an oath that pledges them to uphold the Constitution.

> *The President, the Vice-President, the Secretaries of the Executive Departments, Senators, members of the House of Representatives, and Supreme Court Justices*: **all** take an oath that pledges them to uphold the Constitution.

> *Drugs, violence, poverty, disease, despair* are the familiar afflictions that destroy the fabric of a community.

> *Drugs, violence, poverty, disease, despair*—**these ills** are the familiar afflictions that destroy the fabric of a community.

Use the dash or the colon depending on how formal you want to be.

But notice that we can also switch those long subjects to the end:

> An oath to uphold the Constitution is required of *the President, the Vice-President, the Secretaries of the Executive Departments, Senators, members of the House of Representatives, and Supreme Court Justices.*

> The ills that destroy the fabric of a community are familiar—*drugs, violence, poverty, disease, despair.*

PUNCTUATING MIDDLES

This is where explanations get messy, because to punctuate inside a sentence, you have to consider not only grammar but nuances of rhythm, meaning, and emphasis. You can rely on three principles:

1. Set off with commas, dashes, or parentheses whatever promi-
   nently interrupts the flow of a sentence. Never use a semicolon.
2. Set off with commas, dashes, or parentheses whatever loosely
   comments on or explains parts of a clause or phrase. Again, never
   use a semicolon.
3. Use commas to separate items in a series. Use semicolons if the
   individual elements are long or have commas inside them.

1. Interruptions

The history of every species, **regardless of its apparent success,**
proves that only the most adaptive survive.

This single principle of TV programming, **because it overpowers all
other considerations,** determines what each of us will watch morning, noon, and night.

Better yet—avoid the interruptions. Move the interrupter:

Because it overpowers all other considerations, this single principle of TV programming determines what each of us will watch
morning, noon, and night,

Put commas around short ADVERBIAL PHRASES between a subject and a verb or inside a verb phrase, depending on your ear:

Twentieth-century *poetry*, **in recent years,** *has* become more
comprehensible to the average reader.

Twentieth-century *poetry* **in recent years** *has* become more
comprehensible to the average reader.

Twentieth-century poetry *has*, **in recent years,** *become* more
comprehensible to the average reader.

Twentieth-century poetry *has* **in recent years** *become* more
comprehensible to the average reader.

Use commas if you want to be emphatic. Keep in mind that you can
always move the interrupter to the beginning or end:

In recent years, twentieth-century poetry has become more
comprehensible to the average reader.

> Twentieth-century poetry has become more comprehensible to the average reader **in recent years.**

When you interrupt a verb and its object, you don't have to set that interrupter off with commas if it is shorter than the object:

> In moments of anxiety, we *see* **perhaps too clearly** *the stuff* our characters are made of.

But you might set off this kind of interruption if the interrupter is longer than the object and you want the greatest impact:

> The antagonism between Congress and the President has *created*, **among every group of voters,** *utter distrust.*

2. Loose Commentary

It is difficult to explain what counts as "loose commentary" because what's loose depends on both grammar and meaning. The usual distinction is between RESTRICTIVE and NONRESTRICTIVE MODI- FIERS. (Review pp. 21–22) We always set off nonrestrictive modifiers with commas:

> We had to reconstruct the larynx, **which had received a traumatic injury,** with cartilage from the shoulder.

We use no commas with nonrestrictive modifiers.

> A tax deduction for child support is awarded to the parent **with whom the child principally resides.**

A dash is more casual—and more emphatic—than a comma:

> We had to reconstruct the larynx**—which had received a traumatic injury—**with cartilage from the shoulder.

A dash is particularly useful when the "loose commentary" has internal commas. This is confusing:

> All the nations of Central Europe, **Poland, Hungary, Czechoslovakia, Romania, Bulgaria, and Yugoslavia** have been in the middle of an East-West tug-of-war.

You make the structure clear if you set off the modifier with dashes:

> All the nations of Central Europe—**Poland, Hungary, Czechoslova-kia, Romania, Bulgaria, and Yugoslavia**—have been in the middle of an East-West tug-of-war.

You can do the same thing with parentheses, but they are more appropriate when you want to suggest a *sotto voce* aside:

> The brain (if our theories are correct) is really several little brains operating simultaneously.

Or an explanatory footnote inside a sentence:

> Lamarck (1744–1829) was a French naturalist and pre-Darwinian evolutionist.

> The poetry of the *fin de siècle* (end of the century) period was characterized by a world-weariness and fashionable despair.

Sometimes loose commentary closes a sentence. When you add a phrase or clause at the end of a sentence, separate it from the rest of the sentence with a comma if that phrase or clause is not essential to the meaning and structure of the main clause. Compare:

> Hemingway wandered through Europe, **seeking a place where he could write what he felt he had to write.**

> Hemingway spent his time **seeking a place where he could write what he felt he had to write.**

> All offices will be closed from July 2 through July 6, **as announced in the daily bulletin.**

> When closing the offices, it is important to secure all desks and safes **as prescribed in Operating Manual 45-23a.**

> Those who describe what a splendid future we can look forward to have usually underestimated the effect of minor social changes, **at least in regard to this country.**

> These records must be maintained **at least until the IRS has decided whether to review them.**

Again, this is often a matter of nuance, so depend on your ear.

3. Series

First decide in principle whether in a series of three you are someone who does or doesn't put a comma before the *and:*

> His wit, his charm, **and** his loyalty made him our friend.

> His wit, his charm **and** his loyalty made him our friend.

Both are correct, but be consistent. If any of the items in the series has internal commas, then use semicolons to set off those items:

> In mystery novels, the principal action ought to be economical, organic, and logical; fascinating, yet not exotic; clear, but complicated enough to hold the reader's interest—a compromise that is not always easy to strike.

A SPECIAL PROBLEM: LONG COORDINATE ELEMENTS

Avoid a comma between pairs of coordinated words and phrases:

> As computers have become sophisticated, **and more powerful**, they have taken over **clerical, and bookkeeping** tasks.

> As computers have become **sophisticated and more powerful**, they have taken over **clerical and bookkeeping** tasks.

There are exceptions:

1. For a more intense effect, drop the *and* and insert a comma:

> Lincoln never had the advantage of a formal education and **never owned** a large library.

> Lincoln never had the advantage of **a formal education, never owned** a large library.

> The great lesson of the pioneers was to ignore conditions that seemed difficult or even overwhelming **and to get on** with the business of building a life in a hostile environment.

> The great lesson of the pioneers was to ignore conditions that seemed difficult or even overwhelming, **to get on with** the business of building a life in a hostile environment.

2. To avoid monotony, put a comma between long coordinate pairs:

> It is in the graveyard scene that Hamlet finally realizes that the inevitable end of all life is the grave **and that regardless of** one's station in life the end of all pretentiousness and all plotting and counter-plotting must be clay.

> It is in the graveyard scene that Hamlet finally realizes that the inevitable end of all life is the grave, **and that, regardless of one's station in life**, the end of all pretentiousness and all plotting and counter-plotting must be clay.

3. Put a comma after even a short coordinate element if you want a dramatic pause (something I tend to do):

> These conclusions are rather thin, **and even inaccurate.**

> The ocean is one of nature's most glorious creations, **and one of its most destructive.**

This kind of comma is especially common before a *but:*

> Organ transplants are becoming increasingly common, **but** not less expensive.

4. And finally, put a comma after the first part of a coordination if your readers need a comma to understand the grammar:

> Conrad's *Heart of Darkness* brilliantly dramatizes those primitive impulses that lie deep in each of us and stir only in our darkest dreams but asserts the unassailable need for the civilized values and institutions that control those impulses.

A comma after *dreams* would clearly mark the end of one coordinate member and the beginning of the next:

> Conrad's *Heart of Darkness* brilliantly dramatizes those primitive impulses that lie deep in each of us and stir only in our darkest dreams, **but asserts** the unassailable need for the civilized values and institutions that control those impulses.

Exercise 9-1

These passages lack their original punctuation. Extra spacings indicate grammatical sentences. Punctuate these passages three times, once using the least punctuation possible, a second time using as much varied punctuation as you can, and then a third time in the way that you think most effective.

1. Scientists and philosophers of science tend to speak as if "scientific language" were intrinsically precise as if those who use it must understand one another's meaning even if they disagree but in fact scientific language is not as different from ordinary language as is commonly believed   it too is subject to imprecision and ambiguity and hence to imperfect understanding moreover new theories or arguments are rarely if ever constructed by way of clear-cut steps of induction deduction and verification or falsification   neither are they defended rejected or accepted in so straightforward a manner   in practice scientists combine the rules of scientific methodology with a generous admixture of intuition aesthetics and philosophical commitment   the importance of what are sometimes called extrarational or extralogical components of thought in the *discovery* of a new principle or law is generally acknowledged. . . . but the role of these extralogical components in persuasion and acceptance in making an argument convincing is less frequently discussed partly because they are less visible   the ways in which the credibility or effectiveness of an argument depends on the realm of common experiences on extensive practice in communicating those experiences in a common language are hard to see precisely because such commonalities are taken for granted   only when we step out of such a "consensual domain" when we can stand out on the periphery of a community with a common language do we begin to become aware of the unarticulated premises mutual understandings and assumed practices of the group   even in those subjects that lend themselves most readily to quantification discourse depends heavily on conventions and interpretation conventions that are acquired over years of practice and participation in a community.

   from Evelyn Fox Keller, *A Feeling for the Organism: The Life and Work of Barbara McClintock.*

2. In fact of course the notion of universal knowledge has always been an illusion but it is an illusion fostered by the monistic view of the world in which a few great central truths determine in all its wonderful and amazing proliferation everything else that is true we are not today tempted to search for these keys that unlock the whole of human knowledge and of man's experience we know that we are ignorant we are well taught it and the more surely and deeply we know our own job the better able we are to appreciate the full measure of our pervasive ignorance we know that these are inherent limits compounded no doubt and exaggerated by that sloth and that complacency without which we would not be men at all but knowledge rests on knowledge what is new is meaningful because it departs slightly from what was known before this is a world of frontiers where even the liveliest of actors or observers will be absent most of the time from most of them perhaps this sense was not so sharp in the village that village which we have learned a little about but probably do not understand too well the village of slow change and isolation and fixed culture which evokes our nostalgia even if not our full comprehension perhaps in the villages men were not so lonely perhaps they found in each other a fixed community a fixed and only slowly growing store of knowledge of a single world even that we may doubt for there seem to be always in the culture of such times and places vast domains of mystery if not unknowable then imperfectly known endless and open.

—J. Robert Oppenheimer, "The Sciences and Man's Community," from *Science and The Common Understanding.*

SUMMING UP

A summary would be almost as long as this chapter, so I simply refer you to pp. 197, 198–99, 201.

Lesson Ten

Elegance

Anything is better than not to write clearly. There is nothing to be said against lucidity, and against simplicity only the possibility of dryness. This is a risk well worth taking when you reflect how much better it is to be bald than to wear a curly wig.
SOMERSET MAUGHAM

But clarity and brevity, though a good beginning, are only a beginning. By themselves, they may remain bare and bleak. When Calvin Coolidge, asked by his wife what the preacher had preached on, replied "Sin," and, asked what the preacher had said, replied "He was against it," he was brief enough. But one hardly envies Mrs. Coolidge.
F. L. LUCAS

There are two sorts of eloquence; the one indeed scarce deserves the name of it, which consists chiefly in laboured and polished periods, an over-curious and artificial arrangement of figures, tinselled over with a gaudy embellishment of words, . . . The other sort of eloquence is quite the reverse to this, and which may be said to be the true characteristic of the holy Scriptures; where the eloquence does not arise from a laboured and farfetched elocution, but from a surprising mixture of simplicity and majesty, . . .
LAURENCE STERNE

A nyone who can express complex ideas clearly should rejoice to have achieved so much. But while we might prefer bald clarity to the density of most institutional prose, the relentless simplicity of the plain style eventually becomes dry, even arid. Plainness may have the spartan virtues of unsalted meat and potatoes, but such fare is rarely memorable. A touch of class, a flash of elegance can mark the difference between unremarkable clarity and a thought so elegantly shaped that it not only fixes itself in the mind of our readers forever, but gives them a moment of pleasure when they recall it.

I can't tell you how to be graceful in the way I told you how to be clear. I *can* describe a few of the devices used by writers thought to be graceful. But that advice is about as useful as listing the ingredients in the bouillabaisse of a great cook and then expecting you to make it. Knowing the names of the ingredients and knowing how to use them is the difference between reading cookbooks and Cooking. It's a matter of practice, taste, and maybe a gift.

BALANCE AND SYMMETRY

Coordination

We've described how to extend the line of a sentence with COOR-DINATION (p. 167–172). It alone can grace a sentence with rhythm. Here is a passage by Walter Lippmann and my revision.

The national unity of a free people depends upon a sufficiently even balance of political power to make it impracticable for the administration to be arbitrary and for the opposition to be revolutionary and irreconcilable. Where that balance no longer exists, democracy perishes. For unless all the citizens of a state are forced by circumstances to compromise, unless they feel that they can affect policy but that no one can wholly dominate it, unless by habit and necessity they have to give and take, freedom cannot be maintained.

The national unity of a free people depends upon a sufficiently even balance of political power to make it impracticable for an administration to be arbitrary against a revolutionary opposition that is irreconcilably opposed to it. Where that balance no longer exists, democracy perishes. For unless all the citizens of a state are habitually forced by necessary circumstances to compromise in a way that lets them affect policy with no one dominating it, freedom cannot be maintained.

In my version, the sentences limp from one uncoordinated PHRASE and CLAUSE to the next. But Lippmann uses more than just coordination to shape his prose. Like other especially elegant writers, he balances parts of phrases against parts of other phrases, parts of clauses against other clauses, giving the whole passage an internal architecture of balance and symmetry.

If we extend the notion of TOPIC and STRESS from the whole sentence to internal clauses and phrases, then we can see how this kind of architectural elegance depends on creating balanced topics and balanced stresses even in relatively short segments. I have bold-faced what we could take as topics of phrases and I have italicized stresses. Note that each is a significant word that balances another significant word in its corresponding coordinate phrase.

The national unity of a free people depends upon a sufficiently even balance of political power to make it impracticable

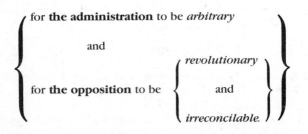

He first balances the opposing topics of *administration* and *opposition,* and closes by balancing the stressed meanings and sounds of *arbitrary, revolutionary* and *irreconcilable.* He follows this with a short concluding sentence whose stresses contrast:

Where that balance *no longer exists,* democracy *perishes.*

Then he again balances the sounds and meanings of internal topics and stress:

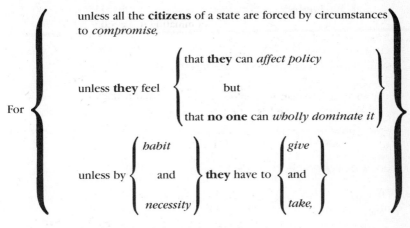

freedom cannot be *maintained.*

He repeats references to *citizens* as the SUBJECT/topic of each clause, then balances the sound and meaning of *forces* against *feel,* and the meaning of *affect policy* against the meaning of *dominate it.* In the last introductory clause, he balances *habit* against *necessity,* and the stressed *give* against *take.* Then to parallel the MAIN CLAUSE of that short preceding sentence, *democracy perishes,* he concludes this long sentence with an equally short clause whose meaning and structure of topic and stress parallel it:

democracy *perishes* ⇔ **freedom** cannot be *maintained.*

This kind of balance depends on parallel length, sound, structure, and meaning within grammatically coordinated sentences.

Uncoordinated Balance

You achieve the same effect when you balance parts of sentences, even when their grammatical structures are not coordinate. Here is a subject balanced against an OBJECT.

$$\left\{\begin{array}{lll} \textbf{Scientists} & \text{who } \textit{tear down} & \textit{established views of} \\ & & \textit{the universe} \\ & \text{invariably challenge} & \\ \textbf{those of us} & \text{who } \textit{build} & \textit{our visions of real-} \\ & & \textit{ity on those views.} \end{array}\right\}$$

In this next one, the PREDICATE of a RELATIVE CLAUSE in a subject balances the predicate of the whole sentence.

A government that is unwilling to

$$\left\{\begin{array}{lll} \textit{listen} \text{ to} & \text{the } \textit{moderate} \text{ hopes} & \text{of its } \textit{citizenry} \\ \text{must } \textit{answer} \text{ to} & \text{the } \textit{harsh} \text{ justice} & \text{of its } \textit{revolutionaries.} \end{array}\right\}$$

Here a direct object parallels the object of a PREPOSITION:

Those of us concerned with our failing school systems will not sacrifice

$$\left\{\begin{array}{ll} \text{the } \textit{intellectual growth} & \text{of our } \textit{innocent children} \\ & \text{to} \\ \text{the } \textit{social engineering} & \text{of } \textit{incompetent bureaucrats.} \end{array}\right\}$$

Here is a more complicated example:

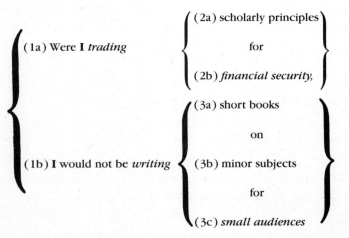

This sentence balances a SUBORDINATE CLAUSE (1a) *Were I trading,* against the main clause (1b), *I would not be writing.* Then it balances the object of that subordinate clause (2a) *scholarly principles,* against the object in the prepositional phrase (2b) *financial security.* Finally he balances the object in the main clause (3a) *short books,* against the objects of prepositions in two following prepositional phrases (3b-c) *minor subjects* and *small audiences.* None of these are coordinated, but they are all balanced.

These patterns can be used to excess, but used prudently, to emphasize an important point or to conclude the line of an argument, they can give prose a shape and a cadence that ordinary writing rarely achieves.

CLIMACTIC EMPHASIS

We create appropriate emphasis when we maneuver our most important words into the stressed position (pp. 146–154). But a sentence can still seem anticlimactic if it ends with grammatically lightweight words. We feel different weights in different parts of speech. Prepositions feel light—a reason why we sometimes avoid leaving one at the end of a sentence. Sentences should move toward strength. Compare:

> The intellectual differences among races is a subject that only the most politically naive scientist **is willing to look into.**

> The intellectual differences among races is a subject that only the most politically naive scientist **is willing to study.**

ADJECTIVES and ADVERBS are heavier than prepositions, but lighter than NOUNS. The heaviest words are NOMINALIZATIONS. They can cause readers a problem at the beginning of a sentence, but at the end of a sentence, we can use nominalizations, particularly paired nominalizations, to close with a satisfyingly climactic thump. Compare these two versions of a sentence from Winston Churchill's "Finest Hour" speech. Always an elegant and emphatic writer, Churchill ended his sentence with an elegant parallelism climaxed by a pair of heavy nominalizations:

> . . . until in God's good time, the New World, with all its power and might, steps forth to the rescue and the liberation of the old.

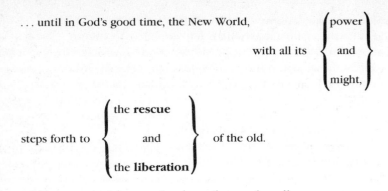

... until in God's good time, the New World, with all its { power and might, } steps forth to { the **rescue** and the **liberation** } of the old.

He could have written more simply, and more banally:

> ... until in God's good time, the powerful New World steps forth to liberate the old.

One more small point: Writers looking for a grand effect combine coordinations and nominalizations at the end of a sentence with prepositional phrases beginning with *of.* That pattern appears at the end of the Churchill quotation. The lightly stressed *of* lightens the rhythm just before the heaviness of a final noun, especially a nominalization.

EXTRAVAGANT ELEGANCE

When a writer combines nominalizations with balanced and parallel constructions, when she draws on resumptive and summative modifiers to extend the line of a sentence, we know she is aiming at something special, as in this next passage by Joyce Carol Oates:

> Far from being locked inside our own skins, inside the "dungeons" of ourselves, we are now able to recognize that our minds belong, quite naturally, to a collective "mind," a mind in which we share everything that is mental, most obviously language itself, and that the old boundary of the skin is not boundary at all but a membrane connecting the inner and outer experience of existence. Our intelligence, our wit, our cleverness, our unique personalities—all are simultaneously "our own" possessions and the world's.
> —Joyce Carol Oates, "New Heaven and New Earth."

Note the two resumptive modifiers: "inside the 'dungeons of our-selves' and "a mind in which we share ..." Note too the doubled nominalization at the end of the first long sentence, "experience of existence" and the coordinate nominalizations at the end of the sec-ond: "'our own' possessions and the world's."

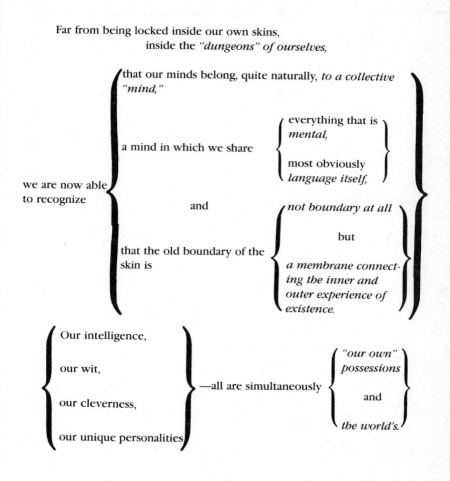

Far from being locked inside our own skins,
                inside the *"dungeons" of ourselves,*

we are now able to recognize

that our minds belong, quite naturally, *to a collective "mind,"*

a mind in which we share
  everything that is *mental,*
  most obviously *language itself,*

and

that the old boundary of the skin is
  not boundary at all
  but
  a membrane connecting the inner and outer experience of existence.

Our intelligence,
our wit,
our cleverness,
our unique personalities

—all are simultaneously
  "our own" possessions
  and
  the world's.

Exercise 10-1

You can develop a knack for this kind of elegance in two ways: Prac-tice writing balanced sentences from scratch or imitate. Imitate a few of these examples. Don't imitate word for word; just follow the general pattern:

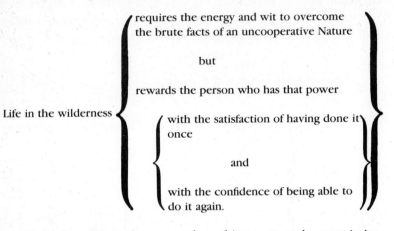

Life in the wilderness {
requires the energy and wit to overcome the brute facts of an uncooperative Nature

but

rewards the person who has that power {
with the satisfaction of having done it once

and

with the confidence of being able to do it again.
}

First, think of a subject close enough to this one to make your imitation easy—the academic life:

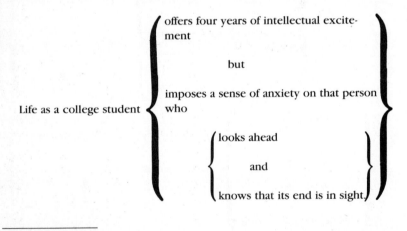

Life as a college student {
offers four years of intellectual excitement

but

imposes a sense of anxiety on that person who {
looks ahead

and

knows that its end is in sight.
}

Exercise 10-2

Here are the first halves of some balanced sentences. Finish them with balancing last halves. For example, given this:

Those who keep silent over the loss of small freedoms will . . .

you finish it with,

> Those who keep silent over the loss of small freedoms are eventually silenced when they protest the loss of large ones.

1. Those who keep silent over the loss of small freedoms will . . .
2. While the strong are often afraid to admit weakness, the weak . . .
3. We should pay more attention to those politicians who tell us how to make what we have better than to those . . .
4. When parent raise children who do not value the importance of hard work, the adults whose children become . . .
5. Too often, teachers mistake neat papers that rehash old ideas for . . .

Exercise 10-3

In addition to other faults, these sentences end on weak adjectives and adverbs or clumsy possessives. Besides editing them for clarity and concision, revise them so that they end on more heavily stressed words, particularly on prepositional phrases beginning with *of.* For example:

> Our interest in paranormal phenomena testifies to the fact that we have empty spirits and shallow minds.

> Our interest in paranormal phenomena testifies to the **emptiness** *of* our spirits and the **shallowness** *of* our minds.

1. If we invest our sweat in these projects, we must avoid appearing to be working only because we are interested in ourselves.
2. The blueprint for the political campaign plan was concocted by those who were least sensitive to what we needed most critically.
3. Throughout history, science has made progress because dedicated scientists have gotten around a hostile public that is uninformed.
4. Not one tendency in our governmental system has brought about more changes in American daily life than federal governmental agencies that are very powerful.
5. In the year 1923 several representatives from the side of the victorious Allied nations went to Versailles with the intention of seeking to dismember Germany's economic potential and to destroy her armaments industry.
6. The day is gone when school systems' boards of education have the expectation that local taxpayers will automatically go along

with whatever extravagant things that incompetent bureaucrats decide to do.

7. Irreplaceable works of native art are progressing into slow deterioration in many of our most prestigious museums for the reason that their curators have no recognition of how extremely fragile even recent artifacts can be.

LENGTH AND RHYTHM

In ordinary prose, the length of a sentence is an issue only when they are all ten or fifteen words long or much longer. One twenty-word sentence after another is no ideal, but they will seem less monotonous than sentences regularly longer or shorter. In artful prose, though, length is controlled and varied. Some stylists write short sentences to strike a note of urgency:

> Toward noon Petrograd again became the field of military action; rifles and machine guns rang out everywhere. It was not easy to tell who was shooting or where. One thing was clear; the past and the future were exchanging shots. There was much casual firing; young boys were shooting off revolvers unexpectedly acquired. The arsenal was wrecked . . . Shots rang out on both sides. But the board fence stood in the way, dividing the soldiers from the revolution. The attackers decided to break down the fence. They broke down part of it and set fire to the rest. About twenty barracks came into view. The bicyclists were concentrated in two or three of them. The empty barracks were set fire to at once.
> —Leon Trotsky, *The Russian Revolution,* trans. Max Eastman

Or terse certainty:

> The teacher or lecturer is a danger. He very seldom recognizes his nature or his position. The lecturer is a man who must talk for an hour. France may possibly have acquired the intellectual leadership of Europe when their academic period was cut down to forty minutes. I also have lectured. The lecturer's first problem is to have enough words to fill forty or sixty minutes. The professor is paid for his time, his results are almost impossible to estimate. . . . No teacher has ever failed from ignorance. That is empiric professional knowledge. Teachers fail because they

cannot "handle the class." Real education must ultimately be limited to men who INSIST on knowing, the rest is mere sheep-herding.

—Ezra Pound, *ABC of Reading*

Or fire:

> Let us look at this American artist first. How did he ever get to America, to start with? Why isn't he a European still, like his father before him?
>
> Now listen to me, don't listen to him. He'll tell you the lie you expect. Which is partly your fault for expecting it.
>
> He didn't come in search of freedom of worship. England had more freedom of worship in the year 1700 than America had. Won by Englishmen who wanted freedom and so stopped at home and fought for it. And got it. Freedom of worship? Read the history of New England during the first century of its existence.
>
> Freedom anyhow? The land of the free! This the land of the free! Why, if I say anything that displeases them, the free mob will lynch me, and that's my freedom. Free? Why I have never been in any country where the individual has such an abject fear of his fellow countrymen. Because, as I say, they are free to lynch him the moment he shows he is not one of them. . . .
>
> All right then, what did they come for? For lots of reasons. Perhaps least of all in search of freedom of any sort: positive freedom, that is.
>
> —D. H. Lawrence, *Studies in Classic American Literature*

In this last example, Lawrence invests his discourse with even more urgency by breaking sentences into FRAGMENTS and what could be longer paragraphs into abrupt snatches of discourse.

Self-conscious stylists can also write one long sentence after another. Here is a sentence describing a protest march.

> In any event, up at the front of this March, in the first line, back of that hollow square of monitors, Mailer and Lowell walked in this barrage of cameras, helicopters, TV cars, monitors, loudspeakers, and wavering buckling twisting line of notables, arms linked (line twisting so much that at times the movement was in file, one arm locked ahead, one behind, then

the line would undulate about and the other arm would be ahead) speeding up a few steps, slowing down while a great happiness came back into the day as if finally one stood under some mythical arch in the great vault of history, helicopters buzzing about, chop-chop, and the sense of America divided on this day now liberated some undiscovered patriotism in Mailer so that he felt a sharp searing love for his country in this moment and on this day, crossing some divide in his own mind wider than the Potomac, a love so lacerated he felt as if a marriage were being torn and children lost—never does one love so much as then, obviously, then—and an odor of wood smoke, from where you knew not, was also in the air, a smoke of dignity and some calm heroism, not unlike the sense of freedom which also comes when a marriage is burst—Mailer knew for the first time why men in the front line of battle are almost always ready to die; there is a promise of some swift transit....

—Norman Mailer, *Armies of the Night*

This long PUNCTUATED SENTENCE consists of several GRAMMATICAL SENTENCES. But it does not sprawl. Mailer opens with a series of staccato phrases to suggest the confusion of the scene, but he controls those phrases by coordinating them. He continues the line of the sentence by coordinating free modifiers (*arms linked, line twisting,... speeding up* ...). After several more free modifiers, he continues with a resumptive modifier (*a love so lacerated* ...), and after another grammatical sentence, another resumptive modifier (*a smoke of dignity and some calm heroism*). A sentence like this makes us feel we are overhearing someone thinking aloud, letting the shape of his sentence lead him from one discovery to the next.

Exercise 10-4

Combine some of the short sentences in these examples into longer sentences like Mailer's. How do they sound? Break up Mailer's long sentence into smaller ones in the style of Lawrence and Pound. How do they differ? Imitate the style of Lawrence, Pound, and Mailer. Then transform your Lawrence imitation into a Mailer imitation, and your Mailer imitation into a Lawrence imitation. It is only by seeing how the same content can be expressed in different styles that you can see how style can seem to change content.

METAPHOR

Clarity, vigor, symmetry, rhythm—prose so graced is a great achievement. And yet, while those virtues might excite admiration for our craft, they do not testify to the reach of our imagination. This next passage displays all these stylistic devices and graces, but it goes beyond craft. If reveals a truth about pleasure through a figure of speech embedded in a comparison that is itself metaphorical.

> The secret of the enjoyment of pleasure is to know when to stop. . . . We do this every time we listen to music. We do not seize hold of a particular chord or phrase and shout at the orchestra to go on playing it for the rest of the evening; on the contrary, however much we may like that particular moment of music, we know that its perpetuation would interrupt and kill the movement of the melody. We understand that the beauty of a symphony is less in these musical moments than in the whole movement from beginning to end. If the symphony tries to go on too long, if at a certain point the composer exhausts his creative ability and tries to carry on just for the sake of filling in the required space of time, then we begin to fidget in our chairs, feeling that he has denied the natural rhythm, has broken the smooth curve from birth to death, and that though a pretense of life is being made, it is in fact a living death.
>
> —Alan W. Watts, *The Meaning of Happiness*

Watts could have written this:

> . . . however much we may like that moment, we know that its perpetuation would interrupt and spoil the movement of the melody . . . we begin to fidget in our chairs, feeling that he has denied the natural rhythm, has interrupted the regular movement from beginning to end, and that though a pretense of wholeness is being made, it is in fact a repeated end.

The two passages are equally clear and graceful. But the first illuminates music—and pleasure—in a way that the second does not. That metaphor of birth and of the smooth, unbroken curve of life into death startles us with a flash of unexpected truth. The figure invites us to look at both things—death and music—in a new way.

Similes do the same, but less intensely, their *like* or *as* moderating the force of the comparison. Compare these:

> The schoolmaster is the person who takes the children off the parents' hands for a consideration. That is to say, he establishes a child prison, engages a number of employee schoolmasters as turnkeys, and covers up the essential cruelty and unnaturalness of the situation by torturing the children if they do not learn, and calling this process, which is within the capacity of any fool or blackguard, by the sacred name of Teaching.
>
> —G. B. Shaw, *Sham Education*

> . . . he establishes something like a child prison, engages a number of schoolmasters to act like turnkeys, covers up the essential cruelty and unnaturalness of the situation by doing things to children that are like torture if they do not learn . . . calling this process, which is within the capacity of any fool or blackguard, by the sacred name of Teaching.

These two passages say essentially the same thing about education, but the first with more intensity.

Metaphor is appropriate not only for reflective or polemical writing. It can vivify all kinds of prose. Historians rely on it:

> This is what may be called the common-sense view of history. History consists of a corpus of ascertained facts. The facts are available to the historian in documents, inscriptions, and so on, like fish on the fishmonger's slab. The historian collects them, takes them home, and cooks and serves then in whatever style appeals to him. Acton, whose culinary tastes were austere, wanted them served plain. . . . Sir George Clark, critical as he was of Acton's attitude, himself contrasts the "hard core of facts" in history with the "surrounding pulp of disputable interpretation"—forgetting perhaps that the pulpy part of the fruit is more rewarding than the hard core.
>
> —E. H. Carr, *What Is History?*

So do biologists:

> Some of you may have been thinking that, instead of delivering a scientific address, I have been indulging in a flight of fancy. It is a flight, but not of mere fancy, nor is it just an individual indulgence. It is my small personal attempt to share in the flight

of the mind into new realms of our cosmic environment. We
have evolved wings for such flights, in shape of the disciplined
scientific imagination. Support for those wings is provided by
the atmosphere of knowledge created by human science and
learning: so far as this supporting atmosphere extends, so far
can our wings take us in our exploration.

—Julian Huxley, "New Bottles for Old Wine," *Journal of the
Royal Anthropological Institute*

And philosophers:

Quine has long professed his skepticism about the possibility of
making any sense of the refractory idioms of intentionality, so
he needs opacity only to provide a quarantine barrier protecting
the healthy, extensional part of a sentence from the infected
part.

—Daniel C. Dennett, "Beyond Belief"

And so do physicists when they are writing about new ideas for which
there is yet no standard language:

Whereas the lepton pair has a positive rest mass when it is
regarded as a single particle moving with a velocity equal to the
vector sum of the motions of its two components, a photon
always has zero rest mass. This difference can be glossed over,
however, by treating the lepton pair as the offspring of the
decay of a shortlived photonlike parent called a virtual photon.

—Leon M. Lederman, "The Upsilon Particle," *Scientific American*

These metaphors serve different ends. Shaw used the prison metaphor to emphasize a point that he could have made without it. But
turnkeys and torture invest his argument with an emotional intensity
that literal language can not capture. Carr used fish and fruit both to
emphasize and to illuminate. He could have expressed his ideas more
prosaically, but the literal statement would have been longer and
weaker. Dennett and Lederman did not require any heightened
emphasis; they used their comparisons to explain.

But if a striking metaphor evidences imagination, it can also
betray those of us whose imagination falls short of its demands. Of
metaphor, Aristotle wrote,

By far the greatest thing is to be a master of metaphor. It is the
one thing that cannot be learned from others. It is a sign of

genius, for a good metaphor implies an intuitive perception of similarity among dissimilars.

Those of us short on genius can still use metaphor, but we have to be careful that we do not hide behind it the idea we want to express:

> Societies give birth to new values through the osmotic flow of daily social interaction. Conflicts evolve when old values collide with new, a process that frequently spawns yet a new set of values that synthesize the conflict into a reconciliation of opposites.

We get the picture, but darkly. The birth metaphor suggests a traumatic event, but the new values, it is claimed, result from osmotic flow, a process of invisibly small events. Conflicts do not "evolve"; they more often occur in an instant, as suggested by the metaphor of collision. The spawning image picks up the metaphor of birth again, but by this time the image is, at best, collectively ludicrous.

Had the writer thought through his ideas carefully, he might have expressed them more clearly in literal language:

> As we interact in small ways, we gradually synthesize new social values. When one person behaves according to an old value and another according to a new, the values may conflict, creating a third value that reconciles the other two.

More embarrassing are those passages that confuse elegance with rhetorical excess—Huxley's passage about the wings of inquiry flapping in an atmosphere of knowledge comes close. Metaphors also invite trouble if we aren't sensitive to the way their literal meanings can unexpectedly come back to life. This is from a student paper:

> The classic blitzkrieg relies on a tank-heavy offensive force, supported by ground-support aircraft, to destroy the defender's ability to fight by running amuck [*sic*] in his undefended rear, after penetrating his forward defenses.

The problem with trying to be elegant is that our failures can be so spectacular. And when we fail spectacularly, we are reluctant to try again. I can only encourage you to accept with good humor those awkward attempts at elegance that all of us have experienced.

A LAST WORD

The satisfactions of style include the pleasure we take in the compliments of our readers. But I also know that for many writers the pleasure of crafting a good paragraph, even a single sentence, lies mainly in its simple achievement. What it finally comes down to, I think, is the responsibility we feel for our language and the private satisfaction we take in meeting that responsibility. It is a satisfaction expressed well, I think, by the philosopher Alfred North Whitehead:

> Finally, there should grow the most austere of all mental qualities; I mean the sense for style. It is an aesthetic sense, based on admiration for the direct attainment of a foreseen end, simply and without waste. Style in art, style in literature, style in science, style in logic, style in practical execution have fundamentally the same aesthetic qualities, namely, attainment and restraint. The love of a subject in itself and for itself, where it is not the sleepy pleasure of pacing a mental quarter-deck, is the love of style as manifested in that study. Here we are brought back to the position from which we started, the utility of education. Style, in its finest sense, is the last acquirement of the educated mind; it is also the most useful. It pervades the whole being. The administrator with a sense for style hates waste; the engineer with a sense for style economizes his material; the artisan with a sense for style prefers good work. Style is the ultimate morality of mind.
>
> *The Aims of Education and Other Essays*

Some Terms Defined

Grammar is the ground of all.
WILLIAM LANGLAND

*There is a satisfactory boniness about grammar which the flesh of
sheer vocabulary requires before it can become vertebrate and walk
the earth. But to study it for its own sake, without relating it to
function, is utter madness.*
ANTHONY BURGESS

*Thou hast most traitorously corrupted the youth of the realm in
erecting a grammar school . . . It will be proved to thy face, that thou
hast men about thee that usually talk of a noun and a verb, and such
abominable words as no Christian ear can endure to hear.*
WILLIAM SHAKESPEARE, *2 Henry VI, 4.7*

What follows is no tight theory of grammar, just a set of useful definitions for the terms in the text. Each has exceptions, but each is serviceable. Important terms are starred. Where something is discussed at length elsewhere, you are referred to the Index.

*Action: Actions include movement, feeling, cognition, creation, etc. Prototypically, an action is expressed by a verb: *move, hate, think, discover.* But actions also appear in NOMINALIZATIONS: *movement, hatred, thought, discovery.* Associated with actions are conditions, typically expressed by adjectives: *able, intelligent, plausible,* etc. But these conditions may also be expressed by nominalizations: *ability, intelligence, plausibility.* (See Index.)

*Active: Distinguish between what feels active and what, by grammatical definition, is a VERB in the active voice. (See Index.)

> Revelation of the project required its termination.

> When the project was revealed, it was terminated.

The first sentence feels more PASSIVE than the second, but it has no passive verbs; the second feels more active than the first, but it has two passive verbs: *was revealed, was terminated.*

A grammatically active verb has as its SUBJECT the doer of its action and occurs in its PAST PARTICIPLE form only after *have:*

> **I have** *broken* the code.

A passive verb has a subject that is the goal of the action of the verb. The main verb appears after a form of *be* and is always in its past participle form.

*Adjective: A word is an adjective if you can put *very* in front of it: *very old, very intelligent, very interesting.* There are exceptions: *major, additional, resumptive,* etc. Since this is also a test for ADVERBS, you can identify adjectives by trying them out between *the* and a noun: *The* **occupational** *hazard, the* **major** *reason, the* **addi-**

tional *problem,* etc. Unfortunately, some nouns occur in the same position—*the* **chemical** *hazard.* (See Index.)

Adjective Phrase: An ADJECTIVE and whatever attaches to it: *so* **large** *that no one could carry it.*

Adverb: Adverbs modify all parts of speech except NOUNS:

> Adjectives: **extremely** *large,* **rather** *old,* **very** *tired.*
>
> Verbs: **frequently** *spoke,* **often** *slept, left* **here.**
>
> Adverbs: **very** *carefully,* **somewhat** *often,* **a bit** *late.*
>
> Articles: **precisely** *the man I meant,* **just** *the thing we need.*
>
> Sentences: **Fortunately,** we were on time.

Adverb Phrase: The adverb and whatever attaches to it: *too* **carefully** *to be accidental.*

*Agent: Agents are a kind of CHARACTER. Prototypically, agents are flesh-and-blood characters, but for our purposes, an agent is the *seeming* source of any ACTION, the responsible entity without which the action could not occur. (See Index.)

> **She** criticized the book in these four essays.
>
> **We** explained the discrepancy by statistical analysis.
>
> **They** supported their claims with accurate data.

Often, the means by which we do something can seem to be an agent:

> **Her four essays** criticize the book.
>
> **Statistical analysis** explained the discrepancy.
>
> **Accurate data** supported our claims.

Do not confuse agents with SUBJECTS. They prototypically are, but an agent can be in a grammatical OBJECT:

> I underwent an interrogation *by* **the police.**

*Character: Prototypically, characters are flesh-and-blood people who act or are acted on. If they act, they are AGENTS; if acted on, they are GOALS. We also count as characters inanimate entities if they are the central elements in a story. Thus we can define as characters anything we talk "about" at length by making it the SUBJECT/TOPIC of several sentences. We even count as characters abstract NOUNS if we are writing about abstract concepts. Thus "cognitive complexity" is a character if we repeatedly refer to it. Other characters might be "statistical significance," "authoritarianism," "impressionism," "upward mobility."

*Clause: A clause has two defining characteristics:

(1) A clause is a sequence of a SUBJECT plus the VERB that goes with it plus anything else that attaches to the subject and verb.

(2) A clause has a verb that agrees with the number of its subject and can be put into a past or present form.

By this definition, these next are all clauses:

I leave/left.	why he leaves/left.	we are/were leaving.
if she left/leaves.	that they leave/left.	whom you see/saw.

By this definition, these phrases are not clauses, because the verbal form cannot be turned into a past tense verb:

for her to **go**   for him to **have gone**   their **having gone**

1. Main/Independent vs. Subordinate/Dependent Clauses
There are two kinds of clauses: *main* (or *independent*) and *subordinate* (or *dependent*). A main or independent clause can be punctuated as an independent sentence:

I left.   Why did you leave?   We are leaving.

A subordinate or dependent clause cannot be punctuated as an independent sentence. It must be attached to a main or independent clause. These would be incorrectly punctuated:

Because she left.   That they left.   Whom you spoke to.

Subordinate clauses usually begin with a SUBORDINATING CONJUNC-
TION such as *if, when, unless,* or *which, that, who:*

> I left **because** she left. I know **that** they left. I did not recognize
> **whom** you spoke to.

2. Adverbial and Adjectival Clauses

There are three kinds of subordinate clauses: nominal, ADVER-
BIAL, and ADJECTIVAL.

A nominal clause functions like a NOUN:

> I know **that you are here.**

Adverbial clauses modify a verb or adjective, indicating time,
cause, condition, etc. They usually begin with subordinating conjunctions such as *because, when, if, since, as, after, while, unless:*

> **Unless** *you leave,* I will take action.

> **Because** *you have not left,* I've called the police.

> **When** *you leave,* close the door.

Adjectival clauses modify nouns. Also called RELATIVE clauses,
they usually begin with a relative pronoun: *which, that, whom, whose,
who:*

> The book **that** *I bought for you* was expensive.

> My car, **which** *you just saw,* is gone.

> A woman **whose** *aunt lives down the street* just called.

3. Restrictive and Non-Restrictive Clauses

We can identify two kinds of relative clauses: *restrictive* (also
called "defining,") and *nonrestrictive.*

A nonrestrictive clause is a clause that the reader does not need
in order to identify the noun phrase it modifies.

> My birthday, **which I keep a secret,** was last month.

Since we have only one birthday, I don't have to identify which birthday I keep secret. Since I need not identify it further, any clause I

attach to it must be nonrestrictive. If it is nonrestrictive, it must begin with *which* (not *that*) and be set off with commas.

A restrictive clause uniquely identifies a particular thing. Most of us own more than one book, so if I refer to a book that I had not yet mentioned, I'd have to "restrict" my reference to a particular book.

Let me tell you about a book **that I just bought.**

In this case, we introduce the clause with *that* (or *which,* but check p. 21 for this sometimes debatable question), and we do not set it off with commas. The following would be odd:

Let me tell you about a book, **which I just bought.**

Once I have identified some particular book, I no longer have to restrict my reference to that book again because it is a concept we now share, and so I use a non-restrictive modifier:

Let me tell you about a book **that I just bought.** This book, **which I paid a dollar for,** is a first edition.

Complement: A complement completes a verb:

Subject	Verb	Complement
I	am	**in the house.**
We	seem	**tired.**
She	discovered	**the money.**
He	began	**to do the job.**

*Compound Noun: You can't tell from spelling when consecutive nouns constitute a compound noun. Some are separate words: *space capsule, retirement home, police station;* some are hyphenated: *mother-in-law, eighty-two;* some are written as one word: *beehive, airport, bookkeeper.* A reliable test is pronunciation: If the first word is stressed more than the second, the word is a compound word: *dóg-hòuse, spáce càpsule, bóok dèaler.* On the other hand, some phrases that seem to be compounds are stressed on the second word: *gàrden páth, stòne wáll, fàther conféssor.* (See Index.)

Conjunction: Usually defined as a word that links other words, PHRASES, or CLAUSES. But VERBS and PREPOSITIONS do the same. (See Index.) It's easier to illustrate conjunctions than define them:

> ADVERBIAL conjunctions: *because, although, when, since,* etc.
>
> RELATIVE conjunction or RELATIVE pronoun: *who, whom, whose, which, that.*
>
> Sentence conjunction: *thus, however, therefore, consequently, nevertheless, on the other hand,* etc.
>
> COORDINATING conjunction: *and, but, yet, for, so, or, nor.*
>
> CORRELATIVE coordinating conjunctions: *both X and Y, not only X but also Y, either X or Y, neither X nor Y, X as well as Y.*

*Coordination: We coordinate grammatically equal elements:

> Same part of speech: *you* **and** *I, red* **and** *black, run* **or** *jump.*
>
> PHRASES: *In the house* **but** *not in the basement.*
>
> CLAUSES: *when I leave* **or** *when you arrive.*

Correlative Conjunction: See CONJUNCTION. Ordinarily, both members of a pair of correlative conjunctions should precede words, PHRASES, or CLAUSES with the same grammatical form:

> Not: He **both** *had the data* **and** *the equipment* to display it.
>
> But: He had **both** *the data* **and** *the equipment* to display it.
>
> Not: We will **either** *arrive on Monday* **or** *on Wednesday.*
>
> But: We will arrive **either** *on Monday* **or** *on Wednesday.*
>
> Or: We will arrive on **either** *Monday* **or** *Wednesday.*

Dangling Modifier: See Index.

Dependent Clause: See CLAUSE.

Direct Object: See OBJECT.

Finite Verb: See CLAUSE and VERB.

Fragment: A string of words that begins with a capital letter and ends with a period, question mark, or exclamation mark, but is either a DEPENDENT CLAUSE or simply a PHRASE, a unit that does not consist of a SUBJECT and a FINITE VERB. These are fragments:

Because I left.	Why you are here.
Although we are here.	For me to leave.
Realizing the error.	A person whom I knew.

These are not fragments:

I left when she arrived.	She left because I arrived.
I know why you are here.	For me to leave is wrong.
Realizing the error, I stopped.	I met a person whom I knew.

*Free Modifier: See Index.

Ready for anything, she walked down the street.

Fused Sentence: See Run-on Sentence.

Gerund: A NOMINALIZATION created by adding *-ing* to a VERB:

He **damaged** me when he **charged** deception.

His **damaging** me was a result of his **charging** deception.

Goal: That toward which the ACTION of a VERB is directed. In most cases, goals are expressed as DIRECT OBJECTS. But in some cases, the literal goal can be the SUBJECT of an ACTIVE VERB:

I see **you.**	**I** underwent an interrogation.
I broke **the dish.**	**She** received a warm welcome.
I built **a house.**	**They** got a long lecture on honesty.

*Grammatical Sentence: (Review CLAUSE) An independent CLAUSE along with all subordinate clauses attached to it.

*Independent Clause: See CLAUSE.

Infinitive: See VERB.

Intransitive Verb: An intransitive verb does not take an object and so cannot be made passive. These are not transitive verbs:

> He **exists.**   They **left** town.   She **became** a doctor.

Linking Verb: A linking verb has a complement that modifies or refers to the same thing as its subject.

> He **is** my brother.   She **seems** reliable.
>
> They **became** teachers.   It **appears** broken.

*Main Clause: See CLAUSE.

*Metadiscourse: Metadiscourse is writing about writing and reading. This includes connecting devices such as *therefore, however, for example, in the first place*; and expressions of the author's attitude and intention: *I believe, in my opinion*; comment about what the writer is about to assert: *most people believe, it is widely assumed, allegedly*; remarks addressed directly to the audience: *as you can see, consider now the problem of.* (See Index.)

*Nominalize: See NOMINALIZATION.

*Nominalization: A nominalization is NOUN derived from a VERB or ADJECTIVE: *move - movement, act - action, resist - resistance, good - goodness, intelligent - intelligence, elastic - elasticity.* (See Index.)

Nonrestrictive Clause: See CLAUSE.

Noun: A word that will fit into the following: *The [ ] is good.* Some nouns are concrete: *dog, rock, car.* Other nouns are abstract: *ambition, space, speed.* The nouns that we are most concerned with are those nouns derived from VERBS or ADJECTIVES that we call NOMINALIZATIONS: *resemble > resemblance, accurate > accuracy.*

Object: There are three kinds of objects:

(1) direct object, the NOUN that follows a TRANSITIVE VERB:

I *read* **the book.** We *followed* **the car;**

(2) PREPOSITIONAL object, the noun that follows a preposition:

in **the house,** *by* **the walk,** *across* **the street,** *with* **fervor;**

(3) indirect object, the noun or pronoun directly after a verb, preceding a direct object:

I *gave* **him** a dollar.

Parallelism: Elements in a sentence are parallel when each element is of the same grammatical kind:

The national unity of a free people depends upon a sufficiently even balance of political power to make it impracticable

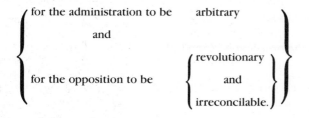

*Passive: See Index.

Past Participle: Most VERBS signal past participle forms with the same form that signals past tense: *-ed: jumped, worked, investigated.* Irregular verbs have irregular past participle forms: *seen, broken, swum, stolen, been,* etc.

I *have* **gone.** Her friends *have* **arrived.** We *had* **been** there.

Past participle forms of transitive verbs also function as modifiers:

a **broken** arm, a **twisted** leg, a **scratched** face.

*Phrase: A group of words that constitute a unit but do not contain a SUBJECT and a FINITE VERB. (See CLAUSE.) There are four kinds of phrases, each defined by the part of speech at its head:

NOUN phrases:	*the little* **book** *on the table;*
VERB phrases:	*may have been* **found;**
ADJECTIVE phrases:	*a little bit too* **small** *to be useful;*
ADVERB phrases:	*very* **carefully.**

Possessive Pronoun: *my, your, his, her, its, their, your,* any noun ending with *-'s* or *-s':* the **dog's** tail.

Predicate: Whatever follows the whole SUBJECT, beginning with the FINITE VERB PHRASE and whatever depends on that verb.

He [**went downtown yesterday**]_{predicate}.

Whatever introduces a sentence that could appear with the predicate is also part of the predicate:

[**Yesterday**] he [**went downtown**]_{predicate}.

Preposition: Prepositions are easier to list than to define: *in, on, up, over, out, under, between, at, with, by,* etc.

Prepositional Phrase: The preposition plus its NOUN OBJECT: *in the house, by the door, without enthusiasm.*

Present Participle: The *-ing* form of the VERB. It can be used as the PROGRESSIVE form of the verb following a form of *be:*

He *was* **running.** I *am* **listening.** You *are* **going.**

As a modifier:

Running streams are beautiful.

As the GERUND form, the form that functions as a NOMINALIZATION (though historically, the participle *-ing* and the gerund *-ing* descend into Modern English from different ancestors):

> **Running** can kill you. **Listening** is important.

Progressive: See VERB.

***Punctuated Sentence:** Whatever begins with a capital letter and ends with a period, question mark, or exclamation point. (See Index.)

Relative Clause: See CLAUSE.

Relative Pronoun: See CLAUSE.

Restrictive Clause: See CLAUSE.

***Resumptive Modifier:** See Index.

Run-on Sentence: A run-on sentence is a PUNCTUATED SENTENCE consisting of two or more GRAMMATICAL SENTENCES not separated by a coordinating conjunction or mark of punctuation this entry illustrates such a run-on sentence there should have been a period between *punctuation* and *this* and between *sentence* and *there.*

***Stress:** (See Index.)

***Subject:** The subject is what the VERB agrees with in number:

> **Two men** *are* at the door.
>
> **One man** *is* at the door.

We can see in these sentences that *there* is the subject of neither.

> **There** *was a* man at the door.
>
> **There** *were two men* at the door.

There is merely a function word that fills the slot that we expect before a verb. The real subjects follow the verb.

Distinguish the "whole" subject from its "simple" subject. You can identify a whole subject once you have identified the verb: Put a *who* or a *what* in front of the verb and turn the sentence into a question. The fullest answer to the question is the whole subject:

> The failure of the city to manage its health care system competently is an accepted fact.
>
> Question: **What** is an accepted fact?
>
> Answer (and subject): The failure of the city to manage its health care system competently.

This doesn't work with sentences beginning with *there.*

The simple subject is the smallest unit within the whole subject that will answer the question. It is also the unit that determines whether the verb should be singular or plural. In the sentence above, the simple subject is *failure* (or *The failure*).

Subjunctive: A form of the verb that we use when we talk about events that are contrary to fact. "If he **were** President...."

*Subordinate Clause: See CLAUSE.

Subordinating Conjunction: *Because, if, when, since, unless,* etc.

*Summative Modifier: See Index.

Summative Subject: See Index.

*Topic: A complicated concept. The topic of a sentence is the unit of information that the rest of the sentence comments on. It is the psychological subject of a sentence. The topic of a sentence is usually also its grammatical SUBJECT (See Index.):

> **China** will eventually become a major industrial nation.

We cannot define topic any more exactly because it may be in an introductory PREPOSITIONAL PHRASE.

> *In regard to* **China,** it will eventually become....

Topics can appear in other constructions, expecially after METADIS-COURSE.

> *I believe that* **China** will eventually become. . . .

> *There is general agreement as to* **China's** eventually becoming a major industrial nation.

*Topic String: A topic string is the sequence of TOPICS through a single passage. (See Index.)

Transitive Verb: A VERB with a direct object. The direct object is prototypically the "receiver" of an action. The prototypical direct object can be made the subject of a passive verb:

> We   **read**   the book.

> The book   **was read**   by us.

By this definition, the verbs *resemble, become, stand* (as in *He stands ten feet tall*) are not transitive verbs.

*Verb: Verbs have four forms:

Infinitive: The base form of the verb: *go, be, have.* The infinitive form follows *to:* He wants *to leave.*

Finite: The verb inflected for present or past: *went, was, were, has, does, sees.* With the exception of *be,* the infinitive form is the same as the finite form when the finite form refers to the present and does not have a third-person-*s:*

> I *see* the book.

> I want to *see* the book.

You can identify the main verb in a CLAUSE because it is also the finite form of the verb. To find out which word that is, change the time that the clause refers to. If the clause refers to the past, change it to refer to the present; if to the present, change it to the past, etc. The word you change is the finite verb:

> He **decided** to leave.   He **decides** to leave.

> He **left.**   He **leaves.**

Perfect (or past participle): Most English verbs use the *-ed* form for the perfect:

He has walk**ed.** I have danc**ed.** You have stumbl**ed.**

But many verbs have irregular forms:

She has s**u**ng. they were beat**en.** we have go**ne.**

Progressive (or present participle): The progressive form always ends in *-ing*: It may appear as part of the verb phrase after a form of the verb *be*:

They *were* danc**ing,** walk**ing,** and sing**ing.**

The present participle may also be an ADJECTIVE-like modifier:

The danc**ing** couples, the sing**ing** birds, the children walk**ing.**

Answers to Exercises

Few of the exercises in this book have a single correct answer. A good many of your answers will be different from but as good as those here; indeed, I would be surprised if many were not better. Trust your ear. If you decide your version is better than the answer here, try to state why: Don't depend on generalities like clarity and precision. Try to say *why* it's clearer and more precise: Is it shorter? Is it more specific? If your answers are less compact and direct than those suggested here, try to decide whether the difference between your version and mine is a significant difference. There comes a point in every sentence where another five minutes spent looking for the most concise and specific version possible is simply not worth the result. It's the first thirty seconds that count.

Exercise 3-8

(p. 44) When you nominalize many verbs, you frustrate what your readers expect—that characters will appear as subjects and their crucial actions as verbs, but when you drop characters out of sentences altogether, you frustrate them even more. You no doubt felt that when you read this version of Little Red Riding Hood . . . I was able to drop Little Red Riding Hood and the Wolf from the story when I nominalized the verb *walk* into . . .

Exercise 3-9

Nominalizations are italicized; verbs and adjectives boldfaced.

2a. *Smoking, pregnancy,* **may lead,** *injury;* 2b. **nominalize, read.**
4a. *Arguments, result, cynicism,* **provide,** *suggestions, dispelling;* 4b. **have claimed, watch, tend, become, able, has demonstrated, be.**
6a. **need, know, are being logged, can save;** 6b. **is,** *need, analysis, intensity, use,* **provide,** *projection, requirements.*
8a. **examine, influence,** *advertising, advertising,* **respond,** *influences,* **create, appeals;** 8b. **is,** *analysis, response, judgments, well-formedness, possession, knowledge, reading.*

Exercise 3-10

Do not worry if your revisions are slightly different from these.

1. There have been arguments by some as to the elevation of global temperatures as a result of carbon dioxide in the atmosphere.
3. Attempts by AIDS researchers at identifying the HIV virus have resulted in the failure of the development of a vaccine that will result in the immunization of those at risk.
5. A discovery by educators of uses of computer-assisted instruction could result in the teaching of subjects of greater complexity and faster learning by students.
7. Many professional athletes have arrived at the discovery that they lack a preparation for life after stardom because of their protection by their teams from problems that the rest of us make adjustment to every day.

Exercise 3-11

2. When pregnant women smoke, they may injure their fetus.
4. Although editorial writers argue that voters are apathetic because they are cynical about elected officials, they have not suggested how to dispel it.
6. We must analyze how intensively students are using our libraries so that we can reliably project what new resources we will require.
8. In this study, we analyze how readers respond to different rhetorical patterns and judge texts to be well-formed when they know the subject matter of the text before they read.

Exercise 3-12

2. President Nixon's aides asserted that he was immune from . . .
4. When the author analyzed our data, he did not cite sources that would support his criticism of our argument.
6. The Pope appealed to the industrialized nations of the world to assist the starving in the Third World.
8. When the participants agreed on the program, they assumed that the Federal Government had promised funds.
10. The two sides agreed that they needed to revise the treaty.
12. The laboratory personnel must thoroughly prepare the specimen sections.
14. Though we were disappointed when the Board rejected our proposal, we were not surprised because we expected that it had decided to delay new initiatives.

Exercise 3-13

2. When you precisely plot the location of the fragments of the vase, you will reconstruct it more accurately.
4. When a student is not socialized into a field, she may have writing problems because she does not know enough about how those in the field construct arguments.
6. When we evaluated the outcome of the programs, we emphasized objective measures, even though we knew that the raters often disagreed with one another.

Exercise 4-1

2. We will never solve the problem of UFOs until we understand better whether extraterrestrial life is possible.
4. In an emergency room, a doctor has to decide on the scene whether to force medication on an irrational patient who is unable to provide legal consent.
6. As we view network television less and cable and rental cassettes more, networks increasingly recognize that our tastes and viewing habits have changed and that they must program accordingly.
8. Recent critics have correctly described how the press has failed to report on the Middle East accurately and fairly. When we compare how

journalists from different countries cover the same event, we see how inaccurately the news is reported by politically biased newspapers. When they omit facts and slant stories, journalists reveal that they have failed to carry out their mission objectively. As a result, because the public does not know the truth, it bases its opinion more on emotion than on reason.

Exercise 4-2

2. OK
4. OK
6. Before Ann Richards was elected governor of Texas, her Republican opponent attacked her as a liberal Democrat who once used drugs, but in her campaign, she also used negative advertising.
8. Schools will improve science education sufficiently to provide American industry with skilled workers and researchers only when taxpayers/state governments/the Federal Government [take your pick] give them more money.

Exercise 4-4

2. The model has been statistically analyzed.
4. We are considering whether we should assemble more extensive data, but we have not yet evaluated how reliable they would be.
6. We intend this book to help readers understand not only how the grammars of Arabic and English differ, but also how Arabic vocabulary reflects a different world view.
8. Tissue rejection was studied by methods developed when it was discovered that dermal sloughing increases when cells regenerate.

Exercise 4-5

2. We now make almost all home morgage loans for thirty years. With inflated prices of housing, you cannot repay a loan more quickly. (eyeball to eye-ball with the borrower)
4. Many Victorian scientists and theologians argued against Darwinian evolution because it contradicted what they assumed about their place in the world. It defined humans not as divinely privileged but as a product of nature. (just to be exact)

6. We can most clearly explicate why smoking is socially significant if we analyze how adolescents interact. In particular, we should study how their social class determines how they relate.
8. We have undervalued how the brain solves problems because we have not studied it in scientifically reliable ways.
9. As you probably have heard, over the last several weeks, some or our students have been racially and sexually harassing other students. Even though on other campuses some students also harass other students, we are just as offended when some of our students harass others here. In most of the 10 to 12 incidents here, students have written graffiti or verbally insulted someone. In only two cases did one of our students physically contact another, and in neither case did that student injure the other one. A commitment exists to providing an environment where life, work and study can take place without fear of racial, sexual, religious or ethnic taunting or harassment. It has been made clear that bigotry and intolerance will not be permitted and that a commitment to diversity is unequivocal. Steps are being taken to improve security in campus housing. There is pride here in a tradition of diversity...

Exercise 4-6

2. The blood pressure of diabetic patients may be reduced if renal depressors are applied.
4. On the basis of these principles, we can formulate rules that allow readers to extract information from narratives.
6. The Federal Trade Commission should enforce guidelines for the durability of tires on new automobiles.
8. When we visited offices and reviewed assessments of what the agency needed for training, we identified issues that we can use to create an initial questionnaire for the staff.

Exercise 5-1

2. Science needs accurate data if its theories are to advance the world safely.
4. Agencies that assist participants in our program have reversed their recently announced policy and returned to their original one.
6. Most patients in a public clinic do not expect special attention because their problems usually seem minor and can be treated with minimal understanding and attention.

8. When investors think that prices will rise, they usually put most of their discretionary resources into art objects.
10. Educators have long wanted to help readers remember information better, but they have not been able to identify the features that make passages differ in difficulty. The first problem is to identify common and different features among comparable passages. Nor have they been able to evaluate the quality and quantity of information that a reader remembers.

Exercise 5-2

[It is the last full paragraph.] You can delete flab if you eliminate the abstractions we discussed in Lessons Three and Four, but you can also write more directly if you cut the wordiness discussed here. Unfortunately, I cannot offer any principles as specific. Wordiness is like the accumulation of specks and motes that individually seem trivial, but cumulatively blur what could have been clear. To write concisely, study your prose, deleting a word, compressing a phrase. It is labor intensive.

Exercise 5-3

2. A second set of rules includes those whose observance we ignore, and whose violation we ignore, as well.
4. While it is unclear what counts as "too many" prepositions, it is clear that when you avoid abstract nouns, you need fewer of them.

Exercise 5-4

2. Stop taking the medicine only if you are free from dizziness and nausea for six hours.
4. Cosmologists disagree on an open or closed universe, a dispute that will likely continue until they compute its mass.
6. If we wish to be independent of imported oil, we must develop oil shale and coal as sources of fuel.
8. The Insured must provide the Insurer with all relevant receipts, checks, or other evidence of costs that exceed $100.
10. Though we are not certain whether life exists elsewhere in the universe, statistical evidence makes it likely that somewhere among its immense number of planetary systems, it does.

Exercise 5-5

2. At the end of his career, Frost used imagery of seasons in his longer poems.
4. The traditional values that once showed us how to be good mothers and wives were self-contradictory.
6. When Freud interpreted dreams, he was mistaken in his assumptions.
8. Order of birth may or may not relate to academic success.

Exercise 5-6

2. In this section, I argue that we must dispense with plea bargaining because it lets hardened criminals avoid punishment and encourages contempt for the judicial system.
4. We cannot assume that ground snakes in unmapped areas are larger than those in mapped areas.
6. Most investigators of life-stages think that mid-life is most critical for our mental health because most of us decide then whether we are winning or losing the game of life.

Exercise 6-1

One of the best skis for beginning and intermediate skiers is the Hart Queen. Its inner core consists of a thin layer of tempered ash from the hardwood forests of Kentucky. Built into its outer construction are two innovations for strength and flexibility. For increased strength, the layer of ash is reinforced with two sheets of ten-gauge steel. For increased flexibility, the two sheets are wrapped with fiberglass. The Queen can be used with most conventional bindings, but the best binding is the Salomon Double. The foot and ankle are firmly cradled in a cushion of foam and insulation that still permits freedom of movement.

Exercise 6-2

2. In their natural states, most animals do not have the power to create and communicate a new message to fit a new experience. They are limited in the number and kind of messages that they can communicate by their genetic code. Bees, for example, can communicate information

only about distance, direction, source, and richness of pollen in flowers. In all significant respects, animals of the same species are able to communicate a limited repertoire of messages delivered in the same way, for generation after generation.

Exercise 6-4

1. Though modern mass communications offers many significant advantages, its also poses many potential threats. If it should be controlled by a powerful minority, it could manipulate public opinion through biased reporting. And while it provides us with a wide knowledge of public affairs through its national coverage, it may accentuate divisiveness and factionalism by connecting otherwise isolated, local conflicts into a single larger conflict when it shows us conflicts about the same issues occurring in different places. While it will, of course, always be true that human nature produces differences of opinion, the media may reinforce the threat of faction and division when it publishes uninformed opinion in national coverage. According to some, media can suppress faction through education when it communicates the true nature of conflicts, but history has shown that the media give as much coverage to people who encourage conflict as to people who try to remove it.

3. When Truman considered the Oppenheimer committee's recommendation to stop the hydrogen bomb project, he had to consider many issues. Russia and China had just proclaimed a Sino-Soviet bloc, so one issue he had to face was the Cold War. He was also losing support for his foreign policy among Republican leaders in Congress, and when the Russians tested their first atom bomb, the public demanded that he respond strongly. It was inevitable that Truman would conclude he could not let the public think he had allowed Russia to be first in developing the most powerful weapon yet. In retrospect, according to some historians, Truman should have risked taking the Oppenheimer recommendation, but he had to face political issues that were too powerful to ignore.

Exercise 6-6

As the Illinois Commerce Commission has authorized **we** are charging you higher Service Charges after November 12, 1990. **We** have not raised rates in over six years, but **we** are restructuring the rates now consistent with the policy of The Public Utilities Act so that **we** can charge you for what **we** pay to provide you with service. **We** are charging you a sum that **we** have prorated over the period during which **we** changed our rates. When **we** pro-rate, **we** base part of the bill on former Service Charges, which **we** identify on your bill as "Old Rate," and part of the bill on the newly authorized Service charges, which **we** identify as "New Rate."

As the Illinois Commerce Commission has authorized, **you** will have to pay higher Service Charges after November 12, 1990. **You** have not had to pay higher rates in over six years, but **you** will now pay rates that have been restructured consistent with the policy of The Public Utilities Act that lets us base what **you** pay on what it costs to provide you with service. **You** will pay a sum that is prorated over the period during which the rates changed. When **you** pay prorated rates, **you** pay part of the bill based on former Service Charges, which **you** can identify on your bill as "Old Rate," and part of the bill that **you** can identify as "New Rate."

Exercise 6-7

You car may have a defective part that connects the suspension to the frame. If you brake hard and the plate fails, you won't be able to steer. We may also have to adjust the secondary latch on your hood because we may have misa-ligned it. If you don't latch the primary latch, the secondary latch might not hold the hood down. If the hood flies up while you are driving, you won't be able to see. If either of these things occurs, you could crash.

Exercise 6-8

Men are less interested than women in talking in class to support friends and in spirited shared discussion. They also feel more at ease with teachers who impose their views on others. Men are seemingly less concerned than women with the teaching-learning process and attend less to the personal experiences of other students. They also ignore the openness and supportiveness of the instructor as a salient factor in determining whether they feel comfortable about talking in class and give less importance than women do to the teacher's attempts to insure that class members feel good about each other.

Exercise 6-9

The people of this village, I have said, hear something from the cathedral at Chartres that I cannot, but it is important to understand that I hear something that they cannot. Perhaps it is the power of the spires, the glory of the windows that strike them; but God has made Himself known longer to them, after all, than to me, and in a different way; the slippery bottomless well to be found in the crypt, down which heretics were hurled to death, terrifies me, along with the obscene, inescapable gargoyles jutting out of the stone and seeming to say that the devil and God can never be divorced. I doubt that the devil enters the villagers' minds when they look at the cathedral because the devil has never been identified with them. But the status which myth imposes on me in the West must be accepted before I can hope to change it.

Exercise 6-10

Four score and seven years ago, **this continent** witnessed the birth of a new nation, conceived in liberty . . . Now **a great Civil War** engages us, testing whether this nation . . . **That war** has given us this great battlefield for a meeting place. **A portion of that field** is ready to receive its dedication as . . . **This is** an altogether fitting . . . But in a larger sense, **this ground** will not let us dedicate, . . . **It** has already received that consecration . . . **The words we say here** will be little noted . . . , but **the actions of the men** can never be forgotten. [You finish the rest.]

Exercise 7-1

Words that provide conceptual connective tissue are highlighted.

2. The next century the situation changed, because after Peter the Great seven out of eight reigns of the Romanov line were plagued by **turmoil** over **disputed** *succession* to the THRONE.

    The **problems** began in 1722, when Peter the Great passed a law of *succession* that terminated the principle of heredity and required the SOVEREIGN to appoint a *successor.* But because many TSARS, including Peter, died before they named *successors,* those who aspired to RULE had no authority by appointment, and so their *succession* was often **disputed** by the boyars, lower level aristocrats. There was **turmoil** even when *successors* were appointed. In 1740, Ivan VI was adopted by Czarina Anna Ivanovna and named as her *successor* at age two months, but his *succession* was **challenged** by Elizabeth, daughter of Peter the Great. In 1741, she defeated Anna and *ascended* to the THRONE herself. In 1797, Paul tried to eliminate these **disputes** by codifying a new law: *primogeniture in the male line.* But **turmoil** continued. Paul was **strangled** by conspirators, one of whom was probably his son, Alexander I.

Exercise 7-2

Your revisions may well differ from these, depending on what you think is most important in each sentence.

2. These studies may produce a new judicial philosophy that could affect our society well into the 21st century.
4. According to everyone in the industry, "turnkey" means responsibility not only for the manufacture and installation of a new piece of equipment, but for its satisfactory performance, as well.
6. Clearly, those who have overbuilt suburban housing developments have in recent years caused widespread flooding and economic disaster.
8. Economically speaking, however, it is feasible to rent rather than buy textbooks for basic courses that do not change from year such as mathematics, foreign languages, and English.
10. Speakers should adhere to the guidelines set forth in the MLA style sheet and the NCTE guidelines for non-sexist language to the best of their ability.

Exercise 7-3

2. The apparent issue here is whether during contract bargaining, management has the duty to disclose the date it intends to close down its operation. The rationale for management's duty to bargain in good faith is to minimize conflict. Though the case law on this matter is scanty, companies are obligated during bargaining to disclose major changes in an operation in order to allow the union to put forth proposals on behalf of its members.
4. One current hypothesis to explain this kind of severe condition is that a toxin elaborated by the vibrio increases mucosal and vascular permeability. In favor of this hypothesis are changes in small capillaries located near the basal surface of the epithelial cells and the appearance of numerous microvesicles in the cytoplasm of the mucosal cells. It is believed that when capillaries become more permeable, fluid is hydrodynamically transported into the interstitial tissue and then through the mucosa into the lumen of the gut.

Exercise 8-2

Again, your revisions will be completely different from these.

2. For the last few years, automobile manufacturers have been trying to meet more stringent mileage requirements, **a challenge** that has tested American ingenuity/**requirements** that Detroit has strenuously tried to change/hoping that new technologies will provide them with a breakthrough in engine design.

4. Most young people today cannot grasp the insecurity that many people felt during the Great Depression, **a failure** that makes it impossible for them to share their grandparents' experiences/**an insecurity** that shaped them for the rest of their lives/believing that the stories they hear from their grandparents are exaggerations.

6. Many Victorians were appalled when Darwin suggested that their ancestors might have included creatures such as apes, **a concept** that offended not only their personal self-respect, but their fundamental religious beliefs, as well/**creatures** that they had seen as utterly different from themselves/choosing to believe instead that they were created by God 6000 years before.

8. Scientific inquiry began when primitive people began to think about the regularities of nature, regularities that were invisible to most such people because they were so familiar but to a few others seemed worth considering.

Exercise 8-3

2. For whatever reason, such conduct is usually prejudicial to good discipline.

4. Given the low quality of elected officials, the merit selection of judges is an idea whose time came long ago.

6. Unless we reduce the emission of carbon dioxide by the end of the century, we will change the climate of the world.

Exercise 8-4

1. An ecological impact statement identical to that submitted the previous year indicates that it will again contain data difficult to evaluate.

3. Because we have reorganized the marketing research division, we can process information more quickly and thereby identify more reliably market segments different from those that we have traditionally aimed at. We will be able to process this information relatively easily because for many markets, we have already accumulated data such as income, spending, etc. We may therefore expect to operate more efficiently than last year.

Exercise 8-5

2. Though we expect to succeed, we will need to resolve immediately the differences that have interfered with communication.
4. After we audited internal operations in the summer of 1988, we audited foreign affiliates that had not been audited by their local headquarters.

Exercise 9-1

1. Scientists and philosophers of science tend to speak as if "scientific language" were intrinsically precise, as if those who use it must understand one another's meaning, even if they disagree. But, in fact, scientific language is not as different from ordinary language as is commonly believed; it, too, is subject to imprecision and ambiguity and hence to imperfect understanding. Moreover, new theories (or arguments) are rarely, if ever, constructed by way of clear-cut steps of induction, deduction, and verification (or falsification). Neither are they defended, rejected, or accepted in so straightforward a manner. In practice, scientists combine the rules of scientific methodology with a generous admixture of intuition, aesthetics, and philosophical commitment. The importance of what are sometimes called extra-rational or extralogical components of thought in the *discovery* of a new principle or law is generally acknowledged. . . . But the role of these extralogical components in persuasion and acceptance (in making an argument convincing) is less frequently discussed, partly because they are less visible. The ways in which the credibility or effectiveness of an argument depends on the realm of common experiences, on extensive practice in communicating those experiences in a common language, are hard to see precisely because such commonalities are taken for granted. Only when we step out of such a

"consensual domain"—when we can stand out on the periphery of a community with a common language—do we begin to become aware of the unarticulated premises, mutual understandings, and assumed practices of the group.

Even in those subjects that lend themselves most readily to quantification, discourse depends heavily on conventions and inter-pretation—conventions that are acquired over years of practice and participation in a community.

2. In fact, of course, the notion of universal knowledge has always been an illusion; but it is an illusion fostered by the monistic view of the world in which a few great central truths determine in all its wonderful and amazing proliferation everything else that is true. We are not today tempted to search for these keys that unlock the whole of human knowledge and of man's experience. We know that we are ignorant; we are well taught it, and the more surely and deeply we know our own job the better able we are to appreciate the full measure of our perva-sive ignorance. We know that these are inherent limits, compounded, no doubt, and exaggerated by that sloth and that complacency without which we would not be men at all.

But knowledge rests on knowledge; what is new is meaningful because it departs slightly from what was known before; this is a world of frontiers, where even the liveliest of actors or observers will be absent most of the time from most of them. Perhaps this sense was not so sharp in the village—that village which we have learned a little about but probably do not understand too well—the village of slow change and isolation and fixed culture which evokes our nostalgia even if not our full comprehension. Perhaps in the villages men were not so lonely; perhaps they found in each other a fixed community, a fixed and only slowly growing store of knowledge—a single world. Even that we may doubt, for there seem to be always in the culture of such times and places vast domains of mystery, if not unknowable, then imperfectly known, endless and open.

Exercise 10-2

2. While the strong are often afraid to admit weakness, the weak often fail to assert the strength they possess.

4. When parents raise children who do not value the importance of hard work, the adults those children become will not know how to work hard for what they claim to value.

Exercise 10-3

2. The political campaign plan was concocted by those with the least sensitivity to our most critical needs.
4. Nothing has changed America more than the power of federal government.
6. Boards of education can no longer expect that taxpayers will support the extravagancies of incompetent bureaucrats.

Acknowledgments

D. H. Lawrence, *Studies in Classic American Literature,* New York: The Viking Press, 1961

Norman Mailer, *Armies of the Night.* New York: The New American Library, Inc., 1971.

From *Science and the Common Understanding* by J. Robert Oppenheimer. Copyright © 1954 by J. Robert Oppenheimer, renewed © 1981 by Robert B. Meyner. Reprinted by permission.

Excerpt from Foreword, *Webster's New World Dictionary.* Second College Edition, 1974, p. viii. Copyright © 1974 by William Collins + World Publishing Company. Reprinted by permission of Simon & Schuster, Inc.

From "The Aims of Education" in *The Aims of Education and Other Essays* by Alfred North Whitehead. Copyright © 1929 by Macmillan Publishing Co., Inc., renewed 1957 by Evelyn Whitehead. Reprinted by permission.

INDEX